theArt of Interior Design

the Art of Interior Design

selecting elements for distinctive styles

Suzanne Woloszynska

CREATIVE PUBLISHING *international*

MINNETONKA, MINNESOTA

First published in the USA and Canada in 2001 by
Creative Publishing international, Inc.

President/CEO: David D. Murphy
Vice President/Editorial: Patricia K. Jacobsen
Vice President/Retail Sales and Marketing: Richard M. Miller
Executive Editor/Lifestyles Department: Elaine Perry

First published in the United Kingdom
in 2000 by Mitchell Beazley,
an imprint of Octopus Publishing Group Ltd
2-4 Heron Quays, London E14 4JP

Art Director: Rita Wuthrich
Executive Art Editor: Janis Utton
Executive Editor: Judith More
Editors: Emily Asquith, Jo Richardson
Picture Researchers: Lois Charlton, Helen Stallion
Production Controllers: Julie Young, Catherine Lay

10 9 8 7 6 5 4 3 2 1.

ISBN 0-86573-149-7

Contents

Introduction

The complex, exhilarating, and satisfying world of interior design is like a vast, colourful map illustrating a whole universe waiting to be explored. Whether you are starting out on a completely new decorating odyssey, without any previous experience, or you are seeking inspiration to revitalize the existing decoration of your home, *Style for Living* provides the signposts, symbols, and languages you will need to guide you on the journey.

A foundation of know-how goes a long way to helping you make the right decorative choices. This book aims to equip you with that information by providing an insight into the history of decoration, the way colour works, how materials can be mixed and placed to best advantage, and what finishing touches you can utilize to bring the whole room together, therefore giving you a sound, overall background in decorating ideas.

Decorating is an emotive art, touched by historical precedent, fashion and global culture, technological advances, and constant media bombardment. There is also a place for individual input, the unique personality and innovation that is part of the decorating game. You will find many suggestions in this book to help you avoid major mishaps, but never be afraid to experiment or make changes to the original idea as you go along. To channel what we see, hear, read, or need into a cohesive, satisfying scheme may not seem easy, but it will always be fun, informative, and ultimately rewarding. Indeed, the whole concept of design has never been so accessible or as widely discussed and exhibited as it is today.

Before you begin decoration there are the fundamental decisions to be made about structural alterations, electrics, plumbing, and heating, and possible changes to architectural fixtures. Once these have been made, with the help of accredited professionals and with planning permission where necessary, you can get to the fun decorating part. The framework of a room is composed of vertical and horizontal surfaces related to the architectural elements such as the windows, doors, and fireplace. The decorative scheme is born through colour, pattern, texture, and lighting chosen for function, suitability, budget, and, above all, personal preferences. Naturally, if you are setting out with an empty new home, you will approach the decorative planning with a different perspective than if you are adapting what is already in place.

The starting point may well be different for each individual, but the stimulus for the project will probably come from a single spark of inspiration. Keep your mind and eyes open to idea sources at all times, because they can appear from anywhere. You might love the colours in a fragment of antique embroidery, an oil painting, or an Indian sari, or even

Opposite Before you begin to decorate your home, look carefully at the room and think about exactly what you are trying to achieve. Choose a style that will complement rather than compete with the existing features. Here, the historical elements of the house have been complemented by using carefully chosen furniture and decorative pieces.

them to a large board in various combinations. Relate each element to its site and application. Look at colour and pattern combinations in their relative proportions. Cut samples to comparative size where possible. Move the samples around, visualizing the effect when different colours and patterns are put together in various combinations. If you prefer a painted finish paper, paint big pieces of lining paper with a number of possible colours and tape them, one at a time, to the wall, scrutinizing each in various lights, from bright sunshine and electric lighting to candle-glow.

Start adding to the design board the secondary ingredients, such as trimmings, cushion fabrics, flooring material, and the vital, subtle decorative accessories. Personal adjustments draw together, highlight, and set off the design. For example, you might paint a thin contrast line below the cornice, move a colourful picture to reset the focal point of the room, or add another table lamp to soften the shadows in a dark corner. Perhaps the sofa needs a luxurious throw for texture contrast, or a pile of gem-coloured silk cushions. Inevitably, these decorative exclamation marks will present themselves as the overall picture comes together.

The greatest design influences have often lain in what is practical, cheap, and accessible. The terracotta soil of Tuscany, for example, is fundamental to the picturesque identity of the area. The Japanese traditionally use local timber, bark, straw, and rice-paper so homes can be easily rebuilt after an earthquake or typhoon, and because of their philosophy to live in harmony with nature. The bamboo plant of Indonesia provides not only a basic building material, but also the source for furniture, flooring, mats, baskets, storage boxes

Above Look around you for design elements and bits and pieces that you find pleasing. Cutting attractive pictures from magazines will help you to discover where your decorative preferences lie. Here, a "storyboard" of materials, fabrics, and accessories in jewel-bright colours has been assembled for inspiration. This eclectic array of items already suggests a coherent design idea.

the textures in a vegetable market. Keep a note of your likes and dislikes as you collect colour and fabric references, swatches, paint cards and tester pots, hard surface samples, and trimmings. Look for decent-sized samples, especially if the repeat is large. Magazines, in-store catalogues, postcards, and photographs all add to the raft of inspiration, but do bear in mind that the colours in magazine photographs are often distorted by lighting and printing. Gather items for inspiration, such as seashells, feathers, polished pebbles, leaves, a straw basket, a tapestry cushion, a patinated jug – anything to stimulate the senses and help you focus on key theme and texture combinations.

Make your first choice of favourite colours and materials for the major components of wall surface, window treatment, and furnishing fabrics, attaching

and other items. Spiritual symbolism also influences many aspects of design detail. Examples are the Islamic motifs that appear in architectural adornment and carpet design, the Shaker use of colour as a reflection of Heaven, and the application of the Zen ideology that creates an aura of tranquil contemplation.

When you choose a decorative style for your home you are participating in a great tradition of interior design that has developed over hundreds of years. The evolution of decorative style has been woven into a rich tapestry of invention, creation, and embellishment, whose progression is shaped by the historical, social, and cultural influences of

Above It is undoubtedly the little things that matter. In this elegant room the correct choice of finishing touches is essential. The sumptuous soft furnishings make the room comfortable and luxurious, and the subtle lighting brings the scheme together in a truly welcoming environment.

Right Whether consciously or not, we are all influenced by the decorative styles of the past, but we are free to interpret ideas in any way we want. This charming sitting room is obviously influenced by traditional floral styles, which complement the high ceilings and tall, elegant windows in the original architecture.

the period. The effects of global trade, for example, led to the intermittent introduction of new dyes. More sophisticated glass production methods allowed larger windows and glazed doors to be produced, therefore affording better natural light and creating scope for more elaborate curtain design. When candlelight and firelight were superceded by brighter, safer and eventually cleaner lighting methods, people viewed and used their houses in new ways, and consequently adopted different colours, furnishings, and materials. The expansion of industrialization and colonialism and more accessible foreign travel and trading, produced an abundance of innovative products. It also brought about a greater interest in other cultures, and an influx of social influences that had a huge effect on the breadth of design and style potential available to an increasingly affluent and acquisitive society.

The *Choosing a Style* section presents a range of historical and cultural styles and will help to give you the confidence to mix these ingredients within a contemporary setting for an integrated look. Do not feel obliged to follow a style too closely – let it evolve and include elements from a variety of eras and sources. A period flavour is not difficult to conjure using key colours, materials, and styling, and there are many historic document designs available. Setting the scene with colour or textural direction can suffice to create a sense of time and place.

When it comes to colour, people have instinctive likes and dislikes. Colour is fundamental to the direction of any interior scheme, so thinking about why you like a particular colour and how it works in association with others will help you to realize its full potential and side-step common errors. It is impossible to adequately describe in words such a subtle visual theme as colour, but you will come across some descriptive terms while putting together your design, in particular hue, intensity, and tone. Hue describes a colour in pure form in the colour spectrum – red, blue, or green, for example. Intensity relates to the brightness or denseness of a hue – the maximum being strong and bright, while its opposite is knocked-back or dulled. Tone defines the graduation from light to dark and from cool to warm. Shades are the darker tones of the hue, and tints are the lighter tones.

The translation of colour depends on the setting, the size of the room, the association with other colours, and lighting. The second section, *Choosing a Colour Scheme*, looks at a number of possible colour combinations for the various rooms in the house. Different perspectives, materials, and surfaces react to light in unique ways. On a vertical, matt surface, you will see a different hue than with a satin finish on a horizontal surface, for example. Obviously, daylight and candlelight create different moods and therefore a room mostly used at night, or a small, intimate room, will favour dark colours that look seductive and comforting when softly lit. Different qualities of natural light also have a profound optical influence. Strong colours in the clear sunlight of the Mediterranean look clean and bright, whereas the same hues in grey Northern light can appear harsh. Likewise, neutral, muted

shades hold their colour better in temperate climates than in sunny ones.

Various materials and paints work differently with light and colour, too. Oily, transparent paints intensify colour, as do lightweight, sheer fabrics, while matt paint and materials are non-reflective and look softer. Optical perception of colour plays tricks, too. A red wall will advance and make a

Below Global influences, as well as historical ones, can be the precursor to a complete room theme. The colours, fabrics, motifs, and details used in this small room are obviously inspired by travel, whether real or through the pages of a guidebook.

room look smaller, while blue recedes and can promote a sense of spaciousness. Yellow yells for attention and is softer and easier when used as a broken effect, such as a colourwash. Choose from warm and cool colours to create the room's atmosphere; greys, blues, and violets are usually cool colours, while orange-yellow, orange, and red are warm. Green tones cover a broad band in the colour wheel and are generally restful and easy to intermix, as in nature. A scheme that uses one colour in various guises, plus a neutral or white, is called monochromatic and is an easily created, effective look. A flash of colour is a professional decorator's trick that will inject a single point of contrast unrelated to the foundation theme.

The way colours are juxtaposed will affect their impact dramatically. Primary colours used together need to appear in different proportions or they will fight for dominance, creating an uncomfortable effect. Colours of the same tonal range or intensity however, can be used together in harmony. Be aware though, that some colours, for example blues, are tricky when there are only two, but if you add a third or fourth they will all tie together, especially when they are partnered with white.

As well as colour, there are also the basic elements of the room to consider when planning your scheme. As walls are the largest surfaces, their treatment is key. Paint is cheap, quick, and versatile and comes in a vast range of colours and finishes, from transparent glazes to chalky, matt textures. Wallpaper provides powerful style identity and can change the geometry of a room. Trailing florals, trellis, scrolling patterns, and all-over designs are all adept at softening difficult architectural lines.

Whether to add architectural details such as picture and dado rails, friezes, and cornices causes much consternation and some mistakes. Check the historical style and room proportions warrant it, and make sure additions are correctly positioned and of appropriate moulding. Today, these details are often used to form a boundary between decorative treatments within the room.

Window treatments reflect the room's style and spirit. Instead of skimping on expensive fabric, use a cheaper material in the right quantity combined with smart detail and, if feasible, contrast lining. Ticking, checks, thin stripes, or a tiny diaper pattern look smart and help to unify the exterior view. Fabric can also be used on the walls, either loosely hung in an informal way or battened and

Below Colour can transform the look of a room like no other element. It is relatively inexpensive to ring the changes by introducing a different hue. The bright ice-cream colours of the chair and woodwork could easily be replaced by muted alternatives for a more relaxed, tranquil look.

finished with braid or gimp. The result is a softly-textured effect that dampens sound. Flooring helps to visually underline and anchor the decorative composition. It is always worth buying the best quality carpet you can afford, where used, relevant to its placement. Rugs are an attractive option and provide a good visual link between areas.

The final section, *Choosing Finishing Touches*, looks at the accessories and details that complete the decorative scheme, from lighting and soft furnishings to vases, frames, mirrors, and collections. The right details can help you to transform a room with a minimum of fuss, and accessories can often provide an inexpensive means of suggesting a particular decorative style. Information is given on choosing and sourcing all

sorts of accessories and how to display them to the best practical and decorative effect.

All three chapters feature detailed text, with colour photographs to illustrate the ideas. The first two chapters include material swatches chosen to suit the type of scheme being discussed. None of the information is intended to be followed exactly, instead, I hope that you will consider the concepts as a means to creating your own style. When designing today's domestic interior we can choose from a melting pot of decorative idioms to evolve a look that suits our environment, fulfils our aesthetic needs, and reflects our lifestyle. What suits one person will not please another, but everybody has within them the spark of inspiration that will produce a characterful and satisfying interior style.

Above The perfect place to unwind at the end of the day. You may decide to choose restful, muted colours to evoke a relaxed ambience in the bedroom. When choosing colours, think about all the functions of the room and pick a scheme that embodies the predominant mood.

Choosing a Style

Traditional Choices

Wherever we look, we are steeped in historical reference and influence. Whether we are consciously aware of it or not, tradition has played a significant part in the development of our surrounding environment and domestic interior. There is very little in life with which we surround ourselves that has been developed without reference to our past through its social and cultural consequences. There are so many echoes of our past which reveal themselves in different guises within contemporary decoration that tradition has unconsciously become part of the fabric of modern life. Everything that has been comes around again in time, often in the most subtle manner, but all design carries lessons of the past into the future and every new design takes its principle from the past.

To use traditional design within the contemporary interior demands an understanding of the elements that have influenced and evolved the period or fashion in question in order to create a foundation of reference from which ideas can be drawn, adapted, and applied. It might sound improbable to suggest devising a Gothic interior, for example, because it would be highly unusual to have the ideal setting for this effusive Victorian style. However, there is no reason why its key design concepts or decorating detail could not be adopted on a smaller scale, such as in styling a bathroom, with delightful results. While you may not be able to acquire Charles Rennie Mackintosh's lineal furniture, you can apply his principles of clean, uncluttered line and lean ornamentation. The best approach is to focus on what is feasible and appropriate to the existing environment and to your lifestyle. Plan out the basic design before progessing any further; careful consideration at this stage will help you to avoid potentially expensive mistakes later on. Don't attempt to mix historical styles, as this can make the room look confused.

At Home with Heraldry

The heraldic style of decoration is drawn from various historic sources: inspiration may be found within the Medieval Gothic period and also within elements of the nineteenth-century Gothic Revival. You can adapt these ingredients to suit contemporary interiors using some of the "themed" fabrics, wallpapers, and decorative artifacts available. There are three principles to follow when establishing a heraldic setting: first, use appropriate motifs for walls and fabrics, second, find the right balance of colours, and finally seek out a few theatrical "props" to enhance the theme. Motifs associated with the heraldic idiom include the fleur-de-lis, which in various forms and countries has appeared on walls and fabrics for centuries; the cypher or monogram which, signifying birth and wealth, was used exclusively by the aristocracy prior to the 1700s; heraldic shields or coats-of-arms; and pictorial representations of mythical beasts and stylized figures. These designs can be found in many colours and shades, from rich reds and greens to faded golds and blues. Make sure that colours are compatible in tone when using several fabrics together. Cover walls with rough, tinted plaster, faintly stencilled with a motif or frieze, or an ornate "tapestry" paper. Stencilled banner hangings are appropriate for stone-effect walls, while natural-fibre flooring makes a comfortable alternative to a Medieval, rush-strewn floor. This dramatic concept is best suited to a sparsely furnished room, such as a hallway or bathroom, where furniture is minimal and low-lighting can be used effectively.

Left An understated use of the ubiquitous fleur-de-lis motif lends a "heraldic" mood to this restrained contemporary room. Here, the stencil motif is applied using bronze metallic paint and then rubbed back with sandpaper to produce an attractive antiqued finish. You can apply bought or homemade stencils of simple heraldic designs to an inexpensive, plain material to make effective window drapes or blinds, bedcovers, or even bed hangings. These touches give just a hint of heraldic flavour to a decorative scheme without dominating the room.

Above For a luxurious, theatrical look, the same material in different colours covers the walls and bed, and is used as a throw over a chair to create an impressive throne. The colours and insignia materials create the heraldic aura and form the focal point of the room.

1. The fleur-de-lis motif represents the Holy Trinity, and has been popular since Medieval times. It can make a bold statement or form part of a subtle pattern.

2. Medieval tapestries illustrated daily life, Bible stories, hunting, and battle scenes and pageantry. Softer, modern tapestry fabric may be used for upholstery, loose covers, and window hangings. Add a border to imitate a real tapestry hanging.

3. The lion and crown are recurring motifs in Medieval and Gothic decoration. Rich colour with hints of gold provides drama and glamour.

4. These floor or wall tiles could be used as an inset among plain tiles or to form a border.

5. This chunky sisal matting creates a raw, rustic look. Use it over the whole floor or as a mat.

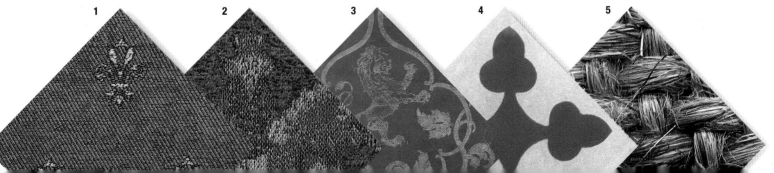

1   2   3   4   5

Gothic Inspiration

There are a number of disparate styles that all come under the name "Gothic". Medieval domestic Gothic style reflected the tone of church architecture with trefoil arches, tracery stonework, and carved woodwork typified by heraldic references, stylized flowers, and fleur-de-lis. As the interiors were sparsely furnished, the architectural elements were decoratively important, with colour being provided by tapestry wall hangings depicting ecclesiastical stories, pageantry, and scenes from everyday life. Colours associated with the period are rich reds and blues, and old gold. Walls were made of unpainted hardwood panelling or raw stone – a look which could be recreated today with reclaimed or reproduction panelling, or wood and stone painted effects.

The mid-eighteenth-century, refined Gothic style was characterized by fanciful "sugar-icing" plasterwork, usually white on a pink, powder-blue, sulphur-yellow, or soft-green background. The Gothic Revival of the mid-to-late nineteenth century is epitomized by ornate, feudal ornamentation, as embodied in the architect Pugin's work for the British Houses of Parliament. Victorian Gothic was strong in drama and weight, taking its reference from the Medieval, rather than the lighter eighteenth-century, period. Colours were dark and strong, with lots of gilt, tracery-design wallpaper, and damask. Furniture was made of deeply carved, dark wood, often featuring an ogee arch, while lavish cornices and fire surrounds typified architectural detail. Flowers, birds, animals, and heraldic motifs were used liberally on wallpaper and fabrics. Arts and Crafts Movement designers admired the craftsmanship and "natural" decorative elements of Medieval Gothicism and incorporated them into their unique interpretation of this style.

Left A finely carved chair, made around 1855, stands in this impressive hallway. Nearly all nineteenth-century Gothic furniture was made of dark wood or was stained to near-black. Stone-effect, trompe l'oeil paintwork or wallpaper could be used to recreate the distinctive wall decoration in a modern home. Generally, when decorating in this style it is best to avoid mixing the different periods of Gothic, as they can vary so much in weight, colour, and decorative focus.

Right A broad collection of Gothic furniture and decorative pieces creates an atmospheric interior. The eye is drawn to the mirror with its ogee arch and to the nineteenth-century chairs. A Gothic frieze would be easy to imitate using paper or stencil. Some Art Nouveau items are included for their aesthetic appeal, such as the candlestick, the hanging light, small lamps, and some vases. Use heavy candlesticks, wall sconces, and religious statuary and pictures to create the Gothic look.

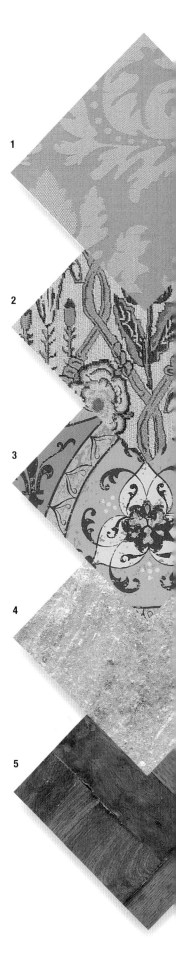

1. The muted tones and lustrous texture of silk damask suits the Gothic interior of either the Medieval period or nineteenth-century Revival. Simply pleat curtains and hang them from heavy wooden or brass poles.

2. Many Gothic designs evolved from religious, political, or mythological symbolism. This fabric shows lilies, thistles, and roses associated with Mary, Queen of Scots. The design also befits the Arts and Crafts Movement.

3. The pattern, texture, and colour of this wallpaper would make a dramatic backdrop for a Gothic scheme. Although wallpapers were not of the period, this ornate style suits the nineteenth-century Gothic Revival.

4. Natural stone adds texture and authentic colour to a room.

5. An alternative to flagstone or plain floor boards, a simple parquet design would be suitable. This geometric pattern, popular since the early seventeenth century, is one of the most enduring.

Classical Lessons

Roman and Greek classical civilizations have had a profound influence on architecture and interior design since the early part of the seventeenth century. Apart from the flamboyant decoration of the Rococo period, classicism has provided the supreme reference for interior design and provides a look which is just as influential today. Initially, Roman antiquity took precedence over Greek. This period relied on architectural dominance rather than on interior refinement, using architectural embellishments such as columns, temple façades, rusticated masonry, and heavy, sculptured Roman motifs. Eagles and masks applied to fixtures, fittings, and furniture help to capture this look.

During the second half of the eighteenth century, the architect Robert Adam elevated classicism into a complete decorative art with light, delicate ornamentation and Italian Renaissance, Roman, Greek, and Etruscan allusions. Rosettes and garlands, urns and ribbons, bands of anthemia (acanthus or honeysuckle), flowers, and birds are all ideal motifs. Apply them to a background of soft green, blue, yellow, or pink. Only the grandest schemes used gilded ornamentation. Silk, damask, brocade, velvet, and embroidery are suitable companion textiles.

Various fashions were sporadically popular throughout this period: the fanciful Gothic style; Chinese and Japanese imports of lacquered furniture, porcelain, and expensive wall-paper panels. When choosing wallpapers and fabrics, look for birds, lanterns, exotic plants, and idealized Chinese domestic and rural scenes. The famous furniture maker, Thomas Chippendale, produced pattern books of hundreds of Chinoiserie designs to complement the fashion of the time. Much in demand from 1770, the pastoral scenes of *Toile de Jouy* are just as charming today as they were originally, and *Toile de Jouy* wall-papers and fabrics are now available in a wider range of colours, making them more versatile and easier to use in the modern home. Traditionally, these patterns were used to cover an entire room, from the walls to the bed linen, but today you are free to use as much or as little of this alluring material as you like to create your own classical setting.

Above Yellow makes a fine backdrop for Chinese porcelain. This porcelain became sought after during the reign of William and Mary (1689–1702). Display the porcelain in bold groups or use it to fill a large, vertical wall space for an impressive look. The Chinoiserie mirror and fine English chandelier fulfil the same decorative purpose here. Muslin is ideal for use as a window dressing without the loss of precious natural light.

Opposite Use one colour in variation, mixed with black detail, to create decorative flow. The deep-buttoned day bed has scroll ends and gilt detail, picked up in the trunk and the chair. A pair of bookcases with columns flank the window, finished with simple curtains hanging from a metal pole. Fixing curtains at the centre creates a pleasing line when they are held in place by tie-backs.

Left You can use an assortment of styles together providing they are balanced in quality and given sufficient space to themselves. Here, there is a c.1750 corner cupboard with classic shell-shaped interior and a Regency gilt-and-ebony chair. The striped damask of the eighteenth-century sofa accentuates the gilt detail. To show a painting to its best advantage, always display it in the deepest possible frame.

1. French *Toile de Jouy*, originally produced in pink only, now comes in several colourways, which makes it easily adaptable to classical and contemporary-style interiors.

2. The antiquarian ruins of Italy and Greece had a profound effect on decorative style. Use this type of detail to recreate the look popular during the last quarter of the eighteenth century.

3. Under-curtains of muslin or voile were popular by the Regency/Empire period, and they are as favoured today. Use classical motifs to bring a hint of classicism to a modern interior.

4. This archetypal classical design would be most suitable for use as a floor border. You could combine it with a rug or a carpet that reveals the geometric border for an authentic look.

5. The pretty coloration and tapestry weave of this elegant carpet is well suited to the curvaceous Rococo decorative style. It provides appropriate, but subtle, pattern.

1   2   3   4   5

By the beginning of the nineteenth century, Neo-classical design was widely popular in Europe, but increasingly looking to Greek rather than to Roman culture for its source of inspiration. Consequently, the style became more refined and practical, and was perhaps the most sophisticated expression of all the classical trends. Both the French Empire and the English mid-Regency decorative periods embraced Greek linear architectural detail. You can recreate this look using reeded or incized pattern, or subtle, vertical surface detail – including classic ornamentation from Egyptian, as well as Graeco-Roman, sources. Suitable motifs of the early French Empire period include laurel wreaths, medallions, winged sphinxes, imperial eagles, and lions. Supplement these with the emblems synonymous with the Napoleonic era, such as the bee, swan's head, and palm tree.

Choose furniture made of mahogany, maple, and rosewood. The Grecian chaise, sofa-tables, and round tables provide an informal, sociable furniture arrangement that was very popular at the time. Tie silk or floral swagged and festooned draperies back from the window to reveal lace or muslin under-curtains or plain blinds. In this period wall-to-wall carpets were used for the first time in preference to floorcloths laid over wooden boards. Lay repeat-patterned, cut-pile and Brussel-weave carpets with a running border. Candle wall sconces are essential light fixtures for both the Empire and Regency styles.

Inspired by the Regency and early French Empire periods, the United States adopted a robust architectural and decorative interpretation of the Classical style of interior design. From 1820 this look evolved via American Federal to Empire and Greek Revival. Both styles remained popular until the 1850s. Signature motifs are key frets, lyres, and egg-and-dart moulding, combined with decorative papers, carpets, and furniture that provide a contrast with the well-defined architectural style. Wall-to-wall carpets decorated with a gold star or laurel pattern are ideal for this American look. Paint walls terracotta, stone, deep pink, or grey, or even hang them with Greek Revival papers and cornice friezes to add a patterned element.

Top Dark and light come together in this minimal, Empire-style bedroom. In an entirely cream-coloured space, the furniture takes centre stage with a fine *lit-en-bateau* draped in silk and muslin, a cheval dressing mirror, and a pair of Graeco-inspired oil lamps on the carved fireplace. Calico curtains add decorative weight without dominating the room.

Above The Directoire period of Napoleon's consulate (1790–1804) was lighter in style than the following Empire. Here, cream paint, no curtains, and bare floorboards act as the backdrop for antique objects, including an elegant stool, a satin-covered sofa, candlestands, and etchings. Contemporary ceramics blend well with authentic pieces.

Opposite This intriguing collection of treasures illustrates the late-Empire decorative style.The marble-topped console table with its animal-shaped legs and patera detailing supports pairs of vases and pots in the Etruscan style, an Egyptian mask, and even a classical torso. The yellow, stencilled paper provides an appropriately decorative background.

1. The rich colouring and luxury of this moiré fabric suits the French Empire and Regency styles. Fabrics were sometimes battened to the wall but wallpaper was becoming more popular and cheaper.

2. The bee is the ancient Greek symbol of order and industry, so Napoleon adopted it as his emblem. This jacquard weave would be suitable for upholstering an ebonized chair or a chaise longue.

3. Ambitious pictorial trompe l'oeil papers were already popular in France, where the best examples were made, and in Britain after 1815. This Greek frieze illustrates the three-dimensional effect that can be achieved.

4. An elegant, hardwood border with a woven acanthus leaf design would be appropriate in a late–Empire or Biedermeier interior (the Austrian and German simplified version of French Empire).

5. A carpet must suit a range of styles without looking out of character or dominating the scene. This example has rhythm and soft colourways, making it kind on the eye and ideal for a classically themed room.

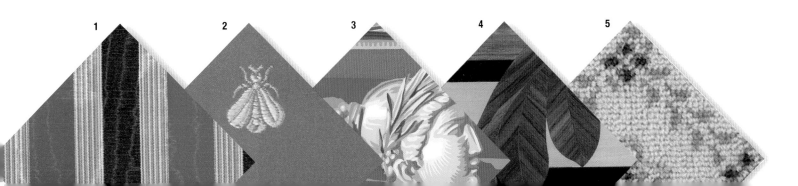

1   2   3   4   5

Victorian Romance

The Victorian era was one of unprecedented commercial and industrial innovation, great social change, and increasing global influence. Extraordinarily, despite these advances in the world around them, people looked to the past for decorative inspiration. This was largely due to an expanding and wealthy middle class who were initially culturally uncertain, and who felt comfortable with interior styles that had previously been accessible only to the upper classes. Colonialism and the availability of international travel also influenced interior-design fashions, and revivals included Baroque, Rococo, Elizabethan, Gothic, even Baronial, Middle Eastern, Moorish, and Oriental. Throughout the 1840s and 1850s, the choice and availability of products, materials, and stylistic influences was vastly increased thanks to the Great Exhibition of 1851 and to the introduction of manufacturers' Pattern Books which gave details of new designs.

From 1830, the Elizabethan phase rose in popularity over two decades, featuring abstract designs of cartouches, brackets, or flowers on banded strapwork designs, shaded to produce a three-dimensional effect. Decorative architectural elements were superficially applied, often using papier mâché instead of plaster decoration. Mass-produced from 1844, wallpaper became the principal wall treatment, with watered silk imitations combined with flowers or dark crimson flock papers proving popular.

To achieve the early-Victorian style, choose glazed chintzes and silk damasks, patterned, formalized flowers and leaves, Rococo-style scrolls, and cartouches in predominantly light colours. "Masculine" rooms should be dramatic – during the Victorian era the dining room and library would often be crimson or bottle green. Stripes and sprigged motifs are suitable for the "feminine" areas, such as the bedrooms and drawing room. Flowers, birds, and trellises are also appropriate. The Gothic Revival instigated a huge variety of dramatically decorative wallpapers, sometimes enriched with gold detail, and usually including a dark-toned background. Other suitable wallpaper patterns include bamboo leaves, naturalistic willow and acanthus, stylized fruit, and large flowers such as dahlias, hollyhocks, and hydrangeas. By 1877, wallpaper with a raised, patterned surface which imitated wood, plaster, or even leather was popular. It is extremely practical as it can be painted or varnished and then washed if required, and so is ideal for areas of heavy use, such as a family sitting room.

Above A truly romantic bed arrangement, furnished with a full tester, and draped, pelmetted, and pleated in grand style. Half-testers are more commonly used and are lighter to fix than four-poster beds.

Opposite An American parlour is given an updated Victorian slant using a pretty chintz material for simple curtains, and to cover a Victorian suite including an overstuffed chair and a charming courting seat. Here, a Victorian couple would sit with the chaperone perched between them. The wicker chair and side table are typical of the type that would be found in the Victorian conservatory. The crocheted tablecloth, heart-shaped wreath, and needlepoint picture are perfect accessories for a room decorated in the style of this period.

1   2   3   4   5

1. This fabric design echoes the Elizabethan style, which was one of the most popular revivals of the early-Victorian period.

2. Choose damasks for the "masculine" rooms of the house, such as the dining room, combined with flock paper and dark, floral carpeting.

3. Keep the decorative flavour of the bedroom light and feminine, using chintz mixes, floral papers, and lace to enhance the effect.

4. To re-create the early Victorian romantic look, use quantities of different laces together, swagged and festooned, frilled and ruched.

5. A range of flooring could be used, including netting, oil-cloth, carpet, tapestry, and tiling. This carpet could be used for a sitting room or a bedroom.

The Victorian era produced such a rich mixture of decorative revivals that often each room would have a different look. In one home there might be a Gothic-Revival dining room, a Moorish boudoir, a Baroque drawing room, and a Baronial hall. Architects and designers loved to manipulate these ingredients, borrowing from here and there to produce a hybrid interpretation, frequently within the same room.

To recreate the late-Victorian look, furniture, preferably mahogany, should be robust, rounded, or even carved with "naturalistic" flowers and leaves. Typical chairs, sofas, pouffes, and ottomans are plump, and deeply-buttoned in sumptuous or highly patterned textiles with extravagant trim. In contrast, delicate papier mâché chairs inlaid with mother-of-pearl or painted with landscapes are also appropriate. After 1830, window curtains became symmetrical and they were often arranged in layers. Choose velvet, satin, or damask with lace under-curtains for winter, and lace, sheers, or muslin for the summer months. Flat, shaped lambrequin pelmets with scrolled, scalloped, or gilded outlines are suitable for an early-Victorian look, while draped or stiffened pelmets finished with fringing and tassels, and gilded or woodgrain poles and rings are appropriate to the mid-to-late years of the Victorian period. Painted floor-cloths were much used until the advent of linoleum and, from 1840, encaustic tiles made from coloured clay patterns were laid in halls and porches. By 1870, close-carpeting was less fashionable than stained boards or parquet, so choose hard flooring and spread it with assorted rugs. Kilims, Paisley shawls, lace, and needlework are synonymous with this period. Rattan and split-cane matting are ideal for use in conservatories and under rugs. Any spare horizontal surface would have held a collection of memorabilia, collectables, and photographs, so take the opportunity to show off your treasures.

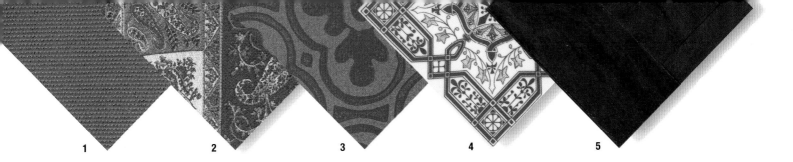

1   2   3   4   5

Left Generous widths of deep yellow silk damask, looped low and breaking in elegant pools on the floor of the room, make a dramatic foundation to a Victorian-style room. Lace or muslin under-curtains make ideal partners for these imposing, heavy drapes, as they bring a light, delicate touch to the window treatment. The variety of cushions and Paisley shawls, the ottoman, the spoon-back buttoned chair, covered corner table, and Persian rug over the carpet complete the look. This interior is characterful and colourful, but the room does not feel too busy or claustrophobic.

Opposite By the late Victorian period, rooms were filled with colours, patterns, and all sorts of decorative objects in a striking style that is instantly recognizable. To achieve this eclectic but attractive look, mix together a variety of chintz patterns and Paisley material, with velvet, flock, and diaper-design wallpapers. You can even include kilim-covered furniture and Turkish and Persian rugs.

1. Dark velvets were much used for sprung upholstery in the late Victorian period, partnered with heavy trimmings and fringing.

2. Originally from India, Paisley shawls were immensely popular, both to wear and to drape over furniture and pianos.

3. All-over patterned wallpaper, as here, or a flock or raised relief paper which can be painted, are appropriate to the late nineteenth century.

4. This design is easier to incorporate than classic Victorian encaustic or majolica-glazed tiles. Tiles were much used in the Victorian period where hygiene was a concern.

5. Stained wooden floorboards or parquet-patterned floors should be left exposed around the perimeter of the rugs. Decorative carpets can be laid on top to complete the look.

Above A beaten copper fireplace incorporates a grate which was designed by the architect Charles Voysey. Copper ornaments, candlesticks, and a story picture in a beaten-copper frame are all typical of the period. However, the pottery and undecorated walls hint at a contemporary setting.

Opposite Here, period furniture and fittings are comfortably accommodated within a modern-style interior, proving that you can recreate an authentic look in a contemporary setting. Always choose colours and accessories that are appropriate. In this elegant room, subtle eau-de-nil paint and a rich blue carpet provide the perfect background to the hand-crafted oak furniture and copper paraphernalia.

Arts and Crafts Style

The opulence and mass-production of the last quarter of the nineteenth century resulted in a new appreciation for hand craftsmanship and a simpler decorative style. This style was greatly influenced by Medieval furniture, together with a belief in the virtue of stylistic unity. William Morris' name has become synonymous with the Arts and Crafts Movement through his wallpaper and fabric designs. In 1859 he commissioned The Red House by Philip Webb, which he built in the modern vernacular manner based on the English cottage and which set the standard for the Arts and Crafts style. This look has remained widely popular around the world, and is not difficult to achieve – many of Morris' timeless designs are still in production today.

The key is to recreate some of the distinctive elements of the style. These include decorative plaster work, Medieval-inspired stained glass windows or leaded cottage casements, bay-window seats, oriental rugs on parquet floors, and fireplace tiles with organic motifs in red-brick surrounds. Use squared panelling up to shoulder height and top it with a shelf, painted flat white, dull green, or green-blue, or even stained dark or varnished, and finish it off with a broad pictorial or floral frieze, or a stencil above. Alternatively, you can use a new-style wallpaper above the dado panel with a design of poppies, sunflowers, willow trails, or other abstract, organic forms. Authentic colours for walls and floors are sombre, including olive or sage green, ochre, deep blue, brown, and black. Heavy drapery was abandoned at this time in favour of simple, gathered curtains, often hung from rings on brass or wooden poles. Decorative objects influenced by the Orient are particularly appropriate, including blue and white porcelain, palm-leaf fans, and Japanese screens. Craft pottery as well as vases and mirrors in pewter, silver, copper, and brass are also in keeping with the style.

1. The muted colours and pattern of this tapestry fabric evoke the Medieval-style designs favoured by the Arts and Crafts Movement. A large cushion finished with an appropriate tasselled fringe would also be suitable.

2. This classic Morris design features fruits and thorns, and could be used to make dramatic window dressings, or in small amounts on cushions for a subtle effect. Morris favoured "flat" designs rather than patterns with a three-dimensional illusion which he considered "dishonest".

3. Arts and Crafts designers' materials were commercialized and many remain in production today. This William Morris design was block-printed using vegetable dyes. Use this design to add some colour to your Arts and Crafts room.

4. Willow-pattern wall- and ceiling-papers were very fashionable, and can be used today to provide an overall, rhythmical background to more elaborate patterns, including pictorial friezes.

5. Ceramic designers of the Arts and Crafts era began the creative process by making realistic drawings on which they based their tiles. This roses-and-trellis design combines pictorial and abstract elements and is typical of the style. This charming natural theme would add a fresh look to a kitchen, or why not use a small number of tiles in the living or dining room to enhance a plain dresser or fireplace?

1   2   3   4   5

In the Mackintosh Mood

Charles Rennie Mackintosh (1868–1928) was one of the most influential architect-designers of his time and the cool minimalism of the Mackintosh style works well with the pared-down interiors that are popular today. He moved away from the hand-crafted medievalism of the Arts and Crafts Movement and the ornate forms of the Art Nouveau style toward a geometric look that included elements of natural form. Mackintosh saw the house as an architectural whole, including the furnishings, and he also discriminated between "male" and "female" areas of the house. To achieve this look use plain or stencilled "feminine" white walls and furniture in the bedroom, drawing room, kitchen, and bathroom, and choose sturdy panelling and furniture for the "masculine" areas – the hall, stairwell, and dining room.

From 1900, Mackintosh designed many items, from house and garden furniture to friezes, stained glass, cutlery, silverware, light fittings, and carpets. Classic signatures of the style are elongated, austere forms, disciplined lineal shapes, Celtic motifs, and Zen-like restraint. In this style, designs are honed to a precise grid form, punctuating walls and floors with geometric, and sometimes Japanese, references. The shapes of ladder- and grid-backed chairs are echoed in the low-relief patterns, carving, and stencils used on walls. Mackintosh frequently used insets of stained or patterned opaque glass, so windows decorated with stained-glass are appropriate. Readily available glass paints and stained-glass kits allow you to transform your windows or glass objects. Curtains are not essential for this look, but if you want to use them, choose simple designs, perhaps headed with a flat fabric pelmet to complete the look.

Opposite Pure white creates a blank canvas for the room. The eye is drawn to the ladder-back chairs and the clean lines of the bed. The storage around the bed provides a solution to the problem of clutter. Pierced decoration suggests the Mackintosh style. Look for chrome artifacts and details with black and white furniture. White, black, grey, and touches of pink work well as foundation colours.

Left The hand-printed design on the curtains is echoed in the rose stencil. These semi-geometric shapes evolved from Art Nouveau forms. The table is Japanese in style and the chairs are composed of ladder shapes. The window seat has built-in book racks for storage. The slim columns have no structural purpose, but they provide a pleasing balance with the window detail.

1. This fabric should be combined with self-patterned materials or plain colours.

2. A wide paper frieze of sinuous design in the colours of Art Nouveau makes a useful addition to a room, placed above panelling or a picture rail.

3. Dark colours and stylized rose-and-leaf forms can add definition to a light colour scheme.

4. Brown, cream, and beige are ideal colours for walls, carpets, and upholstery fabrics. This paper hints at the designs favoured by Mackintosh.

5. Art glass and ceramics were favoured by Mackintosh. This tile's stylized tulip design can also be adapted for a wall stencil or fabric print.

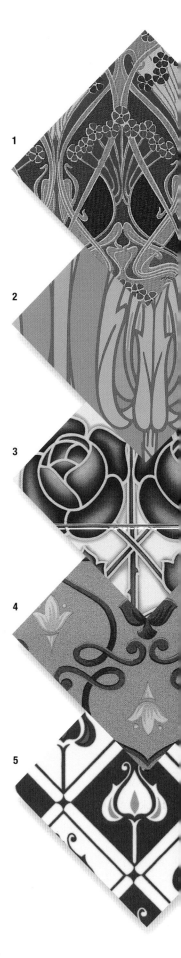

1

2

3

4

5

Country-Home Chintz

The early years of the twentieth century witnessed the building of a great number of large and comfortable country homes, both in Britain and the United States. Styles still hung on to elements of Arts and Crafts design, together with the matured "Queen Anne" look, alongside a touch of Art Nouveau or Rococo. These large houses often had extensive gardens which inspired great enthusiasm, not for the practical aspects of gardening but for the social pleasure that was to be found in walking in the garden. This meant that flowers became very fashionable, not just in the garden itself, but as decorative motifs within the home – a look that still endures today. In an attempt to capture the country-home look, there was a renewed interest in floral fabrics and wallpapers. The interior of the house was gradually becoming less cluttered than its Victorian forebears, displaying a mixture of past influences with a sprinkling of "modern" decorative innovations, such as a fashion for coordinated floral fabrics and wallpapers and the general use of white gloss paint and pastels.

To create the country-home look, use florals which are realistic in interpretation, with lots of bouquet-pattern chintz and cretonnes (unglazed chintz) twinned with matching wallpaper. Roses, lilac, wisteria, and sweet peas are suitable blossoms, especially when elaborately entwined within ribbons, trellis, and stripes. French woven silks embossed with floral patterns and an abundance of lace are also appropriate for this style. Choose upholstery that reveals the framework of the furniture and keep window treatments simple with a short pelmet and lace inner curtains. This gives a much-needed degree of privacy, particularly if the room is overlooked, while also allowing as much light as possible into the room. There was also a reaction against the darker colours which had remained popular over the last decades. Use whites and pastel colours for detailing or as an alternative to patterned wallpaper. Gas remained the main source of lighting, but now the lamps often had dainty fabric shades to diffuse the light and add another decorative element. This provides another opportunity for incorporating the pretty fabrics that are central to the country-home look in a modern setting.

Opposite A pretty floral pattern has been used for the bed, chair, and curtains in this bright, contemporary bedroom. The soft blue wall colour is not typical of the period, but makes an attractive background colour for four flower prints, neatly hung close together, and illustrates how a twenty-first-century twist can be brought to a traditional style. The striped pillowcases are modern, but the quilt is very much of the type seen in an Edwardian country house.

Below This bedroom is very much in keeping with the Edwardian country-house style. Naturalistic floral designs were often used extensively for furnishings, curtains, and bedcovers, together with a complementary wallpaper. However, here the walls are painted two shades of cream and the window curtains are of a different fabric to that used to adorn the bed. The result is a room that captures the flavour of the country-home look while remaining restrained.

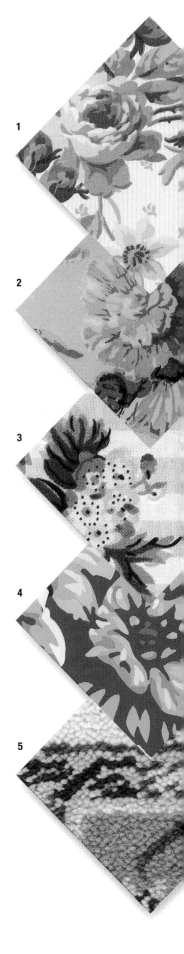

1. Realistically depicted flowers are a key element of Edwardian chintz. They are often held with ribbon and "laid" on a striped or small-patterned background.

2. Country-garden flowers were much in favour. Chairs and sofas were loose-covered and removable for cleaning, allowing lighter weight materials to be used.

3. Fabrics now come in many different colours as a result of more sophisticated chemical dyes and printing techniques. A material such as this can be used for curtains, bedcovers, and chairs.

4. A bold paper frieze was a popular feature of the Edwardian bedroom, and is a simple way of adding a little country-home flavour to a room.

5. Persian-pattern carpets and rugs were very much in fashion during the Edwardian period. Lay them over parquet flooring for an authentic look.

Jazz Age – Art Deco

The term "Art Deco" was coined in 1925 after an exhibition of the art and designs of a new industrial age. Art Deco was an antidote to the ornate curves of the Art Nouveau period and the austerity of the First World War. Also, fashionable, exotic clothing warranted a decorative background. Inspiration was taken from many sources. Early on, it was the Empire style and Chinese and African influences. Later, popular motifs were taken from Egyptian, African, and Aztec cultures, where designs and architectural references were incorporated with the use of pyramid and stepped shapes, stylized sun-rays and birds, fluted columns, and inset plaster-relief patterns and fine inlaid surfaces. The fashion for industrial and utilitarian objects produced new decorative uses for mirror and chrome, and interior architecture was as important to Art Deco as furnishings and decorations.

Use a geometric "Cubist" frieze or mural on cream or beige walls – Picasso and other Cubist artists had a great influence on interior design at the time. Upholstered furniture has exotic wood veneer while black lacquer or ebony pieces have chrome detail, and accessories are slick and angular. Colour combinations include grey, black and green, orange with brown, or cream with green, all with black highlights. Later colours were softer greens, pinks, and yellows. Abstract and geometric forms, especially circles intersected by lines, feature on carpets and fabrics. Parquet, linoleum, or faux-marble floors are ideal. Finish with alabaster, Lalique glass, Clarice Cliff ceramics, opaque uplighters in shell or fan shapes, and chrome globe lights.

Above An Art Deco-style living room shows geometrically patterned upholstery in classic colours of the period. An abstract-form carpet can be laid over parquet flooring. The asymmetric mottled-tile fire surround, stepped mirror, and wall light illustrate the contemporary admiration for design that was heavily influenced by modern industrial building materials.

Right Here, white walls provide the perfect backdrop to this elegant Art Deco dining room. The contrast between the walls and the dark wood is strong, but the room still retains a warm feel. Some decorators created entire rooms that were based on an all-white decorating theme. Recreating this ubiquitous, all-white look gives a room an up-to-date appearance as well as capturing the essential spirit of the Art Deco period.

1. Abstract design with a Futuristic bias related to the new industry and materials of the mid-1920s onward. Keep colours muted, with brown, beige, and white as the mainstay theme.

2. Materials with a sensual quality, such as animal fur, leather, and cut pile, are appropriate. Use a rich gold-and-brown fabric to upholster a sofa or simply as a cushion.

3. There are many fake-fur fabrics available, which can be used to great effect, particularly as spectacular and sensual bedspreads and cushions.

4. Influenced by newly-fashionable safari trips to Africa, animal-skin rugs were in vogue. Use animal patterns to add a note of exoticism.

5. Designs loosely based on flowers, bows, and fans were all popular. A running frieze of these tiles in a bathroom will produce a zigzag effect.

1

2

3

4

5

Above The colours and textures used in this striking living room illustrate the qualities favoured by the Art Deco period and show that this style can be translated in a modern way. Popular colours for this period are chocolate brown, cream, and yellow, especially when used together. Keep wall finishes sleek and smooth. Imitate authentic leather or suede wallcoverings using faux-finish wallpaper. The settee and table are typical examples of this period's blend of upholstery, chrome, and wood. The interior also features an animal-skin rug, which was very much in favour at the time. As the 1930s progressed, this look became increasingly identified with technology and speed, and many designs were based on aerodynamic lines. You can recreate this effect using mirrors, tables, and other items of sleek furniture.

Country Choices

There is no decorative style that conveys a more comfortable and comforting aura than the quintessential country look. When we think of country-style interiors we instantly visualize a warm, comforting hearth, slightly shabby but immensely snug sofas in faded floral chintz, and age-patinated antiques creaking under the weight of faded family photographs and dusty treasured mementos. However, there is more to country choices than just this clichéd picture and a broader spectrum of decorative ideas can be employed to provide a more accessible and contemporary style. When we look at the components of the country look, each has a particular role to play in the overall effect, and choices can be made according to which is suitable and plausible. Choosing appropriate fabrics, particularly florals and checks, provides the foundation for contemporary country style; antiques can be chosen not for their monetary value but for their decorative contribution to a room; and decorative line and colour are intrinsic to comfort or atmosphere, whether you favour the spartan aesthetic of the Shaker interior or the textured earthiness of rustic furniture and fabrics.

The joy of the country look is that there is great potential and freedom to mix ingredients to produce a wholesome entity. Antique decorative objects associate as well with colour-washed plaster walls and rush matting as they do with chintz and panelling; a jolly red gingham and a bright floral fabric make an equally fine pairing with either painted wicker or polished oak; hessian and flagstone, sailcloth and brass, tweed and old pine will sit together in harmony. Make the most of the view from your windows and the natural habitat. Make the best use of whatever is indigenous to the environment around you: decorate your home with pine cones or locally found flowers, or look for driftwood or pretty pebbles during seaside walks.

Antique Inspiration

Using antiques as a purely decorative component of your chosen interior style is very different to acquiring serious pieces that are valuable works of art in their own right. Decorative antiques are valuable as a result of the contribution they make to the overall style of their location. They can be found in the local flea market, in reclamation yards, or at country sales. When choosing objects, decide whether the item will contribute to the atmosphere, whether it looks appropriate in its new home, and if its colour, tone, and texture relate to other "ingredients" that will be placed around it. Small kitchen utensils are ideal for adding a little antique, country flavour as they are easy to place within the room. Look for attractive carved dishes, chopping boards, ladles, and pails. Storage boxes and plate racks, baskets, and bird cages all have interesting shapes and textures, so look out for any everyday accessories with strong visual appeal. Small items can look lost when they are placed in isolation, so group them together to maximize their combined impact, or place them singly within a small area with objects of similar style and quality.

Old wood is a natural and accessible choice for the country interior. The variety of natural wood colours means that it is easy to choose pieces in a shade that will enhance the overall decorative scheme. The subtle patina of wood looks wonderful placed against other rough textures, such as raw stone, granite, and tiling, which are all typical elements of the country interior. Throughout, choose warm, natural colours to complement the antique, country theme. Ceramics provide an inexpensive method of enriching the country interior – the pine dresser overflowing with plates, dishes, cups, and jugs is a quintessential part of the cosy, country look. Pay close attention to the colour and period of the china you are displaying, as careful placement will do much to create a sense of harmonious presentation, especially if the other colours used in the room are linked. Antique textiles will also help to convey the country feel; old French linen, gingham, and traditional tea-towels have an inimitable country quality. Use faded pieces of English floral chintz to create charming light shades, seat squabs, and napkins to complete the look.

1

2

3

4

5

Above The warm, muted colours of this period-style English kitchen make an ideal backdrop to the subtle shades and textures of all the wooden objects and the well-loved chair, which is a focal point in the room. The allusion to time-gone-by is accentuated by the lack of any visible modern kitchen equipment and the integration of antique pieces that are of a similar texture.

Left A broad and serviceable mahogany-grained dresser makes a suitably weighty showcase for a varied collection of platters, plates, dishes, and mugs. There are many different styles and shapes, but all of them have a floral theme and similar colour tones. This provides a dramatic but balanced display, without appearing cluttered.

1. Traditional wool crewelwork is as contemporary in style today as it has ever been because the design is so easy to mix with modern styles. These muted colours are perfect for an antique setting.

2. Medieval tapestries are now reproduced in adaptable cotton. These make appropriate and visually interesting companions to traditional dark wood, pewter, and old stone.

3. *Toile de Jouy* prints are now available in a variety of single colours. They add an historical flavour and mix well with the strong colours of eighteenth-century porcelain.

4. The antique quality of this fabric is helped by the choice of colour as well as the design itself. The muted, soft tones of pink, green, and beige linen in a flowing design would look wonderful used with country-style furniture and rustic rush matting.

5. A hint of green in this sisal matting gives a sophisticated edge to this particular rustic weave, making it appropriate for a hallway or country drawing room.

Shaker Style

Unlike some other religious sects, the Shaker community had contact with the outside world from trading, and interest in their architecture, furnishings, and lifestyle continues to flourish thanks to copies of their exquisitely crafted, simple furniture and utility items, and an interior style that is simple, elegant, and easily copied. Known as "Shakers" because of the physicality of their worshipping, an original band of eight dissident Quakers from Manchester, England, sailed to America in May 1774 and established a community along the eastern seaboard that grew to about 6,000 at its peak in 1850.

The Shaker philosophy of equality, modesty, confession, and faith was built on the foundation that everything was done in the sight of God, and so a chair back should be as perfect as the front; the inside of a drawer as finely finished as the outside. In adopting their vernacular style and eschewing "vain" ornament, the Shakers unwittingly created a new design aesthetic based on tidiness and clever use of natural colour.

To recreate a typical Shaker-style interior, keep the room minimal, uncluttered, restrained, and always scrupulously clean. Everything possible should be put away, folded up, or hung on the ubiquitous wall peg rail. Adhering to the founder of the movement's maxim that "there is no dirt in heaven", multi-drawer storage was usually built into the wall, and chairs were hung upside down so that dust did not accumulate on their seats.

Above The timeless elegance of Shaker craftsmanship is still found in modern copies, which remain extremely popular. Chairs were mostly made from maple, but were also crafted in burr and birdseye woods, cherry, birch, and walnut, depending on what types of wood were available locally. Tint plain plaster walls to a warm biscuit or dusty pink.

Right The peg rail and the authentic-coloured kitchen storage are typical of the Shaker kitchen. The Shakers invented enclosed box or panel stoves, but a range cooker offers a modern alternative. Keep window treatments simple, using muslin or plain cotton. Kitchen equipment should be as basic and well-crafted as possible, and keep clutter to a minimum.

1. Fabrics were only important to the Shaker community for commerce – they sold a variety of woollen cloths, flannel shirts, and knitted socks to the outside world. For added interest, you can use a simple cotton stripe to recreate the plain Shaker style.

2. Use a slub voile at the windows to make short, unadorned curtains. Look for textured, rustic-looking fabrics in plain, natural colours or simple patterns to use in your home. This beige linen has a befitting earthiness, and adds colour without being too showy.

3. Hinting at traditional American homey checks, this interesting cotton sheer fabric adds a restrained element of pattern and alludes to the code of Shaker modesty. Sheers are ideal for adding a touch of subtle pattern to any understated scheme.

4. Greens and blues were possibly the most popular among the palette of pigment colours used by the Shakers for paints, dyes, and stains. Striped wallpaper could be used to recreate the effect of authentic, painted boarding, which was used throughout the home.

5. Grey-green and blue-green paint is ideal for interior woodwork, especially in the window area. The Shakers used it to add embellishment without adding ostentatious decoration. Too much fancy decoration was thought to be sinfully "vain".

1   2   3   4   5

There are a number of items that will make your Shaker-style room instantly recognizable. The Shaker chair design has become a style icon: slightly backward-leaning, with double rungs on three sides, it has three back slats, a rush or wood-strip seat, and turned finials at the top of the rear posts. You can also choose chests of drawers, blanket chests, and storage chests which all exemplify the Shaker cabinet-making skills, or a simple stand to place beside a rocking chair, made with three splayed legs and a round or square top complete with a drawer. The "nice box" is another key object and is invaluable for storing small items in the modern home. It was originally made from steamed wood, with swallowtail detail on the side, and used for storage.

For all the utilitarian simplicity of the Shaker way of life, colour was extremely important. Wood stains were often used, not because of their decorative qualities but because of the belief that there was colour in Heaven. Deep red or yellow ochre and muted colours of blues and greens are all appropriate colours to use. The floor should be plain and uncluttered – varnished wooden floors are ideal – and allow in as much natural light as possible.

Left Elements of Settler and Shaker domestic philosophy are evident in this modern American living room. The cross-boarded walls are painted blue-green – which is typical of the colours favoured by the Shakers. An antique Shaker table with a single drawer stands on the right and a "nice box" sits on the table on the left. The red-painted settee is flanked by a pair of tables covered in simple, tailored calico covers which, along with the many pillows, soften the look. A pair of rustic earthenware jars have been converted into lamps and two antique strip and patchwork cushion covers pick up the colours used in the scheme.

Opposite This simple wooden rocking chair has little adornment but makes a strong impact within the room. Look for single pieces of furniture or decorative objects that will suggest a Shaker theme. This elegant chair and table could be at home in any room in the house.

1. The Shakers enjoyed using colour in a discreet manner. This dark red and buff stripe fits into the appropriate colour range.

2. Use materials in a simple manner with no extra trimming or frills to maintain the Shaker philosophy of plain living.

3. and 4. Use paint to recapture the distinctive colours of the Shaker house. Blue and red were popular for walls and furnishings.

5. The Shakers wove fabric for commercial sale, using natural-pigment dyes. This gives all Shaker colours a desirable earthy quality that echoes their handcrafts.

1

2

3

4

5

Homey Checks

With their charm and versatility, checked and striped materials make easy companions within any decorative setting, whether it has a traditional or contemporary look. However, they are most frequently associated with a particular "country" look which conjures up an informal, homey style that translates into its own decorative language according to its country of origin. From American homespun cottons to French heavy linen checks, from cool Swedish blues in checks and stripes to bright-red English gingham, these materials have historically been the cloth of bonnets and sheets, tablecloths and aprons, bedspreads, and curtains. In a contemporary setting, the huge range of colours and designs allows the creation of a country style that can be as simply minimalist or as elegantly sophisticated as you wish. One of the keys to an effective combination of stripes and checks is to balance the scale of designs and the weight of colour distribution. Checks and stripes are most effective when used in close proximity; for example, one as the curtain and another as the window blind, or one as the bed-spread and the other for the bolsters. It is also beneficial to introduce an unrelated "soft" design – a floral rug or toile tablecloth perhaps – as a visual contrast to the symmetry of geometric lines. It is best to use the simpler designs available, perhaps with the introduction of a flower or stylized motif within the check or stripe, keeping in mind that certain colours and designs lean toward a particular national look.

Right A combination of different designs, from simplest gingham to sophisticated floral stripes, balances colour distribution with areas of neutral white for contrast.

Below left Single-tone blue and white recreates a Swedish interior using a checked cotton rug as the design key. The day-bed is covered in a simple check, with a striped fringed throw, and floral cushion for contrast.

Below The eye is drawn to the window drapes. Accessories, such as the scallop-edged tablecloth and china, provide pleasing colour.

1. When using stripes as part of a "country" look, small, neat designs make an appropriate foil to checks and ginghams. Remember that stripes influence a room's visual proportions.

2. This traditional, two-tone blue check can be dressed up or down to fit in with any scheme.

3. Introducing a floral motif within the check gives the traditional design a new lift and hints at a more sophisticated look.

4. Blue is a cool colour which is affected by the availability of natural light. This should be kept in mind when deciding on colour combinations.

5. A floral stripe is useful for softening the effect of strong vertical and horizontal lines and introducing a third element while retaining visual continuity.

1

2

3

4

5

Faded Florals

Floral materials and papers have provided the inspiration for interior decorative schemes for hundreds of years. The flower has always had a place within the decorative vocabulary, and today we still use some of the same designs and floral references that appeared four hundred years ago.

However, the particular fashion for using faded florals is a relatively modern one. In recent years a number of textiles and wallpapers have been produced that convey the comfort and continuity of the country-home look using relaxed, even slightly shabby, chic. One of the most attractive characteristics of floral chintz is that after years of everyday use and exposure to natural light the glaze wears off and the original colours fade to soft mellowness, which creates a lovely "authentic" country-home effect. The soft outline and colours of these materials are far less strident and dominant than the ubiquitous highly glazed chintzes, and can therefore be more easily blended into a decorative scheme using other patterned materials and embellishments. Antique fabrics are consequently in great demand for country-style decorative schemes, but their rarity can have the effect of making these fabrics difficult to acquire and also relatively expensive. Fortunately more and more manufacturers are now imitating the faded-floral look and producing artificially aged fabrics. It is possible to treat new chintz yourself to achieve the desired effect using a tea bath and a scrub, but this can be a messy process and a good result is not guaranteed, so generally it is better to buy new, pre-aged fabrics.

To make the most of your faded florals it is vital to maintain a muted palette throughout the room, as these fabrics will look drab if they are partnered with primary colours or strongly defined patterns. Keep your paint colours muted as well, using off-whites and faded colours for the best effect. The balance and harmony of colours and design is particularly important when using faded florals. Mix different-sized patterns and interplay these with a stripe or textured material to add visual interest and make the most of your carefully chosen florals. Experiment with patterns from various periods and styles to create your own look.

1   2   3   4   5

1. The soft light of the northern hemisphere suits the faded colours in this linen-and-cotton print, suited to curtains and upholstery. Use contrasting piping for a good outline.

2. An Italian-flavoured linen union in Rococo style could cover a pretty sofa or be made up into large cushions as its cartouche design is very similar to tapestry.

3. A damask design is given a new look with an overlaid soft, stencil pattern. This makes it less grand and more easily mixed with other patterns and colours.

4. This cotton sheer has an unusual, coloured rose design that looks ethereal when the light shines through it and into the room. No other curtaining is required.

5. During the eighteenth century, Aubusson tapestry weavers started to make carpets, and these beautiful carpets are now famous throughout the world. Here, fine patterning is a natural partner for faded florals. You can add a floral touch to your floors using fitted carpets or even a small rug for a more subtle effect.

Left The faded-floral look should mix various periods and styles of chintz, needlepoint, carpet, and wallpaper to create an evolved, lived-in atmosphere, which is rich in texture and glorious pattern.

Above You can mix any amount of floral fabrics but keep the tonal range compatible to build harmoniously layer on layer. Here, cushions made from left-over pieces of material combine with a pretty, faded, handmade quilt for an eclectic look.

Rustic Weaves

Exploring the textural relationships of materials, furnishings, and decorative artifacts is an important exercise in the development of a satisfyingly complete style. Texture adds a sensual dimension to the colour, shape, and proportion of a room's elements and greatly influences its decorative character and aesthetic impact. Often, contrasting textures are put together to accentuate their tactile differences, and weaves make a sensational foil for sophisticated materials. However, for the purposes of the country style illustrated here, it is perhaps more appropriate to explore the essential rustic nature of woven furniture, materials, and flooring, and combining them with muted colours.

One advantage of this style is that the components are inexpensive and there is a great choice of materials available. Wicker, willow, rattan, and cane furniture, for example, is traditionally made in Indonesia, India, China, and England, and the countless different styles suit any given situation. The patterns and patina of these chairs need an artless companion in the form of a heavy material, perhaps linen or hessian. Alternatively, a light, summery contrast could be provided by a seat or throw of simple pure linen or perhaps softly faded floral upholstery.

Natural flooring will also accentuate the rural concept, so use sisal, coir, seagrass, rush, or any other natural woven matting to add to the rustic flavour. Simple split-bamboo blinds or a plain, loose-weave muslin curtain can carry the textured theme to the windows. Accessories such as woven screens, baskets, table mats, platters, and bowls will all help to draw the scheme together.

Left A wicker chair has been given summer clothing with a muslin slip cover which allows the shape of the chair to be visible. The dado has been decorated with a simple and effective checkerboard pattern, while heavy rush matting adds rustic emphasis.

Right The earthy colours and intricate patterns of these wicker chairs are mixed with reclaimed timber walls, a Shaker children's chair, and a table covered in a hessian throw topped with pristine linen.

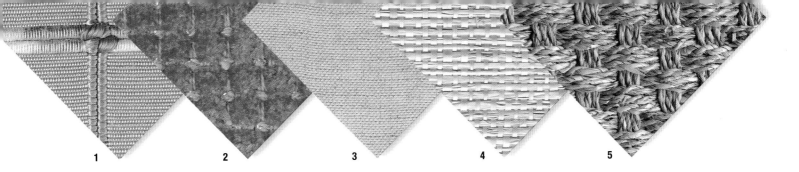

1   2   3   4   5

1. Texture contrasts make a tactile update on a traditional check. Woven in silk, it manages to be simultaneously rustic and sophisticated.

2. This rust-and-putty cut-pile fabric would add a colourful and comforting quality for upholstery or as large, soft cushions.

3. The bee, a symbol of endeavour and of productivity, is very appropriate to the rustic theme for a plain window treatment or even as a bed drape.

4. A natural raffia wallpaper provides a textured and unusual background which needs no other ornamentation.

5. Indian matting has been exported since the late eighteenth century. This grass weave makes an ideal flooring material.

Relaxed Country

The relaxed-country interior owes its popularity to the fact that it looks as if it has evolved over time, rather than having been decorated in one session. This allows you to incorporate favourite country-style pieces without adhering too closely to set rules. Although the style is essentially an "undesigned" one, this is not the easiest way to decorate, as it relies on instinct and on intuition rather than on regular design rules. However, it is fun, adaptable, and flexible. It is possible to mix different ingredients as long as you get the balance of flavours right. As in cooking, experimentation and tasting as you go are the keys to success. First decide on a finish for the walls and flooring which will accommodate other elements of the scheme comfortably. As this is a country theme, exploit any rustic element within the architectural fabric to cultivate the look. If the floorboards are in good condition, they could be sanded, filled, painted, and sealed. If the walls are to be painted, choose a favourite country colour – light green, perhaps, or lavender, or primrose yellow – that will make an impact in sunlight or candlelight, as well as belonging to a contemporary palette. Furniture and fabrics can be as varied in age and style as you like. Embracing country and contemporary style is perfect for mixing a rustic look with glass and chrome, jazzy floral fabrics with a quarry tile floor, or wire-fronted kitchen cabinets with polished steel work-tops. Colours can be many and varied, too, as long as there is an echo of the colour range running through the scheme as a visual anchor.

Above In a small guest room which is dominated by a chunky, custom-made bed, the timber-clad walls are painted a soft blue as a soothing background colour, while the rustic element of wood is accentuated by pine flooring and the unpainted pine bed. A neat bedside-table arrangement on one side and a sculpture and cupboard on the other make good use of the limited space available and add extra visual interest to the room.

Opposite This informal kitchen contains an eclectic mixture of furniture and objects, all jostling together, very much in the manner of the unfitted kitchen. Storage and work space are essential in any kitchen, and this kitchen has them in abundance, provided by various cupboards in plain and painted pine and a pair of Victorian tables – which are now painted cream and blue. The canary-yellow walls provide a jolly background.

1. This is a check with a contemporary twist that is ideal for upholstery or curtains. Using a neutral principal material makes it easier to add more colour elsewhere, if required.

2. This soft yellow check paper has a French look that alludes to summer sun and country kitchens. Use equal colour intensity when combining yellows to avoid clashing.

3. Pictorials are an amusing way of giving a decorative scheme a sense of place and style. However, a little will probably go a long way, so do not over-use this wallpaper design.

4. Dogs and fish make an appropriate design for this earthily coloured upholstery material which would suit a family room. The yellow could be picked out as a background wall colour.

5. Although it is a traditional fabric with a long history, gingham is contemporary and adaptable to any interior scheme, depending on how it is dressed up or down.

1   2   3   4   5

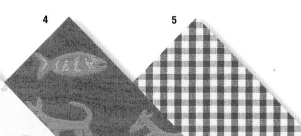

Global Choices

Since the great expansion of nineteenth-century globalism brought easier communication and access to travel for the masses, we have been profoundly influenced by the potential of international design within our lifestyles and home environments. Quite apart from the delightful culinary and cultural effects, we are able to adopt and adapt elements of global design to suit all environments, from the chic cosmopolitan setting to the most spiritual retreat. These influences are partly born from sentiment – a romantic holiday in Tuscany or a safari adventure in Kenya perhaps – but they are also connected with the artistic and individualistic potential they offer to a different culture and locality. Everyone can carry something home from another land and environment whether it be a bunch of dried lavender from Provence, a terracotta pot from Tuscany, an ornate carpet from Morocco, a length of sari silk from India, a lacquered tray from Japan, a bamboo sunshade from Bali, or even the ubiquitous straw donkey from Mexico. These emblems trigger a response to that country's indigenous style which can be used to create a sense of place and style in your own home.

Given that the adopted environment will be utterly different to the source of inspiration, it is important to focus on creating an aura that captures the essence rather than imitates the look of the chosen country itself. Experiment with a variety of colours, textures, patterns, and shapes to find those that exude the desired sense of place. Seek out the quintessential, fundamental fabric that embodies the particular decorative feel of your chosen style. Be creative in your search for the right materials; a clever combination of colours can do much to recreate a particular national look. Exploit the fundamental attributes of the interior in terms of structure, light, and position as a foundation for more exotic ornamentation.

At Home in Provence

What we call the French style has been greatly influenced by the region of Provence. Although this area is drenched in brilliant Mediterranean colours and rich in texture, interiors can be cooler and more temperate in their ingredients when this uniquely French look is translated from the south to other rural and urban environments beyond and abroad. However, there are some key elements that can be used to create a similar character. This style should not look as if it has been studiously decorated but rather that it has come together naturally over a period of time. Balance colours rather than co-ordinating them. You can use several colours in the same room – traditional Provençal cottons mix mustard, cherry red, russet, and blue in a mass of intricate pattern. Apply grey-green and grey-blue matt paint to simple off-white walls for a splash of colour. Checks of all sorts are appropriate used together in several different colours and styles. Keep flooring as simple as possible using bare boards or quarry tiles. Choose accessories that look as if they have been collected or inherited and are well loved and well used. Use country-style furniture – the Bentwood chair is ideal, as are high-backed, rush-seated chairs and dainty, painted bedroom chairs. If possible, include a fruitwood or walnut armoire, stacked with linen or china, and another painted cupboard with fabric panels. In the bedroom, lay iron bedsteads and box beds with bedclothes of lace and flowers, patchwork, and linen, and mix several colours and designs together. A painted-pine washstand and a vase of casually arranged flowers add the finishing touches.

1. Every French house seems to have an unusual check or stripe incorporated into the decoration. This printed herringbone cotton stripe is typical of the kind used.

2. Cushions made from this pretty patterned silk would make a delicate contrast to plain upholstery or checks which have the same background colour.

3. Another small floral motif, this time in wallpaper, picks up on the colours so often seen in French interiors. This paper would suit a bedroom well.

4. Flower and check patterns appear often in French decoration. This pretty cream and pink cotton is suitable for rustic or sophisticated urban schemes alike.

5. A wallpaper design with a typical Provençal pattern. Bright colours need careful placing where the light is strongest to look their very best.

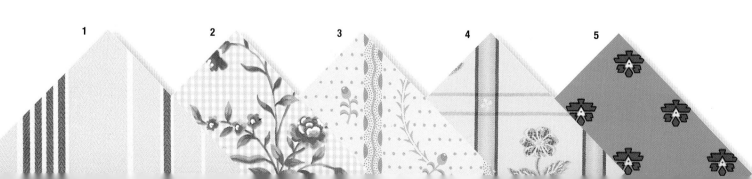

1   2   3   4   5

Opposite The traditional blue-and-white-check linen tablecloth contrasts with a small, red-check cupboard lining and soft sage-green paintwork in this Dordogne dining room. The high-backed chairs are typically French, although these are rather grander than some. The Swedish and Moroccan glasses and ornate antique candelabra enrich the eclectic mixture.

Right Matt-cream colour washed walls contrast with the Mediterranean blue paintwork covering the radiator and dado level. Delicately patterned bedcovers and linen soften the severe lines of the antique bedstead. Instead of a mosquito net, a pretty Provençal cotton could be used. Casually displayed plates, an antique washstand, dressing mirror, and water carrier filled with flowers complete the scheme.

Above Subtle and earthy colours and textures are brought together in an atmospheric dining room. The terracotta walls and tiled floor are key elements, here combined with a sophisticated damask, Italian antique candelabra, and theatrical urns. Elaborate damask curtains add a palatial flourish. To create a simpler interpretation of the theme, choose large terracotta flowerpots, unlined curtains, and rustic candlesticks.

Opposite Often there is no need for window curtains, especially when there are wooden shutters to use in the winter. This simple bedroom features a brick floor and plain, waxed furniture. The antique wrought-iron bedstead is adorned by an Indian bedspread which introduces a complementary mix of colours. The warm glow of the wall colour prevents the setting from looking too austere and unwelcoming.

Travels in Tuscany

The region of Tuscany is one of Italy's greatest attractions and most unique treasures. It has an atmosphere of great serenity in its rich beauty, variety, and history. With its high ceilings and tiled floors, the authentic Tuscan interior is more dramatic than an English country interior and more formal than the French Provençal style, but its colours, textures, and simplicity make it gentle on the eye and easy to emulate.

The Tuscan house is typically low, stone-built with a stuccoed façade painted soft pink or yellow ochre. Green or blue slatted shutters shade the windows and attractive, wavy terracotta roof tiles and a vine-covered terrace echo the curves and colours of the surrounding vineyards. To recapture the look, choose interior decoration led by the warm, comforting colours and textures of the Tuscan countryside: terracotta, yellow ochre, or burnt sienna are washed over rough-plastered walls or applied in layers so that the changing light plays tricks with the colour. Take your inspiration from nature for the paintwork, too; choose grey-green thyme, and grey-blue lavender, and use them in strong, solid blocks of flat, chalky colour. If you use curtains, they should be made of lightweight, floaty, plain fabrics. Alternatively, use stripes in combinations of yellow and blue, or red and green; floral fabrics are rarely used. Look for bedsteads and day beds made from curving wrought iron, or chests and chairs painted a soft, antique yellow with garlands of flowers and ribbons in translucent colours. Tapestry wall hangings and banners portraying a coat of arms are all appropriate.

1. The contrast between rough plaster walls and beautiful materials epitomizes the romantic Tuscan style. Even the simplest banner curtain of silk taffeta will look effective.

2. A red and gold heavy damask would make a dramatic single curtain, long enough to pool on the floor when held by a tie-back.

3. The sinuous pattern on this upholstery fabric brings to mind Italian Renaisssance decoration, grapevines, and antique wrought-iron work.

4. The colour and patina of Tuscan terracotta is provided by the unique local clay. However, unglazed quarry tiles are easily found in many styles and sizes and make attractive, durable flooring.

5. Natural earth pigments tint limewash with subtle rich colours. Generously applied to raw plaster or masonry, limewash gives a matt finish that is bright in good light, darker in poor light conditions.

Moroccan Magic

The distinctive, traditional courtyarded homes of Morocco employ interior colour and ornamentation to create the distinction between the wealthy and humble dwelling. The use of earthily sensual and jewel-bright decorative combinations enriches the exuberant architecture of the typical Moroccan house. In contrast, its façade offers no clue to its hidden domestic character.

Translating the Moroccan style to a contemporary interior in a different climate requires sensitivity, so when you are planning your room think about the overall design concept, balance of colour, and the effect of natural and artificial lighting, as these will all affect the finished look. The interior decoration should reflect the textures, colours, and contrasts of a bustling souk. Paint walls with chalky pigment-tinted limewash, and embellish them using the delicate ornamentation of tile, mosaic, inlay, and intricately painted surfaces. Exquisite decorative plasterwork and screens also embody the style. Ceilings – and sometimes whole rooms – can be made of painted wood. For soft furnishings, choose similarly rich contrasts of colour and texture; robust rugs of complex religious and tribal geometric symbolism make colourful patchworks on the floor and can be used to cover tables and seating. Throw ethnic cottons over low beds and use heavily textured weaves as covers for the essential, lean-on scatter cushions.

Left A curtained bathroom storage area is provided in this theatrical interpretation of an entrance to a stall in the souk. Heavy, dark drapes contrast with the ochre of the inner curtains and traditional rug. Dark-green paintwork, stencilling, and ethnic tie-backs complete the look.

Right A screen wall with a "Moroccan" window sets the scene in this bathroom. Earthy colours and textures are essential, as is detailing. Note the subtle lighting and a choice of decorative ingredients, such as the fretted sconce, painted bamboo table, and natural flooring.

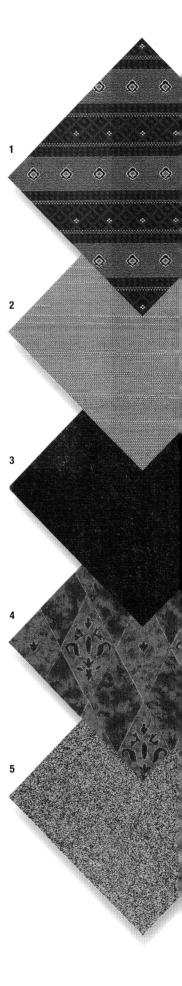

1. Moroccan rugs may be identified by their specific regional pattern, weave, and colour, but for contemporary decorative purposes, earthy colours and strong geometric designs will work well.

2. and 3. Texture is more important than other considerations when making fabric choices. Pure cottons or linens – the heavier and rougher the better – are the natural choices. Mix at least two earthy colours, remembering that dark materials work best in a dark room, brighter colours in a light room.

4. Use a geometric patterned fabric to add visual interest to a Moroccan scheme. Use small amounts for a subtle effect or larger quantities for a more dramatic effect.

5. Tiles can feature in every Moroccan room, from bedroom to living room. In contemporary design, they are best used in a more practical way in the bathroom and kitchen to add a hint of North African traditional style.

1

2

3

4

5

Safari Style

Evoking the tribal spirit of the great plains of Africa in a Western interior might sound implausible, but there are many elements that could be adapted to create a room which is both aesthetically pleasing and practical. The choice of fabrics is crucial to establish this look, and many designers have produced attractive interpretations of tribal African textiles. The most effective of these appear to have been simply hand stamped using natural-pigment dyes on heavy cottons or calicos, in geometric and traditional designs. Focusing on one material and introducing the other decorative elements and objects with discretion is always a successful approach. The primitive exuberance of tribal basketware, pottery, and carving looks equally sensational displayed against a dark, ebonized background or a "muddy" plaster wall. Paint finishes can be chosen which broadly imitate the textures and colours that would be found in a rural African interior, but you might dare to paint a wall in broad earth-coloured zigzags or arrange brightly coloured wirework baskets on a home-made painted corrugated-cardboard shelf. Paint effects should imitate traditional matt, earthy pigments; alternatively, textured wallpapers that imitate grass fibre can be used to good effect. Cane and wicker seating and a fake zebra- or leopard-fur throw will add a colonial touch, while coir matting on the floor is practical and appropriate. Bedrooms simply need an ethnic bedcover, a pretty diaphanous drape in place of a mosquito net, and a pair of storm lanterns instead of candlestick bedside lights.

Left An ebonized ash dresser with copper detail makes a strong backdrop to a collection of African basketware and Afghan pottery. The display allows each item its own space and contribution. The dining table is covered with a raffia runner.

Right The sombre tones of this living room copy the colours of mud walls, ebony, and rush matting. The light from the uncurtained windows highlights the sofa area with its geometric textiles and a table which was once a camel saddle. The striking obelisk is inscribed with Islamic text.

1. Alluding to an ethnic style, rather than trying to imitate it, allows greater flexibility and practicality. This exotic fabric will set the mood.

2. Although you can use strong pictorial or graphic designs in the same room, keep them in separate areas, using plain fabrics and colours between the designs.

3. This textured sheer with a feathered stripe woven through it would make a dramatic alternative to mosquito netting over a bed.

4. Providing a suitably sandy backdrop to the African theme, this subtle colour-washed paper adds just the right depth of warmth.

5. A giraffe-skin pattern on sisal makes an amusing change to traditional matting. Sisal is produced from the Mexican agave plant and produces a smooth, closely woven finish.

Indian Spice

India is a continent full of contrasts. From the Himalayan villages to the scorching heart-land of the Great Plain, and from the green and fertile valleys of the Rivers Indus and Ganges to the hot bustle of its cities, the whole country is a tapestry of overwhelming sound, smell, movement, and shape; it is not surprising that there is a wealth of inspiration to create a decorative kaleidoscope in a contemporary Western setting.

Colour and decoration have always been used to define India's diverse culture, from the richly embroidered luxury of the palace hotels to the tattered bright *ganesh* normally hung over a humble door to frighten the devil. Decorate entrances with richly ornamented surrounds – bannered, painted, inlaid, tiled, or sculptured in terracotta. Cover plain floors with dhurries and add traditional mirrored textiles and fabrics woven with metal thread which illuminate the shadows. In Rajasthan's arid landscape, houses are decked with intricate murals or full of vibrant, make-do ornamentation, vivid textiles, and exotic, symbolic jewellery – a look that can be recreated in any room in the house. The continent that yields exquisite Udaipur miniature paintings also yields the technicolour gaudiness of painted cardboard and lightbulbs, broken china, and tin packaging as ornamentation, so look for objects that you could use to decorate your room. The people of the annually flooded Gujarat district decorate their temporary homes with complex finger moulding made from white clay, while the Orissa people use rice paste as a decorarive white paint to elevate their rice-straw homes into works of art with blossoms, flowering vines, pyramids of grain, and stylized paddy fields. Choose elements from these diverse styles to add some Indian flavour to your home.

Left A modern living room is enriched with a ceiling of traditional wedding awnings called *ras mandel*, which give the room a tented, festive look. The walls are hung with bright, mirror-spangled *ganesh*, normally hung over a door to frighten off the devil. A strip-work rug and crewelwork fabric covering the sofa complete the ethnic decoration. As a cooling contrast, white is chosen for the walls, floor, and some of the upholstery. This is an excellent idea when using hot colours together. "Colonial"-style furniture in natural materials is an appropriate concession for a modern scheme.

Opposite Furniture was introduced for the convenience of the British Colonialists because most Indians sit, eat, and sleep on the floor, bringing out mattresses or charpoys as needed. Here, a thin platform supports the central eating, sitting, and sleeping area, made luxurious with its piles of silk, satin, and embroidered cushions. The warmly coloured walls accentuate the exotic atmosphere along with candles, incense, and 1960s-style posters.

1. A pictorial document fabric in a muted colourway provides an opportunity to create an aura of India without gaudiness. Pick out the deep red and old gold elsewhere in the scheme.

2. This vibrant upholstery fabric will set the scene, combined with lots of different coloured silk cushions. Alternatively, a length of material with added tassels can be hung on the wall or looped from the ceiling.

3. Kashmir crewelwork is beautiful, textural, and adaptable to many interior styles. This version has a classic Indian design and is suitable for curtains, cushions, and bedspreads.

4. Jaipur is known as the Pink City and Jodphur as the Blue City because of the predominant house colours. Natural limewash can only be used on raw, porous surfaces, not over other paints or paper.

5. Indian doorways are often carved in a "peacock tail" design, to which this tile alludes. Indian enamel decoration was traditionally used over whole rooms.

1

2

3

4

5

Asiatic Elements

In all senses, bamboo is the staple building material of Indonesia, the Philippines, Thailand, and Malaysia, so it is quite simple to recreate the look in your own home. In all these countries it is recognised as a versatile material with both practical and aesthetic qualities. In Thailand, for example, the houses are predominantly made of bamboo and thatch. They are built on stilts with a frame of stout bamboo rods with woven mats for walls. Where hardwood is used, it is richly carved or ornamented with painting and gilding in a traditional manner. Choose split rattan, canes, and wicker for blinds, and other items to create moveable, informal partitions. The open, airy architecture sometimes includes roll-up blinds instead of solid walls. This is a useful way of dividing up modern multi-purpose rooms while capturing the Asiatic look. Keep furniture and clutter to a minimum, and choose pieces that are low to the floor.

Ubiquitous woven cane mats are quite easy to find, relatively inexpensive, and extremely versatile. Use them to emulate Indonesian screens and flooring, or even attach them to walls and doors to give the illusion of an Asiatic interior in any home. Look for simple and light materials such as lengths of muslin, together with printed batik, to drape over the bed. Hardwood lattice-work screens are effective and versatile, used as room dividers or even placed in front of a window to create a play of dappled light within the room. Display unglazed earthenware pots and woven baskets or carved bowls and plates on long, low tables to help set the scene.

Left Functional and decorative items give a flavour of the Asiatic style. Java has a long tradition of batik printing, each area having its own distinctive pattern. Instead of being used for clothing, these can make pretty bed covers and throws. The influence of Buddhism and Islam has created attractive ethnic variations using common materials. This is especially evident in the use of bamboo products.

Right This is a modern version of a traditional Indonesian house, which is uncluttered but welcoming. Here, a sofa has been elegantly and simply created from bamboo "logs", as has the table. Textural contrast is provided in the form of an elegant, eye-catching glazed jar and the square-tiled floor. Use woven split bamboo and fine roll-up blinds on the exterior walls to create an authentic look.

1. A roll-up or fold-up window blind made from this semi-opaque sheer cloth would simulate the sort of fine bamboo blinds used as wall and room dividers.

2. Indonesian hot-wax "Batik" with pictorial patterns of buildings, human figures, animals, and birds provides a charmingly ethnic theme for upholstery, curtaining, or bedcovers.

3. Create a cocoon of raffia walls with this natural-fibre wallpaper. Large areas could be divided into sections both horizontally and vertically with split bamboo canes.

4. Add a hard element to a room using ceramic tiles, either on walls or floor. Keep colours muted in keeping with the style.

5. Traditional English rush matting, plaited into strips, makes a sturdy substitute for bamboo or rice-straw matting. It needs regular watering to keep it supple.

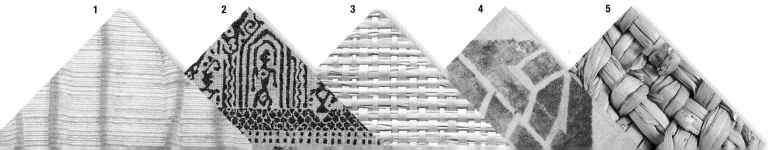

1   2   3   4   5

Zen from Japan

The tradition of Zen Buddhism in Japanese interior style rests in its teaching that all things should exist in harmony. The restrained architecture and calming, uncluttered elegance of Japanese homes is testament to the words the Zen Buddhists use to describe their homes – "astringent", "rustic", and "lonely". Today, we interpret this ideology in a less-disciplined manner, using old and new materials to combine aesthetic qualities and comfort.

Emphasis is placed on the surface areas of the room. Reed mats edged with black borders, called *tatami*, are used for sitting and sleeping on and are laid side by side to cover the floor. The geometric lines of the mats can be echoed in cedar or juniper ceiling struts, sliding doors, windows, and pillars. Blinds and moveable screens (*shoji*) manipulate spaces and views. Hang four paintings – one for each season – in rotating order and display a scroll painting above a low table and cushions. Symbolic of regrowth and regeneration, living plants are an essential element. Cherry blossom and lotus flowers are used singly as acknowledgment of the changing seasons and as a focus for contemplation. Dispense with clutter and keep the accent on natural or rustic textures, neutral colours, and clean shapes. Create a sense of calming continuity and space between the furniture and objects by maintaining the rhythm of colour tone with defined and restrained lines. The eye should be drawn from one area to the next, and everything should be thoroughly clean.

Above Traditionally, a futon would be brought from a cupboard and laid on thick *tatami*. In this modern interpretation, the mattress is elevated on a plain wooden platform. A tall angle lamp is both practical and minimalistic.

The lack of decorative ornamentation is fundamental to the disciplined refinement of the Japanese style.

Opposite The wood is natural, the wall colour neutral, and the flooring practical in this representation of the Zen interior. The fabric half-screen, called a *noren*, could be exchanged for a floor-length division.

1. Water is an essential element in the Japanese design aesthetic, so this simple, light cotton fabric with stylized fish and water ripples is perfect for achieving the desired tranquil ambience.

2. Japanese-style houses do not need many different fabrics, but indigo blue is a traditional colour and this luxurious, dark blue silk has the required quality and texture, perhaps used as a simple bedcover.

3. Lengths of hand-made paper might be used to cover window panes or internal glass panels instead of creating traditional, fragile rice-paper screens.

4. Grass cloths similar to this one have been used in Japan and Korea for centuries. They are made from parallel strips of dried grass or seaweed which have then been glued or woven to a coarse backing paper.

5. Historically, Japanese houses were measured by how many traditional *tatami* mats they could hold. This sisal flooring would make a good substitute.

| 1 | 2 | 3 | 4 | 5 |

Nordic Style

More than any other Nordic country, Sweden provides inspiration for the most familiar Scandinavian interior style. Despite Scandinavia's geographical isolation from Europe, foreign decorative tastes – particularly French and English – eventually shaped Sweden's indigenous style. During the time of the reign of Gustav III (1771–92) the sinuous and ornate Rococo style was extremely popular. After 1818 it merged with the restrained and lean manner of Neo-classicism when Napoleon's Marshal, Bernadotte, became ruler of Sweden.

Although originally influenced by European trends, what we now call "Gustavian" style has a distinctive Swedish slant typified by restrained symmetry, pale colours, and high-ceilinged, light rooms. Hang canvas panels on walls, painted to imitate panelling, columns, and other classic architectural devices. These can be enlivened with garlands, wreaths, ribbons, and swags of flowers. These fashions filtered down from grand houses to be incorporated into the vernacular style of more modest homes, imported there by travelling artists employed to paint furniture and walls with garlands of fruit and flowers, or even "framed" landscapes as an alternative to paintings. Delicate chairs based on Neo-classical shapes and painted in pastel colours are popular in the traditional Swedish home, and are often used alongside traditional furnishings. Originally these traditional pieces were retained in Swedish homes because they were too useful to abandon in spite of a new decorative fashion. Storage is key; ingenious bed designs sometimes incorporated a cupboard at one end for extra storage. Cupboards and tiled stoves fit into awkward spaces and beds are built into the walls and corners, slotted into the eaves and beside the fireplace.

Above A modest window blind and high-backed Gustavian style chairs with checked, upholstered seats add a note of comfort to this simple breakfast room. Rustic furniture makes a natural partner to checked fabrics and, when mixed with lots of matt-white paintwork provides a suitably airy and unfussy quality.

Opposite Hand-painted fabric taken from an archive design makes delicate curtains and bed hangings for this elegant room. The addition of a canopy provides a luxurious element to an exquisitely carved bedstead. Plain floor-boards are essential in the Swedish house, but they are often covered with long strips of carpet to provide extra warmth and comfort.

1. Although the classic Gustavian Swedish style hinges on blue, white, and grey, the warm colours of this plaid cotton are still in keeping with the Swedish style.

2. A subtle shade of green paint will lift a blue-and-white theme and provide a tranquil backdrop to the room.

3. A pretty check voile changes the colour scheme while keeping the ethereal touch.

4. A flower motif always softens an interior scheme, and it is a good idea to introduce warmer background colour, such as cream or parchment.

5. Hard flooring suits the Nordic style well. Pale wooden boards create an uninterrrupted floor area.

1   2   3   4   5

Above A light and airy hallway has a checkerboard pattern painted on the floorboards. This is not very difficult to do and it is a particularly good idea when the boards are narrow. The check is echoed in the design of the box pelmet, which is a simple and effective way to emphasize a decorative theme and add interest to simple curtains. An attractive and practical sturdy storage seat is flanked by exterior wall lamps to give an indoor-outdoor quality that would be very appropriate for a lobby or hallway.

Opposite A sitting room which is welcoming in both summer and winter. Blue, yellow, and white throws provide a summery feel, as do the lightweight curtains which can be changed to a heavier material during the cold winter months. The blue painted floorboards are pretty and provide a colourful contrast to the all-white timbered walls and ceiling. An old painted trunk is dressed with antique cloth and the ceiling light is adorned with a simple, cotton-cloth shade for a softer effect.

In sophisticated houses, the cool, spacious elegance of pure Gustavian decoration dominated interior fashion. The combination of blue and white conveys the period more than any other, and although blue is a cold colour, it can look clean and sharp in the crystal-clear light of the far northern hemisphere, rather than the grey light of temperate climates. Pastel detailing and colourwashes can be applied to walls, while sage-green, grey-blue, and rust-red can be used in fabrics and decorative painted detailing. Painted picture rails and dados, stencils, and trompe-l'oeil panelling are all suitable, but the look should always be under-played. To re-create cool, spacious Swedish interiors, bare floorboards could be given a colourwash of white emulsion, sealed and then topped with traditional long cotton runners or simple rag rugs. Suitable fabrics include the ubiquitous check, as well as all-over patterns of small sprigged or floral designs. Swedish country houses had small windows and little natural light, but with the invention of the enclosed, tiled stove that was installed in every room, windows became larger and provided more light. Using sheer fabrics at the windows or simple, unlined curtains will maximize the sense of airiness and space in the house.

1. In Sweden it is traditional to put up light curtains for summer and replace them with heavier fabric during winter. Striped voile allows uninhibited light while adding a little colour.

2. A pretty check-and-flower paper border would make a charming decorative frieze at ceiling level, or attached to a pelmet board above simple calico curtains.

3. Pale wood floors are a feature of Scandinavian interiors, using a special bleaching technique. Liming paste works well on hardwood floorboards.

4. Swedish interiors often use long strips of white woven carpet, sometimes sewn together, which are then laid on floorboards. This self-patterned wool carpet is an elegant option.

5. Blue and white tiles are an alternative method of introducing the classic Swedish look. Use them as a border or in an all-over pattern.

1

2

3

4

5

Celtic Connections

When Queen Victoria and Prince Albert bought Balmoral Castle in the Scottish Highlands, there was a resulting fashion for all things Celtic. This was epitomized by the Victorian passion for what can be described as the Scottish baronial interior. The early tartans were woven locally into simple checks of limited colours obtained from indigenous plant and pigment dyes. The Victorians documented and adopted existing traditional clan tartans and greatly extended the range of designs, using them not only for clothing but as the pattern for fabrics, wall coverings, carpets, and all sorts of decorative objects. The usefulness of the tartan design comes from its regulated geometric form and textural quality, which can be readily partnered with other tartans and patterns. This is the material for creating a cosy or "masculine" atmosphere and is therefore a good choice for a bachelor apartment, or an introspective environment such as a bathroom or library. A bold tartan could be used as the main focus, with other colours and materials in the scheme picked out from its design, or you can mix tartans using contrasting sizes of checks and textures, while maintaining a sympathetic colour tone. Rugs, throws, and cushions are important accessories to the Celtic look and help to draw the various lineal designs together. For a dramatic interpretation of the Scottish baronial interior, use plain and solid furniture, natural flooring materials, and lots of tartan-design chunky ceramics and storage boxes.

Left Traditionally, the bed would have been placed in a corner, if not within the wall, and provided with thick drapes. Here, contrasting checks allude to the tartan theme and are partnered with natural, woven flooring, a sheepskin rug, and herringbone throw. The cream wood-panelling has been given a lift with a painted dado.

Right A riot of tartans fills this traditional kitchen with a modern slant on a Scottish theme. Carpet, curtains, tiles, ceramics, and accessories create a warm and cosy scheme. The comfortable furniture looks most welcoming beside the range.

1. A rich combination of hearty colours allows numerous options for introducing other fabrics. A strong pattern like this works best when partnered with plain, tonally balanced colours.

2. This traditional Gordon tartan woven in pure silk brings a luxurious touch. Use it for bed hangings and covers combined with lace and white linen.

3. Although not strictly Celtic, this trellis paper hints at clans and castles, and would associate well with many of the softer tartans and plaids available.

4. Showing the colours of the moor, this checked tile makes a cheerful addition in the kitchen, even if only used around the cooker, as in the photograph.

5. This adaptable version of the tartan carpet would look equally handsome in a crofter's cottage or in a sophisticated city apartment.

A Taste of Tex-Mex

The Tex-Mex style mixes Mexican Pueblo native and Wild West rustic in a marriage of raw texture, dazzling colour, quirky pottery, and hand-made furnishings. Timber, stones, or colourwashed plaster form the backdrop for this mix-and-match style. To capture the look, adopt elements that complement each other and that maintain their essential character when placed in a contemporary situation. The key is to find rugs and blankets that have the character of those woven by the Navajo and Hopi tribes. The Hopi wove subtle blue, cream, or black woollen blankets, and the Navajo weavers made bright, striped and zigzag-patterned rugs. These designs contrast well with rough plaster, stone, and wood. They can be used on the floor, over the bed, or as door or wall hangings. Traditional Mexican design employs colour and shape in a riotous display of inventiveness in electric combinations such as acid yellow, cobalt blue, and chartreuse green. Tiles, kitsch statuary, punched and painted tin ornaments, and naively painted fresco panels are typical additions. Use combinations of flat wall colours in solid blocks to create a strong background for homely furniture or carved pieces with an Hispanic influence. Alternatively, take inspiration from fabrics, beadwork, and pottery by painting or stencilling Navajo designs or motifs directly onto roughly painted walls as a frieze or asymmetric embellishment. Tiles with an Hispanic or Pueblo motif can be applied in patterns or blocks as wall decorations.

Above A cowboy look would be a great idea for a young person's bedroom, with painted plaster walls that pick up on the colours in the rugs and blankets. The bed is simply made from cedar branches held together with robust bolts. Cowhides, hats, and stamped leather complete the effect.

Opposite Although this Santa Fe house is newly built, it retains the flavour of a lived-in home. The adobe style walls all have authentic curving edges which are illuminated by bright Native American and South American textiles. Old fittings, such as the strapped and studded door, enhance the ethnic illusion.

1. This richly textured fabric in ethnic cowboy colours will add a dash of log-cabin style, given a flat border and used as a bed cover or sofa throw.

2. This warm, golden fabric is useful for its self-pattern, which will contribute to the colour scheme without dominating any colour that has been used elsewhere in the room.

3. Sometimes the simplest motif material provides the key to a decorative scheme. This little design fits perfectly into the Mexican interior and adds colour and figurative direction.

4. Mexican style happily mixes a wide variety of colours. However, use this vivid red with discretion and combine it with an equally strong colour, always as a flat finish.

5. Suggesting saddlery, sombreros, and sunshine, these "primitive" tiles make a subtle addition to a kitchen, or used as a frieze in an entrance hall. These are suitable for outdoors.

1 2 3 4 5

Modern Choices

Today's contemporary interior looks more toward the elemental ingredients used in design than to an overview of design history. However, classical design concepts form the foundation of all good design from the creation of symmetry within interior spaces, to the harmonious visual transition from one area to another and the arrangement of balanced lighting. The focus of the modern interior favours a mood created by the aesthetic composition of space and light, controlled colour, and an appreciation of subtle and sensual lines and textures. There is less clutter and ornamentation because we need to create a more contemplative, peaceful haven within our homes. In addition a neater, emptier interior allows more flexible use of space and concentrates the eye on the individual qualities within. The Eastern sense of harmony and contemplation where the focus is on the balance between opposites – the yin and yang – has crossed into the contemporary design philosophy where we seek to satisfy both the spirit and the senses.

The alternative idiom of modern decorative style is a bold and unabashed use of colour and patterned fabrics which simply sizzle with dynamic energy. This contemporary use of colour has been inspired by travels to the Mediterranean, the West Indies, South America, and India. It should be used in strong blocks of contrasting colour for maximum impact but it is important to leave areas of neutral colour and space for visual composure. Paint manufacturers frequently produce themed ranges based on a particular regional palette, which help focus choices. Alternatively you could centre your choice around new floral fabrics which are so different from traditional chintz with their clear, lively colours of summer picnic freshness. Sheers, which include voile and organza, have had a face-lift too and can be used boldly in place of heavier window and bed drapes.

Above Colour, and its distribution, becomes the main focus of a scheme when furnishings and objects are strictly limited. The vivid purple screen wall focuses the eye on the strongest colour and also provides a mezzanine wall, a bedhead, and valuable storage space. The large bed area is sleekly fragmented by the striped cover, while the architectural curves and lines of the room are uninterrupted.

Opposite Here, contrasting textures of leather, wood, lacquer, slate, and chrome all make their decorative impact on the room while still maintaining the necessary proportions for this style of room. The soothing foundation of soft off-white walls and wood-strip floor frees the eye to appreciate the quality of the detail in this living room, irrespective of the assorted decorative periods and styles that have been used.

Minimal Mood

The more complex our lives become, the more we yearn for a home environment that is a haven of peace, harmony, and comfort. The idea of using "minimal" style for your surroundings might bring to mind the notion of a look that is bare, cold, and impractical, but this is far from the intention. The pared-down, minimalist look has its roots in the late Art Deco period, when streamlined, industrial decoration became popular. The minimalism referred to here is all about creating a balanced and aesthetically pleasing interior using carefully chosen ingredients which are adaptable and attractive.

First, clear away all superfluous domestic objects and see the effect; you have already created a sense of soothing, uncluttered space. Find a method of storage which is adaptable and easily accessible for you; storing magazines away will create space, but you must know that you can reach one when you want to. Fewer objects and less furniture give greater focus to the room's contents, so store away decorative objects – such as pictures or ceramics – so that you can bring them out in turn. This creates an ever-changing focus that will provide new visual interest and vigour in the room. It also means that quality, colour, and positioning become vital – so every object should be placed to maximize its individualism and decorative or practical contribution. This does not mean that objects have to be expensive – merely characterful and loved. Colour and shape, and the relationship between ingredients are very important. Try repeating one colour or shape within the room to promote an easy visual flow. Use plenty of neutral colours as a foundation between areas of stronger colour and for furnishings. The position of your furntiture can be adapted as required for extra visual interest.

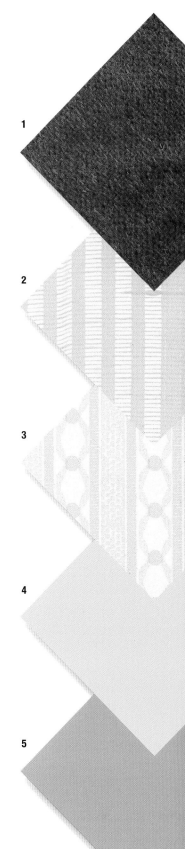

1. Powerful colour in a minimalist interior takes on extra vigour and visual impact. Keep curtains and soft furnishings streamlined and free from frivolous trimmings.

2. The minimal style can be weighted or lightened using different materials. In summer, replace heavier drapes with a light, but sophisticated textural sheer.

3. A subtle vertical stripe visually increases the height of a room, thus adding to the sense of space. Display few ornaments to avoid a conflict of pattern.

4. Always introduce a factor of warm colour, such as this primrose paper, to avoid creating a cold, sparse look in a minimal scheme, and link it in with a small detail elsewhere in the room.

5. Although many blues are considered "cold" colours, when a blue contains some red, as here, it can be used to bring comforting warmth to a sparse, minimal scheme.

Bright and Bold

An inherent love of colour in our lives never disappears, whatever fashion trends may occasionally dictate, because strong colour and form are too stimulating and useful to be set aside for very long. More can be done with colour to manipulate the atmosphere, shape, and character of a room than with any other decorating device – and the wonderful thing is that you can accomplish these goals with relative ease and little cost. The bright-and-bold concept first came into our homes in the 1950s with the advent of mass-produced, moulded furniture. This look should be used dynamically in the chosen setting to produce a truly individualistic statement where colour is concentrated either in one area to focus the eye, paired in balanced combinations, or juxtaposed in a mixed palette of colour and shape for a thoroughly modern, dramatic effect.

This look is sparky, fun, and stimulating rather than calming and restful, and therefore it is a look best adopted for the active areas of the home. The idea works very well in large, open rooms, but it is especially suited to any cramped, dark areas where there is little or no natural light, such as an entrance lobby, interior passageway, or small bathroom. In a tiny room, bright colour creates its own visual interest without the need for space-consuming decorative fillers.

However, you should avoid creating a mono-colour box with walls and ceiling of the same colour, as this would be disorientating and claustrophobic. When you are using several different colours in close proximity, choose colours with equally balanced tones and density to create a sense of harmony. Remember that complementary colours from opposite sides of the spectrum, such as violet and yellow, or green and red, will react positively with each other in a dramatic, vibrant manner.

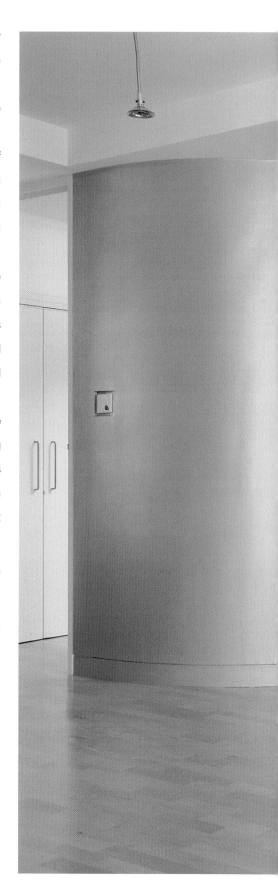

Left Decorating a small room in one colour, such as this bathroom, creates a cocoon of colour and a sense of visual unity, smoothing out angles. The bright yellow is a strong, cheerful colour. However, it is preferable to paint the ceiling a different colour to avoid creating a claustrophobic atmosphere in a restricted area. Here, the shelves have been inset into the door to maximize the feeling of space and lineal continuity.

Right Being the colours of fire and light, orange and yellow make strong, bold companions when used in partnership, as here. The bright orange door slides back to cover a glass panel that allows borrowed light into the internal bathroom, and also reveals the bedroom beyond. The focus of colour is then transferred from the door to the large check, orange and yellow bed linen which creates a visual link between the two areas.

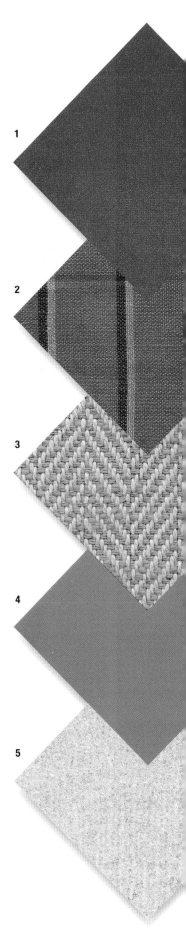

1. Kick off with this dazzling red cotton as a foundation colour. Pure, saturated colours with no white or black content are best partnered with another colour of the same tonality.

1

2. Stripes are always useful for carrying strong colour without monotony, as the line adds rhythm. Finish boldly with a dark trimming to create dramatic contrast.

2

3. A versatile, traditional chevron design in a contemporary colourway will make a bold statement as an upholstery material.

3

4. Hot tangerine and pink work surprisingly well together and create a dazzling effect. Add at least one dulled-down colour to the room, such as charcoal, grey, or beige, to anchor the brighter colours.

4

5. The floor is one of the most dominant areas. Continue the bright-and-bold look by choosing an eye-catching carpet that maximizes the effect of the whole decorative scheme.

5

Using bold shape and colour requires careful thought about the scheme's overall content and balance. For example, an accent of bright colour featured as a single piece of furniture will draw the eye to the dominant colour and take centre stage. Alternatively, such a device can help link areas of bold peripheral colour. To create a sleek, modern scheme, decorative lines, colour, and furniture should all be kept simple while wall finishes can be smoothly reflective, patinated, textured, or even a combination of these. When there are defined areas of colour, the floor becomes an important anchor to hold all the elements together, and a neutral and plain choice is the easiest to work with. Lighting, both natural and artificial, will have a profound influence on how bold colour is perceived. Experiment with the interplay between these two elements before making any final colour decisions. Paint long lengths of lining paper and obtain large fabric samples in your chosen colours, then pin them up or lay them down, looking at them in different lights over a period of time to help you achieve just the right look.

Below A brave colour combination of pink and orange, teamed with cool white illustrates how effective a bold scheme can be when the proportions and distribution of colour are carefully planned. This is fun, innovative, and smart decorating.

Right No less than nine red and white fabrics work together here. The colour scheme is limited, but the shapes and pattern combinations are dynamic with sharp tailoring and an eye-catching pelmet, cushion trim, and pouffe skirt.

1. This stripe creates a bold look on its own, as the contrast between the colours is so strong. Combine this fabric with strong, plain colours or florals in similar shades.

2. Shocking pink works well in small doses as a highlight or with equally vibrant colours such as turquoise, peacock blue, lemon yellow, and lime green.

3. This huge, bold print demands centre stage. The bolder the pattern, the more positive balance it needs, so use blocks of strongly coloured, plain materials.

4. A vibrant wall colour dominates a scheme more than a fabric as it covers a greater surface area within the room. Paint offers a quick and inexpensive method of transforming a room.

5. Bringing together pink and red in one luxurious fabric, this silk damask is hundreds of years old by design, but as modern as you can make it in the right contemporary setting.

1. When using pale materials it is important to include variations of texture and self-pattern for visual interest. This luxurious, velvet-pile upholstery fabric in herringbone has both.

2. The trellis pattern has been employed for centuries in many forms. This is a subtle example in an off-white cotton. Add piping, edging, or fringing for a professional finished look.

3. The natural finish of this linen-and-cotton weave makes an informal, rustic alternative to more complex upholstery fabrics but retains the same restrained elegance.

4. As near to a self-pattern as could be, this subtle floral paper will give an interesting finish to the wall surface without detracting from the overall policy of pure and pale.

5. Alternative flooring, in the form of tiny mosaic pieces glued together, forms a regular-sized tile, making the tiles easier and quicker to lay. The pattern adds important textural variation.

1   2   3   4   5

Purely Pale

Left This room is a perfect example of how to use shape, texture, and space within an all-white interior. The panelling provides architectural interest that needs no other ornamentation. Plain pull-up blinds diffuse the light but do not obstruct the lineal rhythm. The abstract, geometric shape of the upright chairs, side table, and coffee table contrasts with the plumpness of the sofa pillows. Decorative objects centre the eye and add notes of colour and texture.

Right This scheme is serene, beautifully composed and full of interest, while maintaining a limited colour range and few furnishings. The quality of the ingredients, their placement, the attention to decorative detail, and balance of colour highlights is perfect. The sofa and "heraldic" velvet cushions take the focal position, balanced by a pair of neatly upholstered side chairs set against a dado rail that subtly breaks up the large area of white wall. Simple diaphanous calico curtains have a zigzag pelmet for added interest. The decorative artifacts and sculptures are placed for maximum individual effect while maintaining textural flow.

Creating a room using a light, limited palette is a lesson in the delicate handling of white-on-white in order to maximize the sense of calm reflection that such a scheme can achieve. Bright white is very difficult to use because it has a coldness that, especially in the cool lights of a temperate climate, makes it uncomfortable to live with on a dominant scale. It is also unsuitable to combine with off-whites because it can have the effect of making them look dirty. Therefore, if white is given a delicate tint of warming yellow, pink, or brown, it will lift the mood and produce subtle tones that are easy to live with. In a modern scheme based on whites, keep the emphasis on shapes, textures, and spatial distribution of furniture and objects. To prevent the scheme from looking "flat" it is vital to promote visual liveliness and flow. Therefore, as always when using limited colour themes, textural variation is of great importance. For example, an all-white linen sofa needs the addition of cushions in contrasting fabrics such as velvet, silk, and damask. Sheer white curtains will look more interesting with a wide satin border, while a pale bedroom scheme could mix textures to add interest using bedclothes of lace, embroidery, chenille, and even mohair. Plain white surfaces naturally create a play of light and shade with almost abstract sculptural effects, so the constant shifting of natural light and the positioning of electric lighting in the room can have dramatic effects on the overall look. You should also consider the look created by the outlines of the furniture and any decorative objects, making sure their arrangement is balanced in relationship to the room and to each other.

Contemporary Geometrics

Even during the Middle Ages, diaper patterns (all-over geometric designs) were employed on woven fabrics, often taking the form of a trellis base with an overlay of motifs such as lozenges, squares, and formalized flowers and leaves. Checks, diamonds, and v-shaped chevron designs have always been popular. Circles, stripes, and strapwork patterns (twisted and twined bands) have also been used throughout the history of decoration. So, it is not so much the basic design of the material but rather the way it is used and what it is combined with that makes it part of a particular period or style. These designs are equally popular today and innovative weaving techniques have introduced new texture and colour directions. Ethnic weaves from Africa, South America, Asia, and Australasia have added to the geometric range. These can be used as the dominant design in a scheme, or they can be used to link different patterns together with strong emphasis on line and form. In a minimalist interior, you can leave a geometric pattern as the dramatic focus, or introduce other materials that pick out elements in subtle colouring and add quiet variation. When complex curved or floral patterns are used, the introduction of a graphic, geometric design will give a strong lineal element to anchor the scheme. They can also be used to echo an architectural element such as a cornice. Where line, rather than pattern, is the focus, use a geometric design to echo the subtle emphasis of the decorative direction.

Left A pair of eye-catching parterre screens create a strong focal point. Striped curtains hung on tensioned wire, a complementary check fabric on the day-bed, a cool, cream linen chair, and "topiary" ornaments complete the look.

Right Using a single geometric pattern, this predominantly navy and white room is balanced by the introduction of alternative coloured check and plaid cushions. Caramel-coloured boarded walls and white paint alleviate the geometric density of this dramatic room.

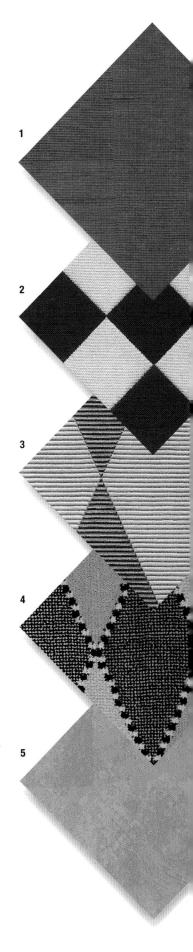

1. A deep and subtle coloured check in slub silk would be suitable for generous window curtains or as a furnishing fabric. Pick out the brown and blue tones elsewhere in the room.

2. This diamond pattern is visually very powerful and will need other dynamic, but perhaps not geometric, fabrics to match it.

3. Boldly geometric but warm and soft in colour, this harlequin design is suitable for curtains or upholstery and would look good combined with a stripe which included the same colours.

4. A richly textured diamond pattern would make a focal point used as upholstery for a chair or sofa. For a more subtle look, use this fabric for cushions on a plain, or self-patterned sofa.

5. Geometric trellis and stripe papers have been used for centuries, but this fresco-style paper in colourwashed squares will add contemporary shape and texture.

Right The serene sophistication of this room relies on contrasting textural effects, not colour, with five different fabric cushions and a luxurious throw, a black lacquered table set off by the velvety cream carpet, and a dark fire surround balanced by plain wooden picture frames.

Opposite Primitive materials and finishes demonstrate the effectiveness of the ethnic theme. Raw, buff-tinted plaster walls make a good backdrop to the rugged driftwood sculpture and earthy African textiles.

New Ways with Texture

Clever use of texture can really bring a room to life. The pleasure of using different textures together should stimulate not only the visual sense, but also the sensual and aesthetic. Making a mix of textures the decorating focus works very well in this modern, pared-down interior. Textures can be integrated with any style, but the subtle differences in texture might be lost within a complex scheme. Therefore, use textures as the dominant decorative force as an alternative to lots of colour and ornamentation. Inspiration can be found in many sources – ethnic or modern, traditional or high-tech. A useful aid to this process is creating an "inspiration board" which brings together all sorts of textural possibilities. Mixing texture is simply a matter of experimenting with the raw ingredients to produce a beautiful, satisfying result. A velvet throw and a generous pile of cushions in contrasting fabrics of similar colour tones are enticing and decoratively effective. Discover the effect that hot/cold and hard/soft components have when played against each other. For example, contrasting elements such as driftwood and lacquer, stone with fake fur, or silk on suede make seductive partners, while earthy, ethnic textiles and objects look equally stunning against a backdrop of rough, colourwashed plaster or polished aluminium sheeting. Pay careful attention to how you arrange the ingredients, as the relationship between them and the rest of the room is vital to the overall success of the scheme. The choice and positioning of pictures, mirrors, flowers, and lighting will all help develop the character of this textured look.

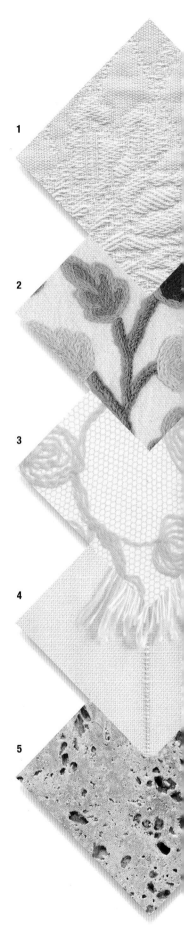

1. This timeless matelassé material is woven to produce a quilted floral effect in a subtle overall pattern that provides luxuriant texture.

2. A form of outline embroidery, crewelwork was traditionally used for bed furnishings and cushion covers but is perfect for the modern interior, too, as curtains or wall coverings.

3. This natural cotton sheer may also be used for curtains as its stylized leaf pattern will filter the natural light into shapes and shadows.

4. This unusual tasselled fabric would make an effective window blind or banner curtain, diffusing the light while creating textural pattern.

5. Travertino marble has a deeply figured surface with neutral but warm colouration, making it an unusual and effective flooring material.

1

2

3

4

5

Florals Updated

Floral patterns are a traditional mainstay of interior design because they are visually stimulating and adaptable with a never-ending variety of pattern size, colour, design, and texture. However, do not be fooled into thinking that florals have had their day – they can be used to create a look that is today's version of country-home style. Even a classic chintz can be given a modern slant by associating it with contemporary elements, or by using it in an unexpected way: for example, instead of regular curtains, use a spectacular floral fabric as a single banner curtain, finished with a wide contrast border and hung from simple ribbon tabs or rings. For this you need a relatively small quantity of material and the pattern will be shown off in its full glory. Take a slant on the Zen interior style and use a simple floral fabric instead of a plain one to make a narrow runner for a rectangular dining table. In a large, multipurpose setting, a mobile room divider is a useful device which could hold single panels of a floral fabric, flat or pleated depending on the size of the repeat. Using cushions is a good way of introducing small quantities of different colour notes and fabrics in one area. A single floral pattern in various colour-ways could be used to make a pretty contrasting array of sofa cushions. Some floral materials are even strong enough to use as a lightweight alternative to carpet, however they should be fitted over underlay and used in areas of light use only. Many updated florals are old document prints which have been re-dressed in new colours, allowing a greater choice from the vast range of modern colours to be used in partnership with them.

1. Finding a floral pattern in neutral colours is not easy for the modern interior. Fortunately this woven "crewelwork" design makes a suitably graphic addition.

2. Although this fabric is in eighteenth-century style, its background colouring gives it a contemporary slant, introducing a vivid range of colour possibilities.

3. This large-patterned and informal fabric in bright, clean colours is ideal for curtains and soft furnishings, or alternatively simply for a room screen or tablecloth.

4. This simple tulip "sprig" wallpaper would complement a larger, more complex floral fabric, linking the two together, yet without conflicting styles.

5. Bold 1950s design updated with a modern palette has given new life to traditional floral papers and chintzes. Use this paper combined with checks and stripes.

1   2   3   4   5

Above Lilac and lime make youthful partners in this floral and striped scheme, focusing on the cosy window seat and its assortment of cushions. As always, stripes, checks, and floral patterns make natural partners.

Right This bedroom glows with fresh colour. Peppermint walls and a boldly checked chair work as a team, while a mixed palette of pinks in florals, checks, prints, and bright accessories complete the updated floral look.

Choosing a Colour Scheme

Neutral Schemes

The only true neutrals are black, white, and grey, but there is an acceptance in decorative language that neutrals also include off-white, cream, ivory, oyster, pearl, beige, taupe, mushroom, ecru, parchment, butterscotch, caramel, and any other description ascribed to this subtle palette. Among the materials associated with neutrals are wood, cane, marble, gravel, stone, hessian, flax, and linen. Neutrals can be warm or cool and can work as advancing or receding colours. Receding neutrals contain blue, blue-green, green, blue-lilac, and some greys. Warm colours that appear to move toward you in this category are the neutrals with a hint of red or yellow, terracotta, or tan. Minute adjustments toward one or the other will be evident, especially when mixing and matching neutrals, so try not to combine warm and cool.

Neutral colour creates a sense of space that relies on texture, shape, and detail for rhythm, pace, and impact. It often acts as a link between other schemes or as a relaxed background to *objets d'art*, richly textured accessories, and architectural detail. To lift and highlight this colour scheme, add accents and textural contrasts. For example, the subtle qualities of bamboo, wood, stone, and wicker look outstanding when their natural qualities are shown against a neutral background. Pattern and texture within the neutrals are important, too. Devouré velvets, knobbly tweeds, loose-woven linen and hessian, mohair and cord, self-patterned checks, and herring-bone all convey subtleness in neutral shades and add visual interest. Sometimes, the addition of a contrasting colour is appropriate when it can be included without upsetting the continuity of the scheme. This could take the form of a brightly coloured cushion, a decorative trimming, or simply a single magnificent blossom carefully placed in the room to act as a focal point.

Neutral Entrance

Neutral colours, more than any others, can diminish hard lines, and therefore naturally disguise awkward angles and a lack of symmetrical proportion, promoting a sense of space and continuity that is perfect for an unusual-shaped hallway. Shades of oatmeal, ivory, or cream will provide an easy, flattering background against which the decorative and textural additions of furniture, fabrics, and ornaments can contribute in a more emphatic way. These colours are especially effective in reflective finishes, such as ethereal ecru silk at the windows, tan leather seating, and polished, pale-wood flooring. Alternatively, to really maximize the sense of space in a small or narrow hall, look toward the cooler, neutral shades and let the surfaces exploit both reflective and matt finishes together. Try oyster and dappled marble white, or mother-of-pearl and flint grey. A combination of "hard" and "soft" or flat and shiny finishes also adds interest to the neutral theme. Try limed wood combined with taupe velvet for chairs, or steel-grey taffeta curtains against matt chalk paintwork.

Where there is no room for furnishings, and no windows to curtain, emphasize the decorative potential of the wall and floor surfaces instead. For example, use an unusual painted or papered wall finish and interesting flooring, such as a satin parchment with natural matting, painted limestone blocks with a blond wood parquet floor, or achieve a grand marble effect with a checkered-pattern tiled floor.

Right The long, lean proportions of this corridor are emphasized by the progression of pale tones and minimal ornamentation, leading the eye through a sequence of lowered door architraves to the salon at the far end. The floor of scored, polished concrete echoes classic stone flags.

Opposite Within this elegant hallway the architectural dimensions and geometric shapes are enhanced by the subtle shades and shadows created by all-over neutral tones, companioned with wood and metal detail and flooring.

Left Subtle colour and line add a note of sophistication while creating a sense of space in this cottage hallway. The wooden panels screen a small utility area as well as acting as a foil for a sculptural, Japanese-style hazel branch.

CHOOSING A COLOUR SCHEME

1. Classical inference is illustrated with an amphora mosaic fabric that could add texture to hall windows. The style might be reflected in a mosaic floor too.

2. A hallway usually has little furniture, so texture in the few fabrics used is important. This material is tactile and has pattern definition.

3. Although originally intended to be painted, Lincrusta paper used unpainted in the neutral scheme has durable and waterproof qualities that make it ideal for the dado panel.

4. A sandstone-appearance wallpaper makes an economic substitute for handpainting the effect over a large area. Stone block lines could easily be added by hand.

5. Let the floor bring together all the aspects of neutral decoration with a mixed birch and oak parquet floor laid in a diagonal pattern.

1   2   3   4   5

Neutral Living

A neutral colour scheme that accentuates a sense of space and light can be used very effectively in a room with large windows and generous proportions, and is therefore highly suitable for a living room, usually the largest area in the average house. The spaciousness can be exaggerated by creating a visual extension of the horizontal and vertical planes. One simple way of achieving this is by introducing stripes from ceiling to floor. Plain banners of inexpensive cloth, such as calico, stapled or battened at ceiling height at regular intervals along a bare wall, make both a lineal and textural addition to the room. Alternatively, broad stripes painted in a subtle variation of the leading wall colour would have the same optical result, but without the change of texture.

Effective neutral colour combinations for the living room should maintain the decorative flow. For example, use shades of soft brown and beige together, with darker shades of the same colours for emphasis. Alternatively, define the contrast between the ultimate, absolute neutrals of black and white, for drama. Mix the textured tones found in tobacco, ecru, and oatmeal matt surfaces and materials to promote a sense of harmony.

The neutral living room is greatly enhanced by the clever use of variety in ornament and texture. It is likely that this room will contain more decorative objects than any other, and neutral surroundings make a great backdrop for them. Ornamental details are very useful when a change of textural emphasis is needed, as they add interest to the scheme using a medium other than colour. Place textured elements in juxtaposition to their neutral neighbours for a tactile finish, such as the partnership of polished stone against slub linen, rough wood against devouré velvet, and wicker against muslin.

Top Despite having no curtains or carpet, there is nothing cold or uncomfortable about this sitting room. Simple cream panelling and boldly framed pictures contrast with the dark-wood floor. Huge, deep couches covered in a self-patterned, quilted cotton (matélasse) look inviting with their big cushions and chenille throw. The wooden furniture has a solid simplicity and patina well suited to these unfussy surroundings.

Above A perfect balance of neutral tones, lineal emphasis, and mixed texture. The cream wool drapes are lined and interlined and banded in black all round, while the tall windows are given extra height because the unusual poles have been placed near the ceiling. The sense of space is emphasized by the clean, plain lines of white linen upholstery, just a few carefully chosen decorative items, and neat bookshelves.

Opposite In this modern living room, cool off-whites and lots of natural light promote an aura of quiet contemplation in a setting that is full of interesting shapes. The sculptured lines of the buttoned chaise longue are softened by a pile of cushions whose square shapes are echoed in the wall panelling. A carved stone fireplace and simple, square tables make strongly geometric contrasts. Details are kept to a minimum.

1. A self-patterned herringbone cotton is versatile and modern, and looks smart trimmed with black or another dark colour for definition.

2. A soft, sensual woollen material for upholstery could be mixed with other textures such as velvet and silk in the form of big, inviting cushions and throws.

3. A paper imitating stained and polished walnut makes a handsome wall covering or screen set within a panel arrangement.

4. Sisal matting is woven from the fibrous Mexican agave plant and will last a long time, but only use this pale shade in areas where there is minimum spillage.

5. Flowers and trellis always make good partners, and this translation into a large patterned but soft coloured carpet will work in any neutral interior.

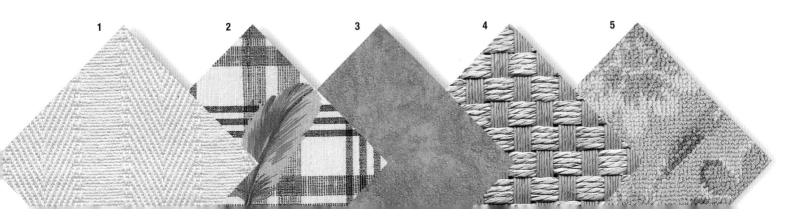

1 2 3 4 5

The neutral scheme should not be allowed to become blurred at the edges, losing the definition of the individual materials, which is more likely to happen in a living room than any other room due to the amount of "soft" materials it usually contains, including sofas and armchairs, cushions, throws, carpet, and rugs. One way to avoid this is to use a contrasting colour to define the decorative flow. As the concept is to maintain a monochromatic effect, it would be pointless to use a true colour, but black or a deep shade of brown will have a dramatic effect on maintaining form and outline. This device might be adopted to emphasize any surface plane, such as edging the curtains to define the vertical, incorporating a darker dado rail or skirting to delineate the horizontal, or edging the carpet with tape or a narrow border to highlight the flat. It is also a good idea to use a slightly darker carpet colour to prevent the scheme from "floating".

A well-balanced lighting plan is so important here. Not only must it be practical and aesthetic for reading, relaxing, and entertaining, but it should illuminate the room in such a way that the sense of space is uninterrupted by areas of shadow, and it is essential that the lighting should not corrupt the subtlety of the colours used.

Below Deepening the neutral tones and partnering them with more rustic elements gives this family sitting room an invitingly rural and cosy atmosphere. Set against painted boarding, the soft brown sofa and chair are upholstered in camel-hair wool which is both hardwearing and comfortable, especially when accompanied by big, soft cushions and a luxurious throw. Jute matting underlines the homely scheme.

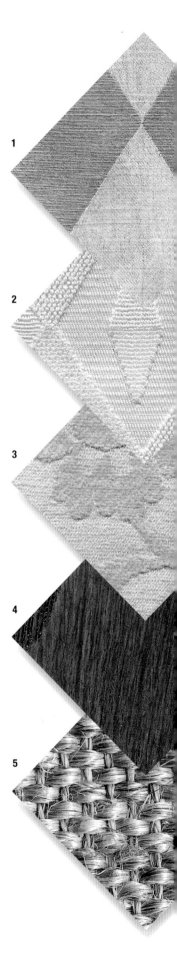

1. Harlequin patterns are always useful as they suit a variety of schemes and period themes. This could be complemented by another neutral to soften its geometric form.

2. A well-defined trellis pattern with textures that imitate velvet, linen, and cord will reflect light from its different surfaces in interesting ways.

3. This woven-pile *gaufrage* can be worked into both period and traditional interiors.

4. The warm and subtle tonal variations of this stained wood make a statement without being intrusive in a subtle decorative scheme.

5. A fine-weave sisal matting is textural and alluring. This sort of flooring can be used all over or made into rugs by adding a strong, broad edging to finish it.

1

2

3

4

5

Above The flat, green paintwork of the panelling in this room provides a good background to buff-linen covered seating. To add contrast and texture the sofa, chair, and footstool have been given seat cushions in a linen check with scatter cushions and a throw in a checkerboard handwoven linen. The natural flooring adds a different texture and neutral tone.

Neutral Bedroom

The neutral bedroom promotes an atmosphere of tranquillity and relaxation. In such a setting there should be no conflicting strong colours to distract the eye or interfere with the calming effect of fluent, decorative rhythm. To avoid causing claustrophobia, ceilings should be as pale as the other surfaces, but never pure white, which is cold and unsympathetic. Soft off-white, on the other hand, harmonizes well with other neutrals.

Keep bedroom colour combinations to those tones of neutral that have a hint of warming pink, yellow, or rust in them, to avoid creating a cold, unwelcomng room, but remember to maintain the same undertone throughout the whole scheme.

There are elements, unique to the bedroom, that promote both the aesthetic and the sensual: essential among these are appropriate bedclothes. Use fine cotton or linen and fat, fluffy duvets or generous, satin-bound blankets. Pile the bed with huge pillows and cushions, using shape and texture to emphasize their individual character, but make sure they are practical as well. The bed's topcoat will contribute greatly to the material mix, whether it be of velvet, mohair, cashmere, fake fur, or a combination of these. Combine ivory and beeswax with a hint of straw yellow, to maintain the sense of warmth and comfort introduced by the fabrics. Alternatively, use warm cream in its natural form for the main bed covering, complemented with suitable highlights, such as cushions in rich burnt umber and yellow ochre. A bedroom can be opulent without being overstuffed and it can be serene without being cold; balance is all.

 **1.** A beige fabric with a warm tone can be used to make bedroom curtains, cushion covers, a simple throw, or even to batten in strips onto the walls.

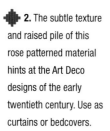 **2.** The subtle texture and raised pile of this rose patterned material hints at the Art Deco designs of the early twentieth century. Use as curtains or bedcovers.

3. An inexpensive damask like this could either be used in generous widths for window curtains, or battened to the wall to give it a tactile element.

 **4.** Neutrals with a hint of warm colour, such as this apricot-tinted wallpaper, should be companioned with fabrics containing colours of similar tones.

 **5.** All-over scrolling patterns like this wallpaper design create a decorative but flexible background that harmonizes with florals, checks, and stripes alike.

1   2   3   4   5

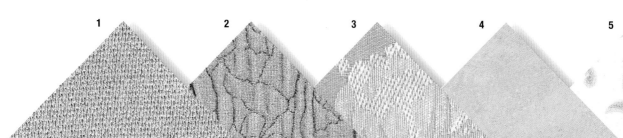

Above A simple, neat, inexpensive idea is to make a bed from scaffolding poles, place it on painted floorboards, add a deep mattress, cotton covers, and mohair blankets, pile up the lacy pillows, and conceal linen-covered storage containers underneath. Other decorative pieces would be superfluous.

Top The strong architectural lines of this bedroom relate it to the view from the large windows. Disciplined use of ornament and the platform structure of the bed create the sensation of floating. The brown tones of the scatter cushions bring in a minimal colour aspect that also adds comfort.

Right In a child's bedroom, an antique bed has been given a soft colourwash that highlights its carved detailing. Creamy-white walls, colourwashed floorboards, and calico curtains sweeping onto the floor combine to create a light neutral theme. The addition of a patchwork quilt on the bed and a linen floorcloth with yellow scalloped edging provides just the right amount of colour highlight and soft comfort.

Neutral Bathroom

The practical, hard components within a bathroom usually dominate the decorative scheme. Although the bathroom suite may be elegant, with rounded corners and smoothly shaped pedestals, the nature of the materials is bound to create harsh lines. Of course, this can be turned to advantage in modern schemes which use glass, chrome, tiling, and colour to define the vertical and horizontal architectural surfaces and emphasize the utilitarian lineal scheme. However, neutral colours are best employed to create a more harmonious and soft bathroom look because these delicate shades help to blend hard edges and surfaces and produce a comfortable mellowness.

If possible, leave pure white out of this scheme, since it will unbalance the overall harmony and make some neutrals look dull. Choose several neutral tints and use them in different areas to build up a subtle and visually textured palette, to ensure the scheme does not look bland. A bathroom is usually fairly small and often the whole room can be viewed at once, another good reason for using a low-key colour scheme. Subtle ornamentation would also work here, such as a restrained, stencilled wall pattern or painted frieze in a monochrome scheme. The neutral colours often found in bathroom materials can help to promote the overall look, such as flecked marble, patinated terracotta, honey-coloured limestone flooring, pale-wood panelling, and so on. Flooring will help to soften and warm up the scheme, so a natural matting could be used as an alternative to tiling or linoleum.

Opposite Shades of off-white, from milk through ivory and parchment, create a warm and subtle scheme. The generous shower drape adds an element of soft texture and indulgence.

Top In this small space beneath the staircase the colours are kept light and clean, while the natural textures of coral, sponge, wood, and hemp provide a tactile element.

Right The high-quality "hard" elements, such as the marble bathtub, double basin unit, and "woven" terracotta floor, are softened by the contrast of extra long curtains at the windows.

1. Appropriate and softening, this voile in white, silver, and bronze echoes the mineral colours of marble, stone, and metal.

2. A special gold-dust paper creates a luxurious patina best used dramatically in small areas. Accompany with antique-gold bathroom accessories.

3. Texture and luxury are represented in this trompe l'oeil, crystalline-effect wallpaper for the bathroom. Accessories should be of high quality and minimalist.

4. Jute matting provides a soft option for a bathroom floor. Use pale, natural colours so that the flooring does not dominate the room.

5. Limestone floor tiles feature variations in finish and colour that will complement other materials in the scheme.

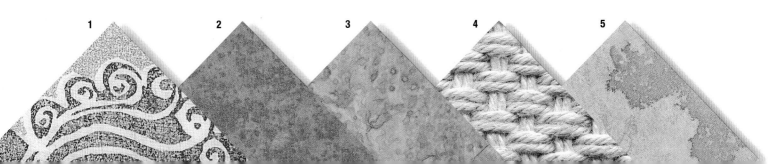

1   2   3   4   5

Neutral Dining

Dining rooms are often decorated in rich, dark colours that suit their traditional, historical, and social associations. However, neutral surroundings in this particular room turn it into a pleasing environment that concentrates the focus on food and conversation without distraction, and is further enhanced by colourful, stylish presentation and table decorations.

Eating is a warmly communicative occasion, therefore neutral tones should not be clinical in the dining room. Concentrate on colours that lean toward yellow or pink, rather than grey or brown. The vital ingredient in this particular colour choice is to have access to lots of natural light, pouring in through large windows and glassed doors to illuminate the interior with gently diffused rays. Sheer, translucent curtains will permit daylight to fill the room with soft light, rather than pure sunlight. Candles create a romantic, introspective island, and in the neutral dining room they should concentrate their light on the table area rather than illuminating unnecessary corners.

To create a grand dining room in the Italian style, paint panels of cool, faux marble, or use a trompe l'oeil wallpaper, accompanied with flat grey woodwork, rough textured limestone flooring, and rust coloured silk curtaining. Reintroduce this warm colour note as a tablecloth for a romantic, candlelit scenario. Alternatively, use the fullness and length of a natural rustic hessian or linen tablecloth as a means of focusing attention on the table, and complete with surprising contrast colours in flowers and tableware, such as purple and terracotta.

CHOOSING A COLOUR SCHEME

1. This versatile, organic pattern might date from the Jazz Age, but can equally be used in a contemporary interior, perhaps as a fringed tablecloth.

2. A woven "bee" material would make amusing and figurative dining chair covers, especially as the bee is the symbol of endeavour and good order.

3. Traditional milk paint is made with natural pigments and skimmed or buttermilk, and has a unique silkiness that can be used on furniture as well as walls.

4. Nearing yellow or mustard, but neutral in essence, this paint colour works well with lighter off-white and smart highlights of black and warm brown.

5. Laying a broad area of neutral colour with this sycamore board floor leaves room for additional colours and textures to be added in the form of rugs and floor cushions.

1   2   3   4   5

Opposite In this dining area, the square pattern of the panelling dominates the interior. Elegant chairs covered with a sophisticated diamond motif share the limelight with a sculptured metal table that adds an asymmetric note to this otherwise disciplined interior.

Above Pale, yellow-beige tones harmonize to create a mellow, diffused look in this elegant dining room. The large, squared pattern in the diaphanous drapes echoes the architectural detail in the panelling, while shedding softly diffused light within. The woven chairbacks and checkered seats echo the geometric detail. This scheme combines many "hard" elements and relies on light and shape for its particular decorative style.

Neutral Kitchen

The advantage of creating a neutral kitchen is that the colour element is relatively easy to work with in relation to all the other materials and fittings that the kitchen has to house.

Adopting a neutral palette involves using a limited range of colour, from creams to greys and browns, blending subtle tints with subtle finishes and leaving aspects of colour to be added by the ever-changing kitchen accessories, including food, pots and pans, and storage jars. Pick out colours that relate to the intrinsic ingredients of the kitchen such as wicker, terracotta, and patinated wood bleached by years of cleaning.

The quality of "hard" materials is pivotal to creating a modern architectural emphasis, and so a neutral foundation should be exploited by using sleek, metallic finishes such as gleaming stainless steel and satin aluminium, or ultra-modern whiteware equipment. These will act as visual accents and embellish the background. Heavy-duty industrial flooring and unusual tiling will lend the scheme visual weight. To create a more rustic look, choose matt materials in shades of oatmeal, bran, and barley. Lighting can be used to accentuate textural elements in the room and to highlight some areas while subduing others, depending on either social or practical use.

1. A motif material, depicting mythical beasts and Medieval symbols, can easily be mixed with stripes and checks for window treatments or chair covers.

2. Using a material with a more sophisticated flavour in the dining area of a kitchen helps to differentiate between the two sections of the room.

3. A plain material, used to make curtains, blinds, or chair covers, in cinnamon cotton could accentuate the colours used elsewhere in the kitchen.

4. This limed-wood-effect wallpaper makes a good alternative to the real thing – saving on time and effort – for a rustic kitchen.

5. Reclaimed limestone floor tiles or ceramic tiles that imitate natural materials go well with "hard" kitchen or bathroom elements.

1   2   3   4   5

Left An example of the strong accent on architectural line and change in surface texture is seen in this neutrally coloured kitchen. The practical area is confined to one side of the room, with two-tier pale wood cupboards. A simple pine sidetable provides further practical working space and adds to the light, neutral feel. A fine antique refectory table is accompanied by modern chairs with curved backs upholstered in natural linen to add a softening note.

Above A miniature interpretation of the open-plan kitchen. Here, the work area is contained beneath the sloping wall of the staircase which makes a natural canopy above it. The stainless-steel utensils are arranged easily to hand while contributing a decorative element that stands out against the neutral backdrop. Softening edges of flowers, wicker, and terracotta are dotted here and there against cream walls and cupboards, a beechwood worktop, and painted wooden floor. The dining area is partially screened from the working area, and here a scrubbed pine table is partnered with elegant, toile-covered chairs and a pewter candelabra that continues the theme from the kitchen.

Understandably, many people regard cooking as a deeply focused and therapeutic activity, and therefore it is important for them to have the well-ordered, soothing surroundings that a neutral approach within the kitchen helps to promote. Out of all the rooms within a home, the kitchen has the largest area and diversity of "hard" surfaces and shapes, and the neutral scheme will accentuate and exploit this element. For example, limed-oak cupboards contrast well with slate working surfaces. The harshness of a marble kitchen table could be partnered with the comfort of wicker chairs. If your gleaming copper or stainless steel pots and pans are on display above the cooker, create an area of variation to this cold material by using an assortment of warm, terracotta storage jars. There is no reason why the neutral kitchen inevitably has to be a hard-edged one when there are so many ways to create textural rhythm. Sometimes the "hard" materials themselves have a soft patina and tactile quality. For example, display old woven baskets holding fruit and vegetables, or earthenware crockery, platters, and cooking pots, and use unvarnished, limed, or colourwashed timber.

When you employ a neutral scheme that avoids colour distractions, the inherent geometry of a kitchen can offer another focus for the design. The squares and rectangles of storage cupboards and whiteware, the circles and ovals of plates and serving dishes, the vertical and horizontal lines of architectural detailing and floor pattern all provide a sculptural element that is clearly outlined against the neutral background, so that the shapes become the main focus of interest.

Right An open-plan loft conversion contains this streamlined, neutral kitchen area which makes a feature of its chrome and stainless steel workstation, shelving, and cooking utensils, sleek push-open cabinets, and oak-strip flooring.

Below The tactile quality and country associations of raw, handcrafted wood are employed to good effect in this kitchen. The finish on the wood is achieved by grit blasting and dry brushing with matt-grey paint. The flat, rustic look is continued with white stained adobe floor tiles, cream rough-plaster walls and ceiling, and a wicker chair furnished with linen cushions and a throw.

1. To help create a rustic, texture-oriented kitchen, include materials that complement the theme, in both tactile quality and choice of colour, such as this fine, soft, brown linen weave.

2. Checks are always a useful foil to plain and patterned fabrics alike. This smart check could be used in both rural and urban kitchens.

3. Trellis is a good pattern to use when you specifically do not want to lose the look of the neutral kitchen's strong definition.

4. A charming stone-and-cement tile adds another element of texture and pattern without disrupting the neutral theme.

5. Invented 160 years ago, linoleum is invaluable today as an inexpensive, multipurpose floor covering. This mottled pattern disguises any accidental spillages.

Hot Schemes

Despite its popularity in twentieth-century decorative schemes, it is important to remember that bright colour is not a modern invention. Hot and strong colours have been used to some degree for centuries, but more particularly since the invention of chemical dyes in the Victorian era. Scarlet is an ancient colour, created from vermilion, red lead pigments, and cochineal extract, but, being expensive, was only used in small quantities for book illustrations and Chinese lacquering. Deepest red was widely used from the mid-nineteenth century with the introduction of alizarin dye. This is a hot, densely saturated colour which looks wonderful in a glazed finish, or as an outstanding background for old gold and black decorative details. Hot pink is really a saturated purplish-pink, once known as magenta and now called "shocking pink". A strong, demanding colour, we associate it with silks and saris and it works well with hot, acid colours such as peacock blue, tangerine, and lime green. Orange-red contains earthy iron oxides as seen in Pompeian frescoes and Persian carpets and is not as dominating as pure scarlet, making it easier to use. Yellow-orange unfortunately featured with brown and purple in the 1970s and has acquired an unfavourable reputation, but, when used with discretion, it can provide a punchy focus or colour link in a large room, or warm a dark area.

Although we generally associate yellow with sunshine and warmth, it can either be cool or warm, depending on the amount of added pigmentation, ranging from chrome yellow to yellow ochre. Hot yellows suggest the colour of sunflowers, egg-yolks, and amber. Using these colours requires a steady nerve and a disciplined scheme in order to balance weight and distribution of colour. However, with a little care you can create an eye-catching scheme that is energizing, but surprisingly easy to live with.

Hot Entrance

The decision to create a hot-coloured hallway needs to be taken early, preferably, in the planning stage of the decorating process, because with this scheme you will need to consider the colour choices for the rooms that lead off the hall. A hallway sets the scene for the flavour of the decoration elsewhere, and it can be visually unharmonious to move directly from very bright colour combinations into muted, cool, or neutral ones. This problem, however, can be overcome. Try placing a toned-down transition colour between the hot colours in the hall and the interior rooms. For example, if the main entrance colours are red and yellow, a lighter shade of yellow may be applied as a wall colour on the stairway. If pink is the dominant hue, try adding a little burnt umber to a linking corridor or as a single wall colour. If your entrance does not feature linking passageways, or the use of a played-down version of the entrance colour is not a feasible choice in the adjoining room, an alternative optical trick is to place a brightly coloured piece of furniture, a large decorative object, or a painting that relates to the entrance scheme in the internal room, providing a visual link between the two areas.

Right A modern hallway relies on its architectural strength with decorative focus created by painting one wall of the stairway bright red. Because other colours and materials are muted, this emphasizes the vertical.

Below Oriental red, earthy and warm, makes a good welcoming colour, used here with ethnic detailing, furnishings, and decorative items from China and Tibet, so that both objects and colour have a sense of place.

1. Renaissance-style fabrics, with their rich patination and deep colouring, add a luxurious quality to any room, and in a hot entrance they will mix perfectly with contemporary and global artifacts.

2. A dramatic, bold design on a fabric requires a long window drop. Alternatively, use it to cover the front door, or hang it like a banner on the wall.

3. Derived from an early nineteenth-century fabric panel, this lavish print could be used framed, as a focal point, in an Indian- or Chinese-style scheme.

4. Given the patina and quality of this deep fresco-wash red, there is no need for other hot colours to partner it. Dark gold, black, fruitwood brown, or cream would offset it well.

5. The design of this paper hints at influences from the Middle East, India, or North Africa. Pick out the colours in luminous silks.

Entrance halls are visually and decoratively dominated by hard lines, rather than soft materials. It is therefore prudent to make the most of this factor and hot, strong colour can be exploited to accentuate the merits of the hall's shapes and proportions. For example, a fine staircase can be framed in a painted archway of eye-catching hot colour to draw the eye up the stairs; alternatively, the rising stair wall might be painted to create a defined geometric shape pointing up the stairs. Using colour on the opposite wall from the entrance doorway draws the visitor into the home's interior. Even if the hot colour is just focused on this facing wall, the effect can be dramatic. For example, paint a wall or panel using lacquer red in layers of shiny glaze to create a magnificently rich backdrop for a decorative *objet d'art* or painting. Particular materials look wonderfully dramatic against hot colour, such as black lacquer furniture and objects against Chinese yellow, deeply polished fruit-wood backed by crimson or bleached wood, and gold or silver metal finishes united with hot pink.

In a small area it is unwise to paint just the side walls, or the ceiling, in hot colours as this will visually shrink the area, creating a claustrophobic atmosphere. Instead, extend the hot definition outward and upward to create a sense of continuity. Hot schemes need a strong flooring design or colour to maintain the theme and provide an anchor. As entrance halls do not contain many decorative elements, it is important that the floor creates decorative interest and focus. Polished, dark wood is a natural choice for entrances. Not only does wood have a warm look and feel, it is also practical to clean in this area of the home that will inevitably receive a lot of wear and tear.

The right lighting for hot colours is essential. Strong sunlight bleaches hot colours, while electric light is tinged with yellow or pink and inevitably alters colours, especially pink, red, orange, and yellow. Only natural daylight bulbs will reveal the "true" colours, but at night these produce minimal ambience. Instead, use uplighters to create an atmospherically shadowed look, or if you have a spacious staircase you could use something truly dramatic such as a pair of electric *torchères*.

Above Asymmetrical shapes of bright colour add to this hall's dramatic open architecture. On a smaller scale, incorporate toned-down colours around the blocks of bright colour to maintain a sense of space.

Opposite A combination of primary colours and white emphasizes the strong outlines in this hall. The red fireplace and yellow wall balance each other in density, while a serene sculpture and spiky cactus draw the eye from one element to the other.

1. Texture replaces the need for plenty of pattern and objects when it is both of good quality and rich in colour, as this natural silk is. Use it in swathes at the window.

2. An elegant fabric like this, with a rich colour and texture, helps to give the hot scheme a sense of timeless place and style, at the same time as maintaining the vibrant feel.

3. Use this warm terracotta paint combined with a traditional pattern, such as a laurel wreath and ribbon, to create a period look. In a contemporary scheme, combine it with fabrics in bright checks.

4. When choosing deep, hot colours, like this red, consider whether to use matt, soft-sheen, or eggshell finishes. Paint out samples and view them in conjuction with various fabrics.

5. Dark-stained floorboards look impressive in traditional and modern interiors, especially when associated with strong, hot colour.

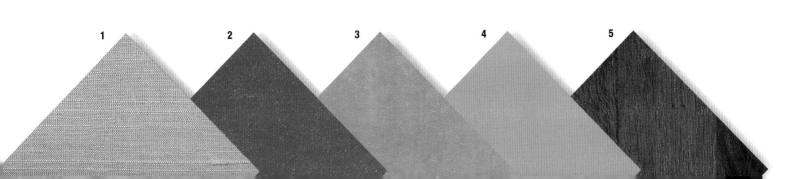

1   2   3   4   5

Hot Living

Living-room style and colour choices are inevitably dictated by size, use, and environment and this is particularly relevant when hot colours are introduced. The first consideration is the living-room setting, that is, which direction it faces, how much light it gets, and how the light comes into the room at different times throughout the day. The dull grey light of the northern hemisphere affects colour, and the way it works with other colours, plus the atmosphere it creates. Bright colours maintain a vibrancy in strong sunlight that is lost under naturally dull light. Mediterranean or Caribbean hues of hibiscus pink and canary yellow cannot be expected to hang onto their indigenous qualities and atmosphere in the subdued light of cooler climes. These hot colours do not respond well when there is extended use of electric light; natural daylight bulbs are an option, although at night-time candlelight makes a good companion to a vibrant colour scheme. Pinks and yellows, in particular, do not work the same magic, but intense reds and oranges can be more easily manipulated to create a successful hot scheme in the cool north. The advantage of using hot colours in a living room is that they promote a sense of enveloping warmth and welcome in the room, lifting the spirits and the atmosphere. Try using unexpected colour combinations such as scarlet, pink, and turquoise, or zesty orange and banana yellow with defining purple detailing. Consider balancing one area of hot colour with another of equal colour saturation, but scale it differently or use it on a separate plane, so there is no uncomfortable optical conflict.

It is important to consider the way that natural light enters the living room since this will have a bearing on how you compose and distribute the colour scheme. In winter the sunlight will enter at a low angle, illuminating the room in quite a different way to the warmer seasons. You can exploit the way the sunshine highlights certain areas, such as around the window or on a back wall, by painting that particular area with a bright, hot colour, such as a sizzling orange, or a strong purple. These hot colours will look stunning when they are caught by the light.

Above Elegant and spare, the effect of focusing on one area of hot colour is demonstrated here where only the fireplace wall is painted flame orange. The royal blue furniture, blue carpet, and wooden table legs add strong colour and lineal contrast.

Opposite Glowing orange walls and good lighting ensure that this room has a comforting glow without being overpowering. Unfussy furnishing and a plain wooden floor help to maintain a pleasing sense of space.

Left Although lilac is really a warm colour rather than a hot one, it fits well into the hot living room as a focus colour, here as a sophisticated background to rustic antlers and informal seating. The high-level dado rail effect adds architectural emphasis.

1. A strong upholstery fabric may be used to make big floor cushions or large sofa pillows for a sumptuous finish to the room.

2. Use a gilt cream or wax to add a touch of sparkle and really bring your hot room to life. Even a small quantity can transform your woodwork.

3. Use this deep violet damask in small doses for cushions, stools, or a tablecloth, with complementary colours such as golden yellow.

4. Luminous orange-yellow needs equally strong companions, but do not forget to use hard elements such as wood and chrome for balance.

5. Hot pink looks good in an ethnic or urban interior. For the first, combine with hot citric colours, for the second, use black lacquer.

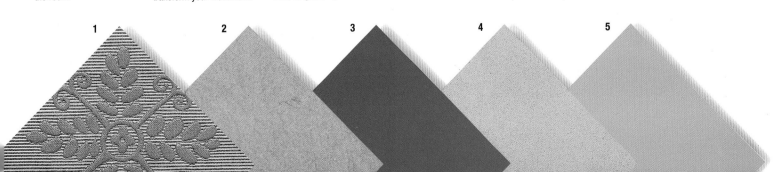

1   2   3   4   5

It is important, when choosing a suitable colour scheme for the living room, to consider how you use it, who uses it, and when. Hot colours create an active environment, whether they are the dominant scheme or a decorative focus. Hot colour is therefore not the right choice for quiet contemplation and conversation, reading, and study. However, if this is the room where family and friends congregate for eating, entertainment, and games, then bright, strong colour will go a long way to promoting energy.

If the living room is large, the various areas of it can be manipulated with colour, but, for visual balance, there should still be cool space in between. The effect of all-over hot colour can be overpowering, so contain it in disciplined, focused combinations, using one strong colour, such as tropical pink, on one wall, and something more muted, such as sandy yellow, on another. Different areas of use could also feature different colour distribution. For example, create an active, hot area where you entertain and eat, but keep the sitting area relatively cool with just a hint of hot colour to link the areas, such as a simple fabric or wallpaper screen, a rug, pots and flowers, or paintings and decorative objects that hint at the hot look.

Right The deep sheen of the walls is matched by the luxurious quantity of colour, texture, and shape, set off by a bold black-and-white floor. Lots of pattern and colour together will intensify the "heat" of a decorative scheme.

Left Double-heighted rooms benefit from warm colour on the walls, fragmented with various hangings and pictures to disguise their expanse. Here, a range of bright cushions centre the eye on the dark sofa, while a bright carpet defines the seating area from the dining area behind.

1. Although the emphasis for the hot colour scheme might be on blocks of painted or papered colour, a bold pattern can really enhance the theme.

2. Using hot colours and patterns together is all part of the fun of creating a scheme. This wallpaper needs the balance of a strong horizontal colour.

3. The ubiquitous oak leaf makes a warm and charming design suitable for the country interior. Create cosiness with hot pink, deep red, and dark wood.

4. You can change the main hot emphasis from red or orange to purple using a vibrant violet wall colour that will mix well with other hot and contemporary shades.

5. Leather tiles make an unusual, highly contemporary flooring material to add another element of luxurious texture to the hot living-room scheme.

1   2   3   4   5

Hot Bedroom

The hot bedroom produces an aura of confidence and vitality. Hot colour makes a creative environment for someone who has their best ideas when comfortably propped up in bed, undisturbed and cocooned in their personal sanctuary.

Hot colour in the bedroom can either be used in broad strokes for walls, curtains, and bedcovers, or concentrated on focused parts of the room, perhaps contained within the bed area alone. Within these parameters, consider a style to adopt. Hot colours cry out to be used in an exotic scheme and the bedroom is the perfect place to realise this. If your preferred look is plush ethnic, seek out hot colours from the earthy Moroccan palette, with blue, green, and pink predominating. Or the silky reds and yellows from the kaleidoscope shades of the Indian colour wheel may appeal. The Mexican taste, too, features an uninhibited mixture of hot colours that puts together yellow, red, pink, violet, and blue in an unselfconscious display. The Medieval period produced some ravishing colours, seen in handpainted manuscripts. These jewelled reds, purples, golds, and greens could be the inspiration for a baronial look, using traditional materials such as purple damask, gold silk, and crimson velvet. To underline the sensual opulence, finish fabrics with theatrical tassels and fringing.

A large bed can create a disproportionately solid mass when completely covered with a bedspread of a single colour. For a more decorative, broken line, layer the bed linen and covers to create a transition of texture and colour. Pile up different coloured pillows and cushions to add texture, colour, and height, as well as luxury.

Opposite The dominating orange tints of the floor and ceiling in this bedroom are tempered with green and blue, while still maintaining the warm glow. The sculptural quality of the bed needs no companion ornamentation.

Right Opposites from the colour spectrum accentuate each other in this subtly lit bedroom. The hot, orange focus of the bed is contrasted with dark cushions and rich blue panels placed like late evening sky as seen through picture windows.

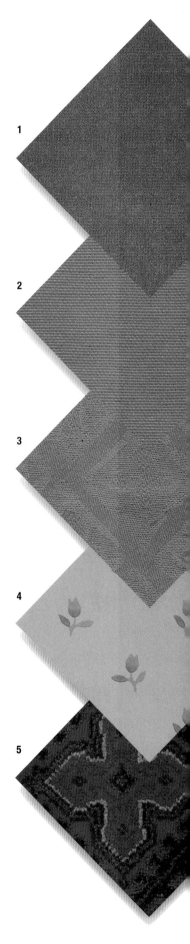

1. Plain colours in lovely materials are always satisfying. This rich red silk is similar in style to fabrics used since the Renaissance period, and mixes well with contemporary patterns for curtains or bedclothes.

2. Shocking pink looks best in strong Mediterranean or West Indian sunlight, but used discreetly with other jewel colours carries any scheme to sunnier places.

3. Luxury could be added with a bedspread made of this sophisticated fabric. Texture and depth will contribute to the overall scheme.

4. A small design in the hot bedroom breaks up the solid blocks of colour and adds a light touch to their intensity.

5. Give a Turkish-style patterned carpet a contemporary slant by combining it with hot, red walls and blue-and-black detailing.

1

2

3

4

5

Hot Bathroom

Use hot colours in the bathroom to create either a cosy retreat or a bright and zany zone. Using reds and pinks in darker shades still maintains the warm theme, while providing a more enclosed and relaxing environment. Enhance this scheme by combining complementary colours, such as dark red with warm green, highlighted with a little antique gold fillet to dado and ceiling level if appropriate.

Tongue-and-groove panelling makes a good decorative finish for bathroom walls, and, painted bright red or pink, can either be used in full height or just along the bath panel. For an exotic touch, make a material drape from muslin dyed a suitably rich, hot colour, to hang from a corona above the bath. Such a device adds the possibility of including more colour and provides an element of softening fabric. An ethnic look might be another preference, with deep yellow, blue, or dusty pink walls and stencilled Moorish motifs. Continue the look with a shaped mirror, or add a cutout painted border in a Moorish arch shape to a regular rectangular mirror. Alternatively, accentuate the dominant hard surfaces, painting the different areas in shimmering colours for a lean, modern look. Try and tie in as many of the hard surface ingredients as possible, from a coloured towel rail to bold tiling on the walls and floor. Since there are not many "soft" elements within the bathroom, make the most of what there is by stacking up towels and accessories in appropriately hot colours to enhance the mood.

Right Warm colours create a cosy, comforting feel in a bathroom. Choose light-coloured textiles, such as the printed voile at the window and the cream bathmat, to prevent the scheme from looking oppressive.

Left A bright and practical treatment uses horizontal boarding painted shocking pink together with a fun, "bathroom objects" wallpaper, from which the accessories all take their colours.

1. Using block colour to fill in when there are bold, hot patterns used elsewhere requires careful matching in both natural and electric light.

2. This sumptuous darkest crimson edges toward blue-red. To keep it "hot", combine with strong pink and tints of warm old gold.

3. Although not strictly "hot", the deep colour saturation of this dazzling turquoise makes it a good complementary detail colour.

4. A sunshine-yellow woodstain would be very effective used on wood panelling in a bathroom, because it is both hardwearing and fun.

5. This vinyl maple flooring makes a change from tiling and provides a visually and physically warm finish for the bathroom scheme.

1   2   3   4   5

Hot Dining

It has long been recognized that warm or hot colours, reds in particular, help to create a convivial atmosphere in which to eat and entertain. Since red became less expensive after new dyes were introduced in the mid-nineteenth century, it has been a favourite foundation colour for the dining room.

For modern-day schemes, colours can either be knocked-back to produce subtle terracotta, burnt orange, deep pink, and maroon, or used in their purer form for a more emphatic look. Deep orange is an especially effective dining-room colour that works well with chrome and violet in the modern interior. Intense, pure colours perform best as glazes, painted in layers over a ground colour. Red is particularly suitable as it can be built up like lacquer for a sophisticated finish. Partner this with details of gold and black for a sumptuous ambience. The potency of candlelight is greatly magnified by these rich colours, especially when they have a slightly reflective finish.

Dining-room colour works best when it is used in a rhythmical way, covering large, unbroken surfaces, rather than distracting the eye with different areas of fragmented colour. The focus for the room is on the social hub at the table and so the peripheral decorations should set the scene and work as an atmospheric backdrop. Unlike other rooms, the dining room does not need to have variations in shape and texture. It is more important that there is continuity within the texture of surfaces to maintain visual harmony, rather than become too distracting.

Right In this large, open-plan apartment, the dining area acts as a screen between the sitting area and kitchen, and has been zoned with hot orange and yellow walls and chairs.

Left With the ceiling painted as well as the walls, the dominating hot-red paintwork is kept in check by the dark blue painted dado and an eclectic mixture of furniture and objects.

1. Even a minimalist scheme needs texture and this glowing yellow moiré, used for tablecloth or curtains, adds lustre and soft warmth.

2. Mix contemporary fabrics and designs with traditional ones to create an evolved warm and confident look.

3. Red and gold have been traditional dining-room colours for centuries, but can look equally contemporary when used today.

4. Drama and hot colour combine in this interpretation of the heraldic theme. Mix with crimson and gold velvet, dark wood, candles, and flagstones.

5. Subtle variations of the same colour are easy on the eye as the foundation for other hot colours of a similar hue. Use with dark green and black as details.

1   2   3   4   5

Hot Kitchen

Hot colours in the kitchen promote a sense of activity and vitality. The hot scheme is a youthful and contemporary choice that is often under-used as the principal focus in the kitchen. We may see small areas of hot colour incorporated as incidentals to the overall theme, such as bright enamelled stoves or displays of jazzy-coloured plates and kitchenware, but to use reds and oranges as the main design focus demands a brave and disciplined hand. It is best not to saturate the entire kitchen with hot colour, given that strong hues visually dominate. Stick to a single-principal colour choice, used in a single area, such as on walls or cabinets alone, and use only cool or neutral colours with them.

A strong sense of lineal or spatial definition is essential in the hot kitchen, since the shape and proportions of the colours used will catch the eye. Curved lines promote a sense of spatial flow, which is essential where space is limited. Lines that are purposefully vertical and horizontal create strong, lineal definition. This directional effect combines with hot, vibrant colours to create a clean, uncluttered, and totally modern look.

Contrasting elements seen against the dominant colour take on great importance: cool materials make good partners to hot colours, so the use of brushed aluminium or stainless steel splashbacks, granite and cement worktops, or glass and metal kitchenware contributes greatly to the decorative ingredients of the scheme. The hot theme could be "zoned" within the working area, while the relaxed eating area might be treated with a more temperate overall scheme.

Above Deep burnt orange makes a spectacular background for cooler materials such as shiny stainless steel, chrome, and glass. Concrete worktops provide contrasting grey colour and texture, while a polished wooden floor not only accentuates the warmth of the theme, but also the strong, lineal definition of the units.

Opposite The efficient use of every working surface has a decorative effect in this small kitchen, where hot colour is tempered with black-and-white flooring.

1. Plain hot materials can appear as a rather solid block, so using one with a contemporary motif adds a little texture and change of colour without spoiling the focus.

2. A geometric check with a difference, this combination has a fashionable retro look that works well when its strong colours are emphasized elsewhere.

3. One of the joys of modern paints is the availability of all sorts of finishes. Notice the difference in the way light affects each one before deciding.

4. Highly glazed tiles add a unique depth to the finished hot scheme. This one has a mottled effect that adds textural interest as well as vibrant colour.

5. Linoleum allows the introduction of any kind of floor finish at an inexpensive price and is a practical choice for the kitchen. This rich colour and texture are timeless.

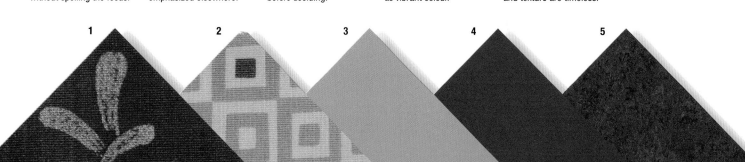

1 2 3 4 5

Cool Schemes

There is more to putting together a cool scheme than simply using colours within the cool spectrum. The idea is to create a room with a feeling of spaciousness, light, and harmony, where discerning use of colour, pattern, furnishings, and ornamentation all contribute to the decorative direction. The colours which can be used to create the look run from black and white to blues and greys of all sorts. Grey is underrated as a decorating colour because it infers dullness. However, there are a whole range of subtle shades from pale dove grey to dark storm-cloud grey that can look wonderful when complemented by the right colours, and grey is very useful for highlighting and toning down other colours. In a cool scheme grey can be partnered with blue and white as a mid-tone transition, helping the other colours not to look too sharply contrasted. Grey works well with palest yellow, too, for a crisply sophisticated and cool look. Grey-blue is an extraordinarily timeless colour that has been used throughout history and is now associated especially with intrinsic Swedish design. It can be combined with lots of white, finished with black detailing or perhaps with a touch of warmer blue, because the "cool" look should never become "cold".

Blues are of course the ubiquitous colours of the cool palette. From the subtlest blue-white to bright turquoise and deep navy, you can use blue to add a sense of calm to a room. Combine blue with white for a classic, timeless look, or introduce black accents for definition. Why not introduce some metallic touches to really bring your scheme to life? A sense of space and rhythm is maintained by limiting busy pattern in a cool interior. Suitable designs include stripes, trellis, and delicate all-over patterns on a white background. Avoid mixing lots of patterned fabrics and wallpapers in a busy way because this will decrease the visual sense of roominess.

Cool Entrance

The quality and use of colour is vital to the initial impression given when a front door is opened into the entrance hall. The cool scheme, using colours that range from simple black and white to a multitude of blues and greys, partners perfectly with the architectural nature of a typical hallway and the commonly used entrance materials such as stone, metal, and wood.

The cool scheme combines controlled colour with lots of space between each element. In the entrance, the open front door gives the onlooker a framed view of the opposite aspect across the hall, so this area is of prime importance and colour should therefore be concentrated here. Cool blues, greys, or greens help to underline the entry view by providing it with a focusing colour framework. Subsequently, if there is a blank wall opposite the door, concentrate the decorative focus, perhaps by placing a large pot filled with fantastic flowers outlined by a blue-and-grey painted wall that acts as a frame. If the staircase is opposite the front door, flank it with a pair of white, grey, or marble-effect candlestands or accentuate its architectural lines by extending the cool hall paintwork right up the staircase.

Allow the architecture to dominate in the cool entrance, using simple blocks of colour or geometric patterns. Stripes and strong, lineal furniture shapes help to achieve a broken but structured look. Blue-green and grey-blue are particularly proficient at conveying cool informality for an understated entrance hall. Chalky Swedish blue with glossy black and white creates a well-defined cool scheme. Bear in mind that too many decorative bits and pieces distract the eye and muddle the intrinsically cool look.

Opposite Coolness and earthiness combine forces to create a harmonious picture with blue stripes and flaky paint and a narrow table decked with plants and handy storage boxes.

Above Using black, blue, and white together creates strong, lineal emphasis and frames unfussy objects and architectural elements. The Mackintosh chair is pure, cool elegance.

Below A lesson in controlled colour from the Shaker sect is learnt in this cool arrangement of white and blue colour, minimal, sturdy wooden furnishings, and polished good order.

1. A sophisticated and cool, yellow-grey and grey-blue silk stripe makes a smart window blind, door curtain, or luxurious wall fabric.

2. Cream and black stripes will accentuate the height of a room, so maximize the curtain drop by fixing the heading well above the window.

3. Add a softening note to the hallway and promote the sense of space and light by using a diaphanous fabric at the window.

4. Black paint with a high-sheen lacquer finish can be used on door frames and skirting boards for a defining decorative touch.

5. Experiment with different finishes available in a deep blue paint, best combined with a lighter, brighter shade for a balanced scheme.

1   2   3   4   5

Cool Living

The range of colours for the cool scheme extends beyond the simple blue-plus-white equation, since a greater range of colours and non-colours can be employed, including black and white, and grey and cream, but blue still provides the broadest and most useful colour scope.

Blues, blue-greys, and whites are natural partners for creating a relaxed and harmonious living space. This is because they help to promote a sense of calm and airiness, and provide the cool scheme with strong definition and character. The success of the combination is obvious, having been favoured traditionally and internationally in various ways, from Scandinavian style to Chinese and European ceramics, all of which can be used as the inspiration for your scheme. The cool grey-blue and white combination continues to be associated with the Swedish style today, and is an immensely popular look.

The cool blues can be interpreted in various tones for different effects: grey-blues look smart and sophisticated; aquamarine works well with purest white and silver hues; dark blues are best used in broken patterns to avoid looking heavy. To successfully maintain the scheme it is always worth remembering that cool blues mix well with silver and off-white. In the living room, however, coolest glacial blue could be partnered with stronger tones to prevent the look becoming rather cold and insipid. Alternatively, combine different shades of grey with lots of white.

Above Maximize natural light and exaggerate vertical space by using striped materials at the windows in a simple way, without pelmets. Palest blue walls, bare floorboards, and a simple blue rug enhance the spaciousness.

Opposite Simplicity and lightness of decorative touch are illustrated in this cool seating area with striped walls and blond-wood flooring. The cool blue and white of the cushions is contrasted with an elegant aquamarine painted table.

1. Inexpensive, a good mixer, and very versatile, cotton ticking can be dressed up with smart trimmings or used simply as a contrast lining for curtains.

2. A glassy blue background with eighteenth-century style classical motifs on silk makes a handsome, cool reflective finish for upholstery.

3. An aqua and diamond pattern paper, first seen in the seventeenth century, provides a cool background lifted by the hint of gold in the design.

4. A modest motif-design wallpaper is useful when you do not want to use a particular design theme, and where there is a large area of blank wall surface to cover.

5. Woodstains make flooring effects much more versatile and are available in many shades. Here, a light oak satin finish transforms ordinary softwood.

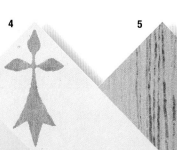

1   2   3   4   5

Avoid an overload of mixed pattern in the cool living room, as this will detract from the airy spaciousness of the theme. However, where pattern is used, scrolling and trellis designs will keep the look light and clean, using, for example, a grey-green background with a sharp, white applied pattern. Stripes always promote the illusion of extended space, particularly when used vertically and juxtapositioned with dark and light colours such as grey and silver, or Chinese blue and porcelain white.

The distribution of colour and decorative additions in the cool living room need to be balanced and uncluttered. Therefore, the blank areas between focuses of colour and furniture are important to the overall composure of the scheme. In the living room especially, where furniture and furnishings fill the room and a mix of colours and patterns can become overpowering, it is a good idea to include elements of broken or lightweight colour, such as an open-style bookcase featuring just a few, simple ornaments, or plain white or cream cushion covers.

Apart from the decorative content of a cool-coloured living environment – wall colours, sofas, cushions, curtains, carpets, and rugs – the interpretation of "cool" is also determined by lighting, both artificial and natural, the proportions and size of the room, and its global location. The yellow of some artificial light bulbs makes certain shades of blue appear much greener, or much warmer. A very pale, cool wall colour will be lost in a large room and promote a neutral rather than cool feel, while a darker shade will bring the walls inward. Therefore, when deciding on cool shades, decent samples should be experimented with all over the room, to test the effects of natural and electric light on colour and pattern when seen in situ.

The right choice of flooring should be utilized to promote and anchor the chosen theme. In the cool living room, bleached or colourwashed floorboards make an effective foil, perhaps including a simple painted border line to bring in one of the room's dominant colours. Alternatively, for a sleek, modern interior, floor tiles would effectively promote the cool look. Most natural flooring is cold underfoot, but limestone and terracotta retain the ambient temperature.

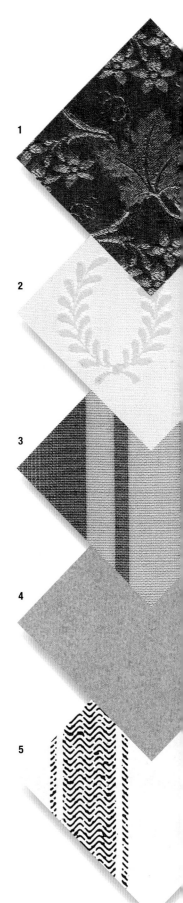

Above Blue-and-white stripes, checks, and a single floral pattern make natural partners for the cool living room, here combined with lots of dazzling white and cool, dark blue paintwork.

Left Line and space create a cool look here, with slimline furniture and angular architectural dimensions. The strong blue wall, white ceiling, and elegant painted floor complete the spacious feel.

1. Monochromatic fabrics and wallpapers are easy to mix and provide a good patterned foundation colour.

2. Sheers are always useful for creating a light and cool feeling, and can be used either as a simple banner curtain or in generous widths.

3. Shades of blue highlighted with palest yellow make an unusual silk fabric that is easy to match with other blues.

4. The stippled effect of this paper creates a lighter finish than flat paint and will make a sophisticated background.

5. An unusual use of the ticking design, this wallpaper should be used with restraint, rather than all over a room.

1

2

3

4

5

Above A striped armchair fits under a sloping ceiling and a bed, stacked with cushions that match the curtains and mattress, and becomes a second seating area. The blue-and-white theme and mix of stripe and pattern evoke cool symmetry.

Opposite An uncluttered, cool look is created in this awkwardly-shaped bedroom by surrounding the royal blue focus wall with "blank" areas of white and natural wood, and by keeping ornamentation and pattern to a minimum.

Cool Bedroom

Whatever decorating scheme you choose, the greatest endeavour should be made to ensure that the bedroom will always be a place of sanctuary imbued with individual personality and comfort. Happily, the bedroom is potentially one of the most decoratively flexible, creative, and individual areas in the home because it is contrived solely for personal, rather than public, gratification. Within the bedroom environment, the cool look creates an atmosphere of harmony, reflection, and peace.

The aspect of the room is one of the first considerations when deciding on what ingredients will best empathize with the spirit of the style. If the room has large windows and faces toward the sunshine, then this is the principal factor on which to base all other ingredients. Exploit the fact that the room is blessed with lots of natural light by using ethereal or subtly patterned fabrics. Be generous in the quantities to engender a sense of luxury, but keep the curtain design unfussy and rhythmical: there is a vital balance to find when using cool colour, maintaining an open, cool look while not mistakenly creating a sense of bleakness.

The bed's solid bulk is the visual core of the room, and as such should be fully included within the overall scheme, rather than treated as a separate entity, as so often happens. Include at least one deeply upholstered chair or chaise longue, if there is room, and provide plenty of storage space to exclude mess.

1. Combine a simple ticking with charcoal and plain blue materials for a versatile combination that is suitable for window and bed dressings.

2. If pattern without colour is what you desire, then a sheer like this is suitable for an adult's or child's curtains, with its stylized trees and cavorting animals.

3. Although this is a historical document wallpaper, it looks equally contemporary today, especially when combined with modern bedroom furniture.

4. A very matt paint finish has a texture and depth that makes it the perfect companion to softly finished materials in the bedroom.

5. Perfectly appropriate for the bedroom, this star-struck carpet is modern, softly smooth, and comfortably warm underfoot.

1
2
3
4
5

Take full advantage of the combinations of "hard" and "soft" surfaces for the cool bedroom: bedrooms contain a lot of soft furnishings, while the bedframe, wardrobes, and other storage items provide ample hard surfaces. It can be the pivot for a blue and silver, or white and aquamarine scheme, leaving the "hard" areas of floor and walls as the clean-lined backdrop in white or palest blue. While hard flooring certainly contributes to the cool atmosphere of a room – painted floorboards, for example – it is a good idea to combine this with rugs and curtains to soften the sound. Woodwork could be painted to pick up on the focus of colour around the bed. If the fabric focus is to be held on the bed area, an easily created four-poster effect can be made by attaching light material curtains onto tape and fixing the four corners to hooks screwed into the ceiling.

The cool theme, especially in the bedroom, must never be a clinical or cold one, so you will need to make concessions here and there. Either use subtle variations in colour so that the look is not too "empty", or use full, on-the-floor curtains in cool grey-blue and white, or aqua-green and silver, that help to maintain a soft edge where appropriate.

Naturally, white walls accentuate cool space, but in the bedroom it is best to include areas of colour – soft blues that retain the cool feel – especially around the bed to define that focus, perhaps by painting the bedhead wall.

Right Combining lots of blues is easier than harmonizing two. Despite the use of different fabrics, coolness is the result here, because of their similarity and tonal balance. The addition of curtains would be too much.

Far right Although in a basement, the room is kept light and airy by painting the ceiling, tiling the floor, and leaving lots of white space around the bed's strong blue focus.

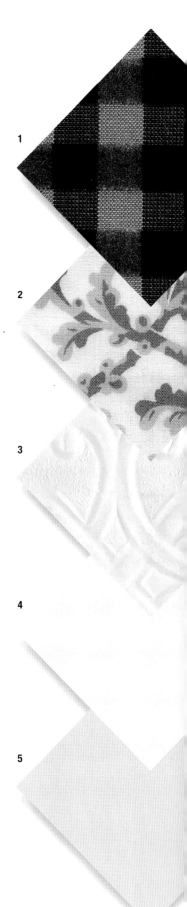

1. Tactile materials lend another decorative texture to the cool scheme. This velvet-pile check is both cool and sensual, ideal for the bedroom.

2. Try using sheers in other ways, not just at the window or as bed drapes. Perhaps a delicate overspread on the bed would complement the room's theme.

3. A different, although once traditional, way to add form and texture to the walls is to hang a raised-relief paper like this one. Paint with solid colour or apply a colourwash over the top.

4. Exploit the fact that modern paints can imitate any finish in either water- or oil-based composition. A matt finish is soft and absorbing, silk is washable and softly sensual, while gloss reflects light.

5. A light coloured paint in a special milk finish creates a light and cool environment that can be companioned with stronger colours.

1

2

3

4

5

Cool Bathroom

Good bathroom design exhibits innovation and practicality, enticing new finishes for glass, tiles, and flooring, comfortable bath shapes, and state-of-the-art shower units. The cool look is unsurprisingly extremely popular for bathrooms. The idea of a cool bathroom conjures up images of a spotlessly clean, uncluttered room, decorated in watery, calming colours that will wake you in the morning and provide a haven in which to rejuvenate after a long day.

This look centres on the hard materials within the bathroom for style focus, emphasizing this lean and pared-down direction. Uniquely, the bathroom's horizontal and vertical surfaces can be unified by using tiling or mosaic, creating a streamlined finish. Clad the walls, floor, panelling, and shelving of a small bathroom in unified tiles, or perhaps add a little detailing in another colour as a frieze around the cornice level, edging the floor, or framing the mirror area for extra visual interest. To maintain the cool lines, minimize any obtrusions in the room such as cupboards and shelving and maximize the potential of natural and electric light. Lighting needs to be clear and bright, leaving no shadowy areas or harsh hot spots. Preferably, use draw-curtains which can be pulled right away from the glazed window area to allow maximum light into the room, or use shutters or blinds instead. Consider options other than white bathroom equipment; grey makes a smart alternative and provides a change from the usual large blocks of harsh white. Grey looks cool and clean partnered with flashes of white and blue, or black and white.

Above It is not just the colouring that helps to create the cool look. Here, deep-blue mosaic covers the practical area, neat stepped cupboards add architectural merit, and a bleached-wood floor maintains the cool theme.

Opposite A tiny bathroom is given a neat, sleek finish with tiny blue tiles and pure white paintwork. Most is made of the space with out-of-the-way high shelving and a boxed-in cupboard concealing plumbing.

1. Although the cool look is sleek, a fabric, such as this soft blue cotton, adds another decorative dimension.

2. Use this marine-themed fabric to add some pattern to the room. It would be ideal for window dressings.

3. With a finish like deep, tropical seawater, these tiles will bring a deeply relaxing aquatic feel to a bathroom.

4. Nothing could be cooler than a light-reflective white tile. Combine these with a blue or grey detail.

5. Combined with white and silver-grey walls and detail, this dark, pearl floor tile will give a bathroom great character.

1   2   3   4   5

Cool Dining

Naturally, the focus of the dining room is centred around the table, and therefore the onlookers will not be giving as much attention to the decorative detail as they would in the living room, for example. Accordingly, the starting point for planning the design should be the wall treatment, as this is the largest area within the room and thus the most dominant feature. Think a little about the other colours used in the room, the crockery and table decoration for example, and choose favourable shades of cool colour for the walls – duck egg blue with cream, baby blue with primrose, denim with salmon pink, or mint green with butter yellow. Link elements of the table ensemble with aspects of the scheme other than the walls, such as the tablecloth or some chair covers. China and glass are also relevant to the rest of the decoration, because the success of this look is based on balancing tone and texture.

Informal and contemporary, the cool scheme is best when good natural light enters the room, because the greens, greys, and blues associated with the cool dining room need natural light in order for the subtlety of their colours to be best appreciated. Good strong light will enhance the spaciousness and alfresco feel; this is the scheme to use when you entertain informally during the daytime, when the colourful food is the main decoration. To warm up the look at night, be generous with the candlelight on the dining table and leave the walls to darken in the shadows, making the room more intimate.

Right Intensely blue walls and unpretentious furniture, shelving, and objects create a pared-down simplicity and balance of colour, shape, and texture.

Below Cool grey-green paint covers plaster and brick alike, leaving the focus on the table and the abstract landscape painting. Flowers and napkins add hot notes here and there.

1. Plain materials can convey a cool, lean look better than patterns. This self-stripe natural fabric can be used for curtains and upholstery.

2. Striped wallpapers have been associated with dining rooms since the Regency period, but this example has a contemporary colouration.

3. A whisper of pale grey-green creates a tinted backdrop for blues and greys to be brought into the scheme.

4. This turquoise milk paint has an opacity of colour that is unrivalled by modern paints.

5. A dining-room carpet is useful for deadening the echo of voices, and this lapis short-pile carpet will tie in with other cool decorative elements.

1   2   3   4   5

Cool Kitchen

The kitchen is probably one of the easiest rooms in the house in which to use the cool scheme successfully, because there are already many "cool" components which must inevitably be included to form the functional framework of this practical room. Here, the look is not only expressed through the use of cool colour, but also through the line and composition of the kitchen units, cooking station, work table, chairs, and so on. Much of the kitchen is composed of "hard" materials, with metal machinery and cooking utensils, stoves and wash basins, wooden cabinets and worktops, natural surfaces such as granite and stone, and reflective glass and tiles. To maximize the cool look, focus attention on these elements. Use cool colour detail, or simply focus colour in one single area for a change of visual texture. Colour combinations should reflect the nature of the "hard" components: silver and aquamarine with satin aluminium, blue and white checks or stripes with chrome and glacier blue, and diaphanous white with frosted glass and blond wood.

Use samples and illustrations to see how combinations of colours, metals, tiles, specialist paints, cooking utensils, and so on work together. Reflective surfaces are "cooler" than matt finishes and this can be emphasized throughout the scheme. Maximize the potential of "industrial modernism" and make the greatest play on clear, clean lines and smart, shiny surfaces.

One way of approaching the cool kitchen theme is to focus on a particularly effective material, such as metal, and combine it with one single colour, such as metallic blue paint, to produce a streamlined finish, displaying as few visual extras as possible. Alternatively, soften the presentation by introducing fabrics and patterned tiles, special paint effects, and curvaceously sculptured work units. Just because this is a cool scheme, it does not mean you have to do away with all fabrics, but maintain the rhythm by avoiding large patterns, and keep the tailoring sharp.

Above A strong horizontal emphasis is produced by layering materials, from the shiny steel to sea-green tiles, and finishing with a Shakeresque stainless-steel rail.

Opposite Steely finishes and snow-white paintwork, combined with wood-strip flooring and slender furniture, make an uncluttered, modern, and airy kitchen.

1. Add a fabric dimension to the cool and hard kitchen environment with this silver-grey silk in the form of a blind or chair covers.

2. Unfussy material choices are important in the cool kitchen, so use simple fabrics in simple ways, such as this natural-coloured linen.

3. Use simple patterns, such as this restful blue-and-white stripe, to maintain the cool, streamlined look in the kitchen.

4. A trompe l'oeil vinyl flooring that imitates rough-cut slate would suit a country-style kitchen, mixed with white and blue-green.

5. When the decorative emphasis is on "hard" kitchen materials, incorporate the flooring into the scheme, too. Use a liming paste to give wood a cool look.

1   2   3   4   5

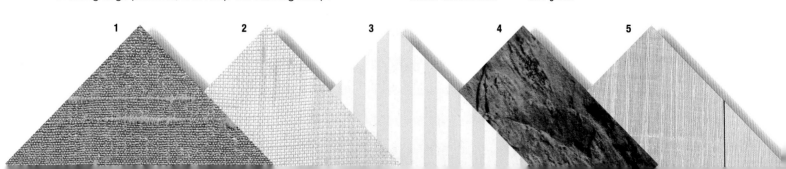

Fresh Schemes

The concept of fresh might mean different things to different people, because colour terminology is not an exact art and is open to interpretation. In this context we allude to fresh as the style that encompasses a range of lively colours, such as spring green, rose pink, lilac, and primrose yellow. These colours are youthful and light-hearted, restorative and unintimidating. Look to the world around you for inspiration. Imagine the colours of fresh fruits invitingly displayed outdoors on a sunny day and how bright and vital they look. Use blue and green together to recreate a partnership that is so successful in the natural world. When developing a decorative scheme, fresh describes a youthful, lively feeling as much as any particular group of colours.

How to use your fresh colours depends on the situation and the use of the room, but for the purposes of the fresh scheme, it is best to use only one colour as the focus, bringing in touches of another here and there for contrast. To create a truly fresh quality, the colours should be associated with lots of white or cream so that they are well separated and the pattern density is not overpowering. Fresh relates to the type of pattern used as well. If you choose a floral design, it is preferable to use just one mixed with a simple stripe or check rather than combining several dense patterns which might undermine the delicate airiness of the scheme. The same applies in your choice of window dressings and furnishings. In order to make the most of natural light and increase the sense of space, window curtains should be kept light and modest, covering as little of the window area as possible. Furnishings should have a lean look with comfortable but well-tailored upholstery or covers, without fussy trimmings or frills. Bed dressings, too, need to be part of the scheme, using layers to lighten the bed mass and crisp edges rather than gathers and frills.

Fresh Entrance

The fresh entrance scheme should convey all that the word does; colours are light and bright without being overpowering, the sense of space is exploited to full measure, natural light is seen to best advantage, and the use of pattern and furnishings is underplayed and innovative.

The perfect situation for such a scheme relies upon having enough ground area to create a roomy atmosphere, while making the most of natural light to maintain true fresh colours and a generally sunny feeling. This scheme does not require a lot of colour, merely the right sort of colour mixed with lots of pale space. Fresh colours – spanning a range from watery blues to sage, fern, and peppermint greens, fuchsia pink, and gerbera yellow – always associate well with white and off-white. Place the chosen main colour alongside cool white and its effect will be intensified. Make the most of a generous open staircase or high ceilings by painting the tallest wall in a fresh shade of yellow or green, and let the other walls, painted cream or apple white, frame the distinctive aspect.

Given that the entrance hall, rather like the kitchen, does not usually contain many fabrics and soft elements, the focus for promoting the fresh quality will rely on the distribution of small quantities of colour, such as spring-green pot plants or a tall vase of sunflowers placed in a safe position on the floor. Alternatively, a striped or checked floor, in suitably light, fresh colours, undoubtedly featuring white, will anchor and extend the theme.

Above Lots of white paint creates a spacious vacuum for this scheme with a pretty aquamarine checkered flooring extended into the kitchen beyond, picked up in the light-handed detailing.

Opposite Within this hallway's subtle, off-white shell, the detail creates a fresh, innovative direction, using a "notice board" of old documents and a duo of painted chairs covered in calligraphy and red, white, and blue silk.

1. Link decorative ingredients by using a calligraphy voile at the window and document photocopies on the walls.

2. This heavy cotton weave could be used as entrance "banners" on the walls of an Oriental-themed hallway.

3. Visual continuity within the hall and up the stairs is important. The link is easily made with paint detail.

4. A bold and crisp floor design in black-and-white tiles is a good baseline for colourful, fresh materials.

5. This striking motif gives a fresh, natural feel to the tile, and provides an alternative to more predictable floral patterns.

1   2   3   4   5

Fresh Living

The choice of colour scheme for the living room is more likely to relate to how the room is used than to other criteria. If the room is large and combines sitting and dining areas, then each zone can be used to illustrate the fresh look by using different combinations of the chosen colour scheme, or by separating them entirely. Colourwashes are effective at maintaining the light, fresh feel. For example, clear, spring green could be applied to the walls in a soft colourwash, linking the different areas, while the furnishings and ornamentation can be used to define each area. Blues work well when several shades are used together, so paint dining chairs, or combine blue and white on upholstery. Bring in the wall colour again for a tablecloth, edged in a darker, defining colour, such as a deeper tone of green or a contrasting blue. The sitting area could be furnished using a different contrast, such as off-white alongside the same blues and greens.

Pattern in the fresh colour scheme is flexible and can be directed toward bright and light checks, stripes, geometrics, and florals, as well as foundation plain colours. Cheerful modern florals provide a useful means of bringing together the room's principal colours in various mixes. Try them in dusty pink and spring green, lilac and cream, or primrose and zesty yellow-green.

Fresh colour combinations help create a lighthearted, young aura that relates to easy and informal living, where the colours are light and true and the atmosphere uplifting. Against a background of these delicate hues, pick up a contrasting colour or two within limited elements, such as flowers and china.

Left Soft green walls begin to set the fresh tone, partnered with white cloth and wicker, touches of stronger and brighter green, and a neutral carpet. The long shelf allows flexible positioning for objects and pictures.

Right Light cream matt-finish walls set the fresh essence of this expansive living room, furnished in a harmonious style in a green-and-cream plaid that sets off the lean, wooden frames. Touches of deep pink add interesting highlights.

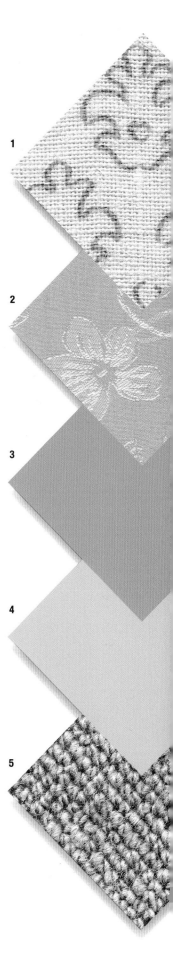

1. A small pattern on a fabric helps to break up bulky horizontal or vertical surfaces, without dominating the interior story. Use it to freshen up a large, solid sofa, for example.

2. Keep patterns light and bright, without bringing in too many distracting changes of colour or scale.

3. Areas of paint should be relative to scale, so that the scheme does not become saturated with one colour. Keep large blocks of solid colour to a single wall in a small room, for example.

4. Use paint to create visual continuity and subtlety by using two different tones of the same colour.

5. Sometimes a carpet can be key to bringing a scheme together and anchoring the various elements. A light, almost neutral shade with a hint of colour will not over-power the whole effect.

1
2
3
4
5

The fresh living room needs to make the most of the concept of spaciousness. To do this, distribute chosen elements of either furniture, curtaining, or carpet to create areas of light or neutral colour, using materials that are white, off-white, or the very palest insinuation of your main featured colour. To further the sense of freshness, keep decorative detail and ornamentation simple, clean-lined, and related to the room's colour theme. Here, where less is more, the focus is placed on the composed areas of fresh colour – lime green, primrose yellow, rose pink – combined with lightweight, simple objects, plants, flowers, and furnishings. Understandably, pattern and ornamentation must also maintain this lightness and freshness, therefore intensely patterned or heavyweight fabrics, such as damask or traditional chintz, are too oppressive to use. Likewise, decorative objects, pictures, and accessories need to reflect the same harmonious colour and lightness of quality as the rest of the room.

Natural light helps elevate the fresh quality of colour; greens and yellows become sublimely luminous in clear sunlight, while pinks and violets take on extra vibrancy.

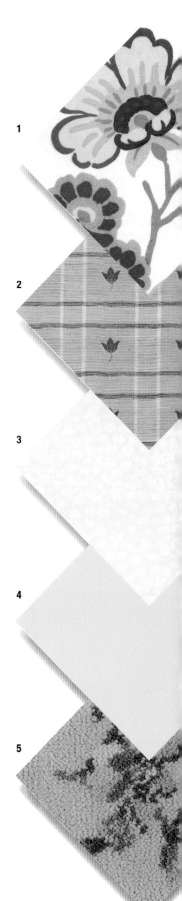

Left This living room is dominated by the solid block of a spring-green sofa, while the fireplace and roof line are painted white and cream to reflect the flood of natural light via the sloping glass roof.

Below A potentially traditional corner is given a new slant using a white slatted shutter that filters natural light to illuminate and refresh the various leafy chintzes and neutral materials.

1. A big, bright pattern should be used with discretion as a single banner curtain, or perhaps on a room-divider screen.

2. Small designs on fabric are always useful as mixers. This pretty check contains several colour possibilities.

3. Create a delicate striped background patina using a subtly coloured wallpaper.

4. A delicate shade of yellow will make the room feel as if the sun is always shining.

5. A pretty floral-design carpet can lay the foundation for the room's decorative scheme.

Fresh Bedroom

The fresh bedroom is lighthearted and airy, making the most of what space and natural light have to offer. This style uses colour with a gentle touch, so yellow will be creamy, aqua will be watered down, and pink should be soothing, not hot. The fresh bedroom has an uncluttered definition that allows each element to fit harmoniously with its neighbour, rather than shining in its own right. This look requires a disciplined use of line and finish that maintains a balance and a link between each area, while retaining a sense of space.

The fresh bedroom scheme should be youthful and modern, simple in interpretation, and restrained in ornamentation. To promote these concepts, use springtime colour combinations such as hyacinth pink with primrose yellow, and hints of moss green for contrast and detail. An alternative scheme could include apple green and lilac with magnolia as a neutral link, or, for a more subdued but consistently fresh look, experiment with shades of straw, butter, and cream.

Introduce pattern with discretion, using crisp floral designs and smart checks and stripes within a limited colour range. Lightweight fabrics and areas of single colour separated by lots of white space will keep the look exuberant but balanced. Because these fresh colours are airy and bright, complement them with a minimal amount of elegant accessories to maintain the sense of uncluttered harmony and style, and give thought to the style of bed dressing in order to reflect the room's style.

Opposite The warm and soft colours in this bedroom create a harmonious quality using cinnamon brown, sand yellow, and egg-yolk yellow combined with cream shades. The layered curtains and the tactile cable-stitch cushion make wonderfully novel contributions.

Above The delight of this bedroom lies in its lack of pretentiousness. Pale blue walls provide the backdrop for pretty double curtains, encompassing a simple pattern, and a check-based bed, complete with light tester drapes and a plump feather quilt.

1. Exquisitely feminine and elegant, this creamy yellow and light red floral document fabric is perfect for the fresh bedroom scheme.

2. This sumptuous patterned material could be used for upholstery, or to make a pretty bedspread or luxurious cushion covers.

3. Fresh coloured stripes, combined with a single simple floral, will make handsome partners, whether traditional or contemporary in style.

4. The bedroom takes pattern better than any other room and a background paper with a small design is easy to mix with other elements.

5. Traditional motifs like this laurel design stand the test of time and can be updated alongside contemporary fabrics and papers.

1	2	3	4	5

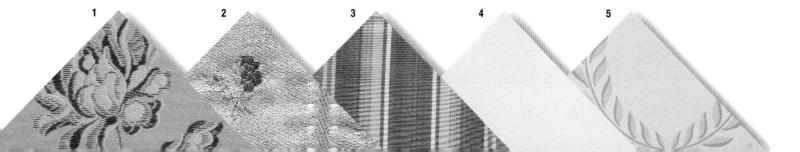

Fresh Bathroom

Imagine how enlightening it feels to swim in crystal-clear, turquoise seawater, or to dive into the deep-blue depths of a swimming pool. This is a sensation that can be created in the privacy of the home, too, in the form of a "fresh" bathroom. The right choice of colour goes a long way to promote this feeling of freshness in the limited confines of the shower stall or bathroom: aquamarine, azure, pearl, and crystal all help instil the desired atmosphere.

The fresh-look bathroom should always provoke a sense of space and light, with an open and bright quality, rather than a cosy and sensual one. Colour and line accentuate this feeling, so use sea-coloured tiles to cover large areas, creating a platform of uninterrupted colour, alongside a generous use of transparent materials and glass. It may be possible to replace a whole wall with glass to eliminate solid visual obstructions, and to install sleek bathroom units in gleaming white or a fresh aqua shade, with minimal visible plumbing. Paint the ceiling in a suitably pale hue and keep the floor light in colour and pattern to further promote the atmosphere of fresh spaciousness.

The inherent hard lines, angles, protrusions, and changes in levels confined within the small space of the bathroom distract from visual harmony. Try and minimize unnecessary angulation and changes in texture by limiting the range of colour featured in materials, fabric, and bathroom services. Choose just one or two closely related colours for walls and tiling, a choice that may be based on the colour of your existing bathroom service, then try to ensure that blinds, shower curtains, towels, and other pieces of bathroom furniture blend in with the main colour theme.

Sympathetic lighting is essential to any bathroom scheme, both for practical and aesthetic purposes. In the fresh-look bathroom creative lighting can be used to enhance the watery effect of the colours and materials that decorate the room. For example, strategically placed spotlights shining through rippled glass and reflecting on the shiny surfaces of the tiles will create the optical illusion of sunshine dancing on water. Alternatively, carefully direct neat, swivel-headed downlighters so that they create fields of light on aqua surfaces.

Above An understairs area has been converted into a neat and bright bathroom, with a window "framed" by stepped tiling, through which the natural light illuminates the watery blue tiles.

Opposite A sense of comfort and freshness is conveyed in this bathroom by the use of aqua and green combined with lots of clean white. The screen replaces curtains, affording privacy and elegance.

1. Including a touch of the unexpected, in a colour that complements the room, adds another fresh design element.

2. A blue-on-white, West Indian pictorial fabric helps to create the story of gentle breezes, warmth, and water.

3. A patterned fabric that picks up on the colour of the walls could be used to make a simple material screen.

4. Versatile green-and-blue tiles with the lustre and dimension of deep water can be used on walls or floors.

5. Inexpensive vinyl flooring has the added advantage of being easy to install and surprisingly warm on the feet.

1   2   3   4   5

Just as with the real thing, the sea colours of turquoise, azure, and crystal become incandescent in sunlight. Use this idea to create a flexible lighting system that can be manipulated to promote these qualities, using natural daylight where possible, perhaps filtered through slats or transparent voile to soften the reflections. Where there is a strong source of natural light in the bathroom, use transparent fabrics in yellows, blues, or greens to dress the window and enhance the effects of daylight, allowing the option of drawing a gossamer veil to filter the light when neccessary. Continue the water-and-light theme by using colours and textures that are associated with this combination; ripple-surfaced aquamarine tiles alongside smooth, thick glass; sandy yellow fabric against a sea-green mosaic; and, for a feminine touch, the subtle sheen of mother-of-pearl floor tiles partnered with a pretty floral voile in blues, pinks, and greens.

Left A triangular shower stall features aquamarine mosaic and clear glass panels to maximize light and space. To accentuate the illusion of submersion in water, plumbing fittings are recessed and extras kept to a minimum.

Opposite Using space economically, placing the bath to catch the natural light, creating curved shapes and bright, smooth finishes extends the illusion of space, light, and freshness.

1. This classic, fresh striped paper is ideal for use in a traditional bathroom, without making it look dull or dated. Use stripes in fabrics as well as on the walls.

2. A green-and-white fabric adds a touch of colour and elegance to the harder outline of bathroom services.

3. Create the illusion of crystal water and sea creatures with these glass tiles that have a fresh, translucent quality.

4. For a plain look paint the walls a fresh aquatic colour. Combine painted walls with patterned tiles or fabric.

5. If the walls are plain, then the floor can pick up a pattern for added interest. These mosaic tiles merely suggest pattern.

1

2

3

4

5

Fresh Dining

With its palette of springtime colours, the fresh concept in the dining room creates an atmosphere of informal lightheartedness. Dining-room furniture is often somewhat sombre and heavy, but a distraction can be provided with the addition of pretty, fresh colours. These may be used to create a Provençal quality with single colour florals – a pink *toile de Jouy*, for example, perhaps accompanied by a cloth for the table and slipcovers for chairs in a complementary check, finished with contrast piping and edging in an "off" colour such as beige or grey, to prevent the look from becoming too feminine. Blue and green together convey the fresh style particularly well, perhaps because the combination works so well in nature. Use this analogy to visualize the pleasing associations between flower and leaf, seen with bluebells, irises, and love-in-a-mist. Stripes and checks in mixed blues and greens can be easily united with other patterns, if required, without creating an overworked look. If pattern is used for the curtains and tablecloth, then, to maintain the spacious, airy, fresh look, keep the wall colour plain, perhaps using a slightly lighter shade of the main fabric colour. Alternatively, simply paint the walls white if the room has good natural light, to maximize the sense of space. Experiment with unusual paints such as milk paint or limewash for a soft sheen or matt finish respectively.

Dining accessories also contribute to the fresh scheme, so use colourful crockery, crisp napkins, bountiful bowls of fruit and vegetables, and bright informal flowers.

Above There is a balance in this dining room between the openness of the natural light and the cosiness of the rustic setting. A traditional toile pelmet is used alongside two red checks and a diaper-pattern wallpaper. The matting makes an effective base for the fresh scheme.

Opposite Clear, fresh colours work well when mixed in a simple, unornamented manner, as in this contemporary dining area in an open-plan living space. The spring-green background and pale wood of the table and chairs form the foundation of the scheme.

1. Checks and flowers together help to give the dining-room scheme an informal, fresh, French quality.

2. Keep materials for seating and curtains lightweight in texture and pattern, and use them in an unstudied way.

3. Silk taffeta has a luminous quality that reflects the light and adds a touch of luxury at the window or table.

4. The ubiquitous dining-room stripe can be used in a fresh way, as this pink, candy-stripe wallpaper illustrates.

5. However light and airy a scheme is, a darker carpet can be a good colour anchor to aid visual reference.

1   2   3   4   5

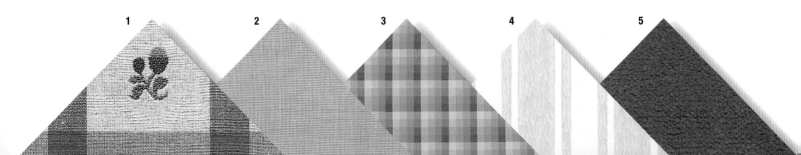

Fresh Kitchen

The use of the word "fresh" associated with the kitchen is thoroughly appropriate. Fresh fruit and vegetables could become inspirational for the fresh kitchen colour scheme with apple green and pineapple yellow, lime green and lemon yellow, strawberries and cream, or raspberry and mint, all taken from the fresh-fruit menu. Add a pinch of chilli, cinnamon, and saffron here and there for colour variation and detail variety, and present this lively decorative recipe on a platter of patinated wood or earthy, textured tiles to complete the look.

The business of cooking requires a great deal of time and effort spent in an environment that contains a lot of practical, hard equipment which produces stressful noise and heat. Therefore, it is enjoyable, if not essential, to have an area of the kitchen which is entirely different in composition to the working department. This may be semi-partitioned by a broad kitchen utility unit, an arched false wall, or a simple and adaptable hinged screen. The latter is a useful device that allows the introduction of another material to further the fresh look. Fill the frame or cover the panels with a bright, patterned fabric, or paint paper or wood panels using one or two of the room's colours. The idea of the partition is to create areas of individual identity while maintaining architectural unity and, very importantly, social contact.

When you are creating a conversation or dining area in the kitchen, the use of fresh and zesty colours and fabrics helps to set the tone for spontaneity and informality. Choose a couple of favourite colours from the scheme and introduce them in a different form than elsewhere, to give identity to the area without divorcing it from the rest of the kitchen. Experiment with combinations of colourwashed paint or bold stripes, or piles of multicoloured crockery on the table. Alternatively, clad the walls around the dining area with tongue-and-groove boarding painted unusually in bright yellow or fresh green, depending on the other colours used in the scheme. If you want a decorative focus on the table, tie the whole kitchen scheme together with a suitably eclectic mixture of ceramic tableware, napkins, glassware, and serving dishes to reflect the fresh mood.

Above In this Californian kitchen, the eating area is linked to, but separate from, the working area. Visually, the arch and window link the two, as do the terracotta floor tiles. The cooler colours in the foreground give way to the fresh, hand-drawn, Mexican-style pattern running like a frieze around the wall. The colours are echoed in the flowers and painted chairs. Natural light is maximized by keeping the window free of curtains.

Above In a comfortable corner of a white-painted clapboard kitchen, a light table can be placed or easily removed to provide additional eating space. The pretty floral banquettes and bolsters are partnered with check fabric cushions and make a charming window seat, too. The window itself has a simple and lightweight valance treatment and the fresh theme is accentuated by the window box of herbs and flowers, ready to hand.

1. When there are so many hard and dull materials in the kitchen, it is fun to be able to use a really bright and fresh fabric in contrast.

2. An alternative scheme uses checks as the foundation, mixing bright green, blue, and white in a fresh medley.

3. In a small space, confine pattern to a limited palette. This pretty floral would make a feature as a tablecloth.

4. Notes of darker colour will lift the light wall paint, so pick out materials in a darker tone and use them as highlights.

5. Crossing the centuries and continents, this terracotta, slate, and stone mosaic flooring adds depth and style to any kitchen.

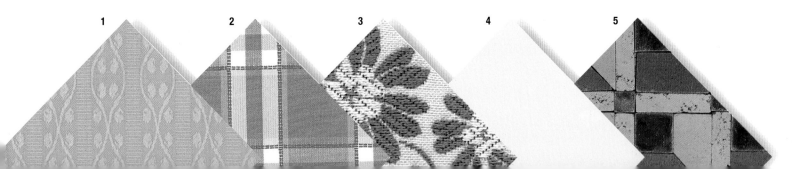

1   2   3   4   5

Muted Schemes

Seen in isolation from the interior scheme and from each other, muted colours might initially be regarded as sombre or even dull. However, when they are used in combinations with each other and with "lifting" highlights of light colour, they create a handsome and mellow scheme. Colours that fall under the collective description of muted include sage green, mustard, tobacco, mushroom, dusty pink, damson, and pewter. Because these colours are devised from subtle and complex combinations of hues and tints, there is no definitive range as there is with other colour themes. Rather, these muted shades are known as "knocked-back" – colours which tend toward the darker tones. As they are close in tonal range, viewing these colours in juxtaposition will maximize their subtlety. They are particularly effective on vertical surfaces where their effect is more noticeable, especially as matt paint on walls and slub cloth curtains. This is a colour range that does not reflect light as some colours will, so the essence of the scheme relies on exploiting played-down colour together with soft, flat materials. To add highlights and touches of brightness, choose soft creams which will lighten the look without interrupting the gentle colour scheme. Silver and gold work well as highlights, so choose picture frames and other accessories that will add a subtle touch of sparkle, and wooden furniture and flooring looks beautiful set against muted colours.

Although these shades have been associated with historical interiors, they are perfectly adaptable to today's style and can be used in a country or city environment. The balance of colour needs careful consideration and off-white, rather than pure white, is more appropriate as a "service" colour on woodwork and ceilings. Alternatively, paint the ceiling a paler shade of the dominant muted colour to create visual harmony throughout the scheme.

Muted Entrance

Muted colours are comforting and deep, companionable, and timeless. In the entrance hallway they can be used to convey the larger scheme of the rest of the house, or period-style values. They can act as an overall background colour or a key that joins various elements and details of the scheme, from furniture to artworks. The tone can be set outside by using a dusky paint colour or effect on the front door. Instead of painting it high gloss, it could be given a patinated, antiqued finish in grey-blue or flat green, undercoated in dark red or charcoal. Inside, continue the theme with muted panelling to dado level, or echo the exterior door colour in an impressive painting or fresco.

The muted style encompasses objects and furnishings as well as base colour, so these should be included in the overall illustration. Fortunately, muted shades make a wonderful background colour to all sorts of other materials, fabrics, and textures, especially when they are featured as contrast highlights. The look should include a balance of the muted tones featured within the various decorative items, including paintings, statues, flowers, and furnishings. Lighting, as always, will create its own aura and change the way the colours and artifacts are seen, depending on time of day and manipulation of electric light. Dramatic uplighting, soft picture lights, or subtle candle illumination all add to the illusion and warrant considered placement. Flooring should help to anchor the other decorative elements; therefore, a natural material, such as wood or a wood effect, is an excellent choice.

Above A sophisticated and ordered entrance hall, arranged with symmetry and colour coordination, reveals smoky-blue paintwork, design prints, and urns overflowing with heather. The keynotes of the design are focused low down to underline the decorative theme.

Opposite From the moment the antique painted door opens, the decorative style of this hallway is revealed, with simplicity and grace. A collection of statues and walking sticks, a grand painting, and a footbath filled with leaves all contribute to an informal, muted look.

1. A muted damask covering the front door or a window conveys subtle pattern and both silk and matt textures.

2. This moss green and buff linen union would complement antiqued paintwork in similar tones.

3. Knocked-back colours, such as this green-grey, make a good, solid background to strong detail.

4. A coloured, striped sheer at the window will filter the light to accentuate the muted entrance theme.

5. Fit a laminate floor that imitates colourwashed wood and you will not have to paint the floor yourself.

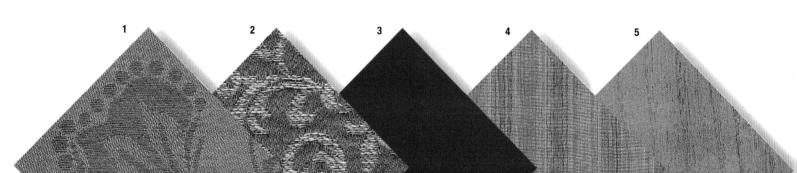

1 2 3 4 5

Muted Living

Potential muted mixtures for the living room include dusty rose with grey and sage. Introduce the rose-and-sage combination as a floral pattern in flat linen or unglazed cotton. Paint the walls above dado level in either sage or rose and add flint grey below. Furnishings can follow the colour combination in any manner, but introduce a lighter note of off-white here and there to keep the scheme lively. Damson with old gold and black makes a very handsome scheme. Apply the damson to the walls in a matt paint, finished around the architectural outline with a fine painted line of dark gold. Against this place black-painted furniture and putty and damson fabrics. Mushroom, grey-blue, and silver is a trio of smart muted colours. Cut lengths of mushroom-coloured felt to make unstitched banner curtains slotted onto silver rods. Provide a strong, sophisticated backdrop using a satin paint finish in mushroom glaze, layering it over an undercoat of grey-blue for underlying colour depth.

Historical and earthy colours come within the muted colour range, too. Flat, organic dark green, for example, very popular in the eighteenth century, works just as well today alongside its complementary colour of ox-blood red. As these are powerful hues, give them their own space, perhaps using one as a solid background colour, while the other features in a bold pattern incorporating some neutral tones such as stone and straw. Another good colour to use, much associated with the Arts and Crafts movement and William Morris wallpaper, is olive green. This is an earthy, intense colour that comes to life when it is highlighted with old gold and off-white. Historical muted shades are best utilized as the foundation colour on the walls, in dead-flat finishes to underline the knocked-back colour theme, and partnered with one other main colour, within a pattern or solo, to assert visual balance and rhythm.

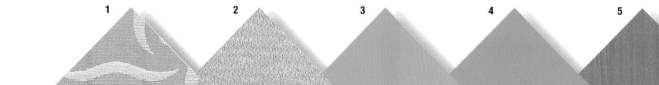

1   2   3   4   5

Left Muted greens on the walls and fire surround provide the background colour to a living room that is rich in subtle tones and textures including faded pink, lacquer, and antique gold.

Below Placed within a neutral shell of cream, parchment, and terracotta, the blue and mustard Madras-cotton curtains make a dramatic addition, accentuating the height of the room.

1. This luxury silk weave in modernist style has a muted, retro look suitable for upholstery or as a sofa throw.

2. Muted blue and mustard work well together as contrast notes or as foundation colours on upholstery.

3. A subtle paint colour, between blue, grey, and green, makes a good background to a colourwash.

4. Try using a mustard or tobacco paint in a decorative paint effect that softens a strong base coat.

5. Woodstained planking could be used to create an unusual panelled wall finish as well as flooring.

A muted theme requires the right situation and interior embellishments. Naturally dark rooms can never be made to look lighter with light colours, so why not choose darker colours to create a comfortably introspective interior. These colours need the contrast of decorative highlights, whether provided by trimming detail, or more generally within the pictures, ornaments, cushions, and so on. Muted colour makes a spectacular background for pictures and furniture of all kinds. When gilt, silver and black, or red lacquer are placed against olive green, brown-red, aubergine, and cool blue, the result is a beautiful visual symbiosis. Wood of all sorts somehow takes on extra glamour and patina against these colours, too. The effect of the contrasting characters of these materials can be further emphasized by using non-reflective textures such as dead-flat paint and textured, unglazed fabrics, against which the reflective elements become even more luminous. To keep the scheme from becoming overweight, change the tempo here and there with highlights of cream, rather than white, and touches of really bright colour which will also give a fillip to the muted tones. Even if there is not the right situation to make the most of an all-over muted scheme, using focused areas in these colours against a broader background of neutrals adds a strong design direction without detracting from the main foundation concept.

Left Quiet comfort is conveyed with the focus around the fireplace, centred on the traditional Welsh-wool quilt, comfortable checked chair, and subtle-patterned kilim.

Above In this living room, the muted aspect relates to leather and subtle-textured furniture, combined with a bronzed screen, khaki wool curtaining, and pared-down art and artifacts.

1. Old pink makes a change to the green-and-blue muted look without being too pretty.

2. It is important to incorporate pattern to break up solid blocks of colour and add contrast.

3. Dead-flat or matt paints are unreflective and convey the muted finish superbly.

4. Muted green is given a lift when associated with off-white and antique gold detail.

5. For a light touch with comfort, this olive-and-khaki carpet suits all muted styles.

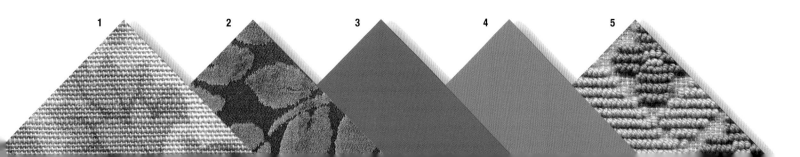

1   2   3   4   5

Muted Bedroom

Within the bedroom context, muted shades create a sense of depth and calm and act as a foundation for texture and highlight colour. Manipulating the atmosphere of a bedroom is particularly rewarding and relatively easy, because there are so many decorative facets to play with. Starting with the wall treatment as the base, first choose the muted colour that you like and then decide on the application. Suitable combinations for the bedroom include warm cinnamon with cream, grey-blue partnered with old gold, or sienna brown and sage green. These relatively masculine base colours can be accentuated using strong, solid blocks of colour and well-defined pattern such as bold stripes or checks. Alternatively, combine them as part of a floral pattern and introduce highlight colours to brighten the scheme.

A suitable muted wallpaper for the bedroom would be plain with a textured finish, such as a grass weave or moiré effect. A flat or matt paint finish looks best in the bedroom because it does not reflect light and therefore creates a soft, cosy ambience. Whether it is real or trompe l'oeil, panelling always looks handsome in this range of colours, calling to mind the traditional use of knocked-back greens and reds.

The bedroom's muted theme needs to use materials generously to generate the necessary sense of warm luxury. Window curtains could feature a coloured or diaper-pattern lining that underlines the muted look. The bed itself should echo the room's background colour, but lightened and defined with brighter notes and cream or off-white highlights.

Above The theatrical approach in this bedroom features a bed raised on a checkerboard stage against plain-painted brick walls and dark-stained floorboards. The bed dressing and artifacts surrounding the bed underline the muted, but texturally rich, arrangement.

1. This fabric conveys a delicate floral rhythm without being a strident, dominating pattern.

2. A contrasting matt and reflective fabric, like this checked silk, extends decorative interest.

3. For a luxurious finish, trim this lustrous silk with old gold and dark red edging.

 **4.** Define light walls with strong colour accents for skirting, woodwork, and contrast edging.

5. With such a wide range of finishes, versatile linoleum makes an alternative bedroom floor.

1   2   3   4   5

Right Muted classicism across the ages is illustrated in miniature with blue-green panelling, a period four-poster bed, a luxuriously embroidered bedspread, together with an eclectic mixture of ornaments.

Muted Bathroom

There are no restrictions dictating the most suitable atmosphere for a bathroom; it can be made to feel warm and cosy, or move in the opposite direction to create cool, minimalist surroundings. The muted bathroom can be manipulated to fall into either category. For the comforting option, choose the warmest hues in the muted range – plum, mulberry, damson – and combine them with wooden cladding, antiqued paintwork, brass detailing, and soft matting. To evoke a cooler, fresher atmosphere, turn the focus toward hard materials, such as marble, glass, and tiling, that emphasize grey, mushroom, or olive. Alternatively, the muted look is equally effective if aspects of the warm and cool are combined. For example, deep sea green looks smart with old gold metals and cream paintwork, and slate grey and aubergine team up handsomely.

The muted style especially suits an internal bathroom, or one with poor natural light, because the colours used, such as grey-blue, sage green, browns, and greys, are particularly effective when illuminated by the glow of a well-arranged electric light system, to produce an urbane and welcoming environment.

Bathroom design relies heavily on "hard" components for its decorative direction and colour input. The muted scheme features a subtle, easily mixed palette of colours that suit being used as part of the structural components within a bathroom. For example, tiles take the darker shades of green and blue glazes well, while the variations in muted types of marble and stone can be chosen to colour-relate to paint and tile finishes.

Right In this monochrome scheme of grey and white, the beautiful marble dominates the sleek, muted look. Black and white photographs of classical buildings underline the theme.

Below Green and cream make naturally handsome muted partners, seen here in the gloss of tinted glass, the splashback, and bath panelling against the matt finish of the paintwork.

1. This marble-effect fabric at the window will soften the hard elements in the bathroom, but still underline the overall muted scheme.

2. Simple pull-up blinds are most appropriate in the bathroom because they are less likely to suffer from damp. This muted check incorporates the softer element of a repeated small floral motif.

3. A smart and contrasting gloss paint in antique grey is perfect for woodwork and metalwork, especially against matt textures.

4. Try to use as much natural texture as possible, by contrasting stone, tile, glass, and ceramic finishes.

5. This hard flooring picks out muted colours and textures.

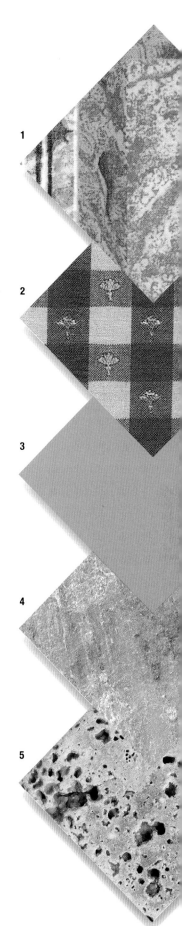

1

2

3

4

5

Muted Dining

There are many ways to manipulate the atmosphere of a decorative scheme, but certain design constituents are more adaptable or more influential on the look than others. Colour is an essential focus within the dining-room scheme, primarily because the room's function prescribes a standard disposition of arrangements. Given that a typical dining room has a central table and upright chairs, a fireplace or display unit on one wall, and windows on another, the decorative colour for curtain fabric, flooring, walls, and tableware is crucial to providing individualism.

Muted colours have historically been associated with the dining event, from the Medieval baronial hall, where the walls were adorned with tapestries, to the over-ornamented Victorian dining room, with its darkly rich embossed leather or damask papers and heavy velvets in green, red, black, and old gold. Today, the combination of ingredients used should create a harmonious balance between colour, object, and style.

As the largest area of decorative surface, let the walls dictate the atmospheric direction, making the most of a solid block of muted colour: spinach, plum, and tobacco are three appropriate colours that make strong key tones into which other decorative elements can be diffused. Strengthen the theme with the impact of well-directed detail. For example, use contrasting borders for curtains and carpet, emphasize the outline of painted walls with pewter or antique gold detail, or contrast-line the curtains with an appropriate muted colour, such as silver grey or deep blue.

Above The combination of matt forest-green paint, soft gold and floral framing, and the rich patina and colour of polished wood makes a pleasing, comfortable dining-room theme.

Opposite Scale and balance work well here, with dark plum walls and splash-patterned curtains, which augment the natural fabrics and earthenware, the wood and bay tree, and the metal and candle wax.

1. A spaghetti-squiggle weave makes practical and elegant dining-chair upholstery.

2. The hints of red in this fabric can be echoed elsewhere as a change of colour direction.

3. Stripes are timeless and distinctive, providing lineal definition, especially at tall windows.

4. A soft, cut-pile, monochrome floral contrasts well with geometric patterns.

5. Use an imitation walnut-effect paper to present a sophisticated panelled background.

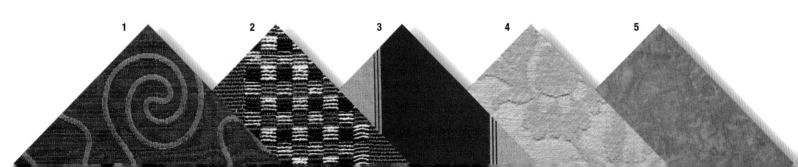

Keep in mind that the surfaces surrounding the dining table will remain a backdrop to its focus, so consider table decorations as well as wall colours. The dining table may be treated as the centre of attention, somewhat removed from the perimeter decoration, although it should always relate in some way to the rest of the scheme, usually by reintroducing a flavour of the main ingredient. There should be light touches, too, because the toned-down scheme is distinguished by attention to subtlety and needs the input of highlights, whether they are neutral and light or distinctive and bright.

One way to interpret all of the above advice is to choose one defining colour, use a second as a subordinate hue, and pick out details in a third light, bright, or neutral shade with a different highlight. Suitable combinations include: cinnamon and dark blue highlighted with off-white; deep maroon and lead grey with antiqued silver gilt detailing; or aubergine and olive green with black and gold contrasts. The highlight colours will glint in the light while the background shades look rich and mellow.

Certain patterns seem to suit the dining room particularly well, so consider using a large diffused pattern, such as a damask, a flowing floral or scroll design, or, for an alternative to traditional vertical stripes, try broad horizontal stripes – if the smooth, uninterrupted wall surface allows. If pattern dominates as a tablecloth or curtains, then paint the walls plainly in a matt, satin, or colourwashed finish.

Left Muted shades of tobacco, green, and blue create an informal dining-room environment, enhanced by tartan curtains and seat cushions, an eighteenth-century display cupboard and collection of china, and an assortment of Windsor chairs.

Right Illustrating the importance of neutral highlights and texture within the muted scheme, the cinnamon-painted walls make a lovely background for ironstone dishes, an Orkney chair, and polished wooden floor. A pinoleum blind and chintz curtains complete the look.

1. This patterned green fabric is a useful material for either curtains or chair upholstery, but, because of the size of the pattern, avoid using for both.

2. A large repeat pattern fabric in knocked-back tones might be used for curtains or as an unusual, striking tablecloth.

3. A dining room used predominantly at night-time can exploit the notion that candlelight works wonders on dark, muted colours such as this rich red.

4. Casein or milk paints have a unique opacity of colour and a soft texture, and can be used on woodwork and furniture.

5. An alternative to the traditional carpet or wood flooring in the dining room, these cork tiles come in a variety of different colours.

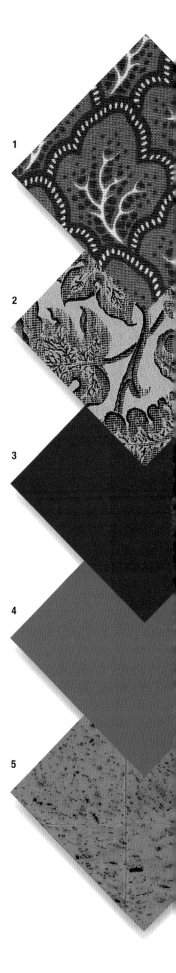

1

2

3

4

5

Muted Kitchen

Putting together the elements for the muted kitchen involves using both limited colour and well-defined structural design. This requires discipline and subtle use of shape, tones, and materials so that the result will be muted in all senses, from colour to lighting, materials, and ambience.

The muted colour scheme underlines the functionalism of the kitchen, incorporating disciplined but not cold coloration. Such a kitchen might be any size, large or small, in any location, but it must be functional and fit the cook's requirements perfectly. Experiment with unusual combinations of shape, material, and colour, such as smoked-glass cupboard panels and granite work-surfaces, lightened by a patterned green and cream voile at the window or a narrow checked linen table runner, to add a softening touch to the eating area without losing the sharp decorative edge. Combine matt and shiny surfaces in natural "mineral" colours of slate and stone, and make checked patterns using rust and green unglazed tiles. The textural effect of a splashback and working surfaces in satinated steel or polished concrete sets off the silkiness of blue and aubergine tiles or mosaic against the flat look of naturally pigmented paintwork.

Easy access to the *batterie de cuisine* is essential, and this can also become part of the muted look, via the contribution of wood, steel, copper, and iron, either hung from well-ordered display racks and hooks, or stacked on shelves in casual array.

Lighting should be diffused over the entire working area, so that it illuminates the textural surfaces and eliminates areas of shadow. Except for touches of fabric at the windows and on the table, there are very few decorative objects, because everything should have a practical function.

Finishing details maintain the visual muted theme through minimal furnishing, such as ultra-plain cupboard handles. Storage, materials, walls, and flooring are kept within a controlled range of colour, which could be dominated by a single muted hue such as grey-green, flat beige, or blue-grey.

Above Strong, geometric lines and a solidly symmetric arrangement set the tone for this practical kitchen. Materials and surfaces are kept within a well-defined range of colour and sourced objects; sleek wood under-units are topped with a streamlined worktop, which in turn has an easy, non-reflective backplate. The window shelving is a novel and practical way of using space and creating an interesting screen, and could be adopted in any kitchen where space is at a premium, or simply because it provides an interesting effect on the play of natural light coming though the window and onto the objects within.

Above White paint and terrazzo tiling dominate this serviceable kitchen. Everything is easily at hand thanks to an open steel rack holding frequently used essential items, including a well-placed wine glass holder. Although there is limited colour used here, the design effect of such a scheme is evident in the concentration on lineal harmony and pared down "ingredients". The emphasis here is centred around the practical, lean lines rather than additional decorative detail and colour.

1. As a contrast to the usual hard kitchen materials, use a soft velvet pile like this for upholstered chairs.

2. Add a lighthearted element – the muted look is not meant to be dull – using a pictorial fabric in approriate shades.

3. Sleek and muted, this dark green, soft-sheen milk paint would look good alongside shiny chrome accessories.

4. Use this subtle, clean colour with darker shades of green in conjunction with strong architectural elements.

5. A natural stone effect on linoleum is a cheaper alternative to real stone tiles, but the effect is just as attractive.

1   2   3   4   5

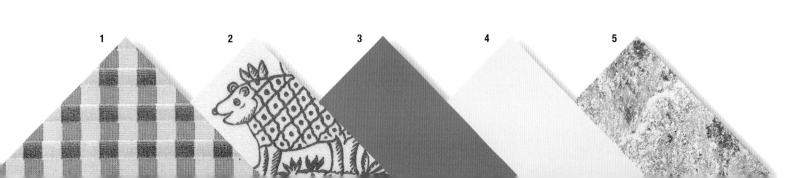

Choosing Finishing Touches

Lighting

The way a room is lit is fundamental to its mood. To make a room look inviting, the style and distribution of lighting is crucial; even the most beautifully thought-out and well executed decorative scheme will be diminished, if not ruined, by not giving enough thought to the lighting arrangement. Apart from candlelight, which is romantic and attractive but impractical as the sole source of light, the most congenial, flattering light is given by table lamps distributed evenly around the room. An additional reading light, swing-arm bracket, or floor light could also be included as required. Unfortunately, however beautiful a chandelier is, or however practical down-lighters are, they do not provide a mellow, regular spread of light in social or "conversational" areas of the home. However, there are places appropriate for alternative types of lighting. Some uplighters contribute to discreet illumination for hallways or passages, while pictures, bookcases, and other displays of treasured items provide an excellent opportunity for including additional sources of light. Think about the nature of what you want to light. For instance, glass reflects and distributes light in a unique way, so lighting a collection of glassware could help to reflect more light into the whole room.

Lighting can be manipulated by selecting lamp shades with care; lining the interior of the shade with special gold paper warms the light, while silver cools it. For variety, mix styles and sizes of shade, from punched parchment to pleated silk, being careful to use the right size for the lamp and keeping in mind that dark shades always create a more dramatic look than pale ones. Wires and flexes are never attractive, so try and hide the flex and, if the skirting board is painted, paint the plug as well to minimize its intrusive effect. Take time to choose the right lighting for your home, and you will be rewarded with rooms that look their best in every situation.

Traditional Candles

Historically, beeswax candles were an expensive luxury beyond the means of most people, and even in the wealthiest households they were only used on important occasions. For hundreds of years the ordinary home used tallow candles, which smoked and blackened the walls and ceilings, smelled, and emitted a very meagre light. Thankfully the candles available today are far less pungent and can be used decoratively to create a convivial atmosphere. Households also used oil or pitch rush lights and lamps but they generally relied on the hearth fire for the main source of illumination. To maximize the light, chandeliers and wall sconces were often reflective, made from gilt brass or ormolu, and mirrors were much used to further reflect the light. These devices can be used today to enhance a period-style room or to bring a little traditional flavour to your home. Georgian candlesticks were often styled on classic architectural detailing of that period such as balusters or columns, and large candelabra were made from gilt brass or ormolu. These were favoured for use on the dining table while glass candlesticks were placed on the sideboard or beneath a wall mirror or overmantel to reflect as much light as possible. To create a romantic oasis of light in one area, arrange candlesticks of several different period styles together to accentuate their individual decorative merit. Alternatively, to generate a soft blanket of balanced candlelight, place individual candles around the room at different levels. Choose tall, slim candles for an elegant look or broad church candles to evoke a Medieval or Gothic feel. Even a single beeswax candle shimmering in its crystal candlestick provides an inimitable, timeless aura.

Opposite bottom A simple antique tea-towel is used as a foil to a pretty French candelabra, antique clock, and red roses in crystal decanters. This would set a truly romantic atmosphere, especially in a traditionally "feminine" room such as a bedroom.

Opposite top left A host of candlesticks and candelabras from several different periods gleam against lacquered paintwork. The light from the candles creates an intimate atmosphere so you can use a group of candles as a focal point within the room. Earlier candlesticks had a simple design but became more ornate during the late nineteenth century.

Opposite top right This delightfully simple "wheel" illuminates the dining table without interfering with the diners' line of sight. This method of lighting also saves table space, although you must use good quality candles to avoid pools of wax falling onto the table.

Above In this simple sitting room, the elegant gilt decoration on the furniture is complemented by the three different gilt candlesticks. This is a simple but effective way of introducing a little sparkle to a room. The bright, gold colouring produces a strong visual effect when placed against a cool white background.

Above right A plain background of polished panelling suits this ornate candelabra, which dates from the late nineteenth century. Allow dramatic pieces, such as this bronze cherub on a marble base, plenty of space in order to make the desired visual impact.

Right Solid ecclesiastical candlesticks containing plump candles are used in this masculine *mise-en-scène* which is easy to imitate. All the elements used here are created from robust, single-tone materials with limed wood, metal, and a simple white pitcher complementing the elegant black and white photograph above.

Traditional Electric Lighting

Today, we take the existence of convenient electric lighting for granted, but it is important to remember that electricity was not in general use until well into the twentieth century. This being the case, it is not surprising that there are many more candle holders in existence today than antique electric lamps and lights. When oil, and then gas, was introduced as the principal source of lighting, it sparked a revolution in the way the domestic interior was viewed and used. From that time, all sorts of antique lights have been adapted to use electricity, allowing us to use lighting that offers just the right style to suit any historical scheme. If you are using antique light, always bear in mind that the addition of a lampshade, wiring, and light bulbs will radically change the original outline and use. Many contemporary manufacturers also offer a good range of attractive period-style lights that will help you to recreate the desired look.

Apart from candle, oil, or gas antique lighting artifacts, there are other decorative conversions available for you to use such as china vases and storage vessels, tin storage jars, and even soda syphons. Rather than buying an adapted light, it is a good idea to search out potential objects and have them converted to order. This gives you an opportunity to use your creative skills in seeking out the right piece, and allows you to have a light fitting that is truly unique. When trying to achieve a period look, it is important to use the most appropriate fittings – white plastic bulb holders and electric wiring will ruin the effect of a pretty porcelain vase. Likewise, the choice of lampshade is vital. Make sure that the shade suits and is in proportion to its partner and that none of the electric fittings, including the bulb, are showing. Choose an appropriate material for the shade: silk, parchment, material, and glass will all suit different periods and styles.

Above left A late-nineteenth-century gas wall bracket is easily converted to electricity. These lights were often incorporated with the overmantel mirror ensemble and fitted to swivels so that the light could be reflected in the glass. Today, it is best to use tinted light bulbs to soften the glare.

Above right This gilt light fitting would make an impact in any room. The strong background colour is echoed in the fabric shades.

Above Here, an antique tin tea caddy is topped by a well-shaped simple shade. Try to place your pieces against an appropriate background so that it does not compete with their patina and style.

Above Porcelain vases and containers have particularly fine colours and proportions which can be matched to suit the period, decorations, and colours within a room. Here, the rich blues and red highlights of a columnar vase add a strong visual and lineal element to this eclectic arrangement of Italian, Chinese, and French pieces presented in a modern apartment.

Top right These gilt Rococo candle brackets have been converted to electricity using a ceramic "candle" fitting shaded by a suitably dainty fine linen shade with a skirted cut. This is attached to a wire under-shade to hold it away from the light. This style of candle lighting would have been in use in the early eighteenth century.

Middle right This original electrified lamp is a fine example of one of the first table lamps, dating from around 1880. These were often based on classical outlines – this one is a bronze column on an ornate plinth with an "alabaster" glass and bronze shade. Here, it is suitably placed alongside other bronze works of art, a contemporary print, and an Art Nouveau tablecloth.

Right A charming, bronze three-candled stand has been given a central electric adaptor so that its decorative effect is undiminished but its practical purpose is enhanced. The delicate card shade has been covered with a piece of antique embroidered linen which diffuses soft light through the fabric and shows off the embroidery.

Country Lighting

An instinctive thought about what lighting is appropriate in a country setting is that, as with all decorative choices, it should echo the style of the house and its surroundings and evoke the flavour of your local habitat. Traditional lighting in a city environment is usually constrained by its urban and often formal situation, whereas country-style lighting can be related to a far broader scope of influences. For example, if you are lucky enough to live close to the sea, it would be natural to accentuate the theme with sympathetic lighting that makes the most of the materials to be found nearby, such as driftwood candlesticks, candle lights in scallop shells, and the simplest electric lights with shaped, tin "fishy" shades or pearly glass globes. The country-cottage scenario requires equally sympathetic lighting in the form of wood, rather than silver, and wrought iron rather than crystal. Choose dramatic candleholders or iron lights to make an impact in a Gothic-style home, and use simple, metal candlesticks for a charming look in a Georgian setting. Electric lighting can be used as well as candles; fabric shades are a good way to introduce appropriate colours, patterns, and textures. Increasingly, people are opening out rooms and relating their decoration to what is happening outside, which gives scope for including some "natural" chandeliers and candlesticks woven from woody materials, candles set into terracotta pots and moss-covered baskets, and lanterns that look good inside and out.

Opposite top Perfect for the ocean-orientated scene, these four simple antique brass candlesticks become part of the seascape, gently illuminating while adding period authenticity.

Opposite left Small details help to draw a scheme together, such as these charming

French-style pleated candle shades sitting comfortably with the florals-and-checks look.

Opposite right Modern and adaptable, these pretty shell shades are perfect for the updated seaside cottage. Look for suitable materials to use for lights in the things around you.

Above This charming chandelier is made from stiff wire, sappy twigs, fruit, and leaves. Make sure that candles are secure in their fixings.

Top right This metal candleholder looks suitably rustic and hand-made and would cast an attractive light over the room.

Right Not so much practical illumination but rather a naturalistic art form, with fairy-lights replacing the ubiquitous chandelier. You could use this idea to create "lamps", too.

Global Lighting

When you are looking for "global" lighting for a room, remember that the aim of a global decorative scheme is to establish a sense of place. A truly satisfying ethnic look can be alluded to by using plausible "global" ingredients through colour, pattern, shape, and ornament, and this applies as much to lighting as to any other form of interior decoration.

Lighting can be used to great effect within the global scheme because there are all sorts of "authentic" ethnic lamps and lighting systems that are available. Be sure to place the lamps or lighting installations where they will have maximum visual impact, both for the illumination they provide and their style. Consider what your lights will look like when lit, and also during daylight hours. Appropriate table lamps and hanging fittings will have decorative value even when they are not being used. If you are unable to track down any other light fittings with an appropriate theme, you should combine your chosen "global" piece with the plainest style of lighting you can find. This will ensure that there is minimum conflict of character between the different light fittings and will prevent your room from looking too "confused".

Trying to match the perfect lamp base with just the right shade needs careful consideration, because the wrong style and size will ruin the look. This can be frustrating, but do persevere as lighting that really complements the decorative style makes the room look complete, and is well worth the effort. Think about whether you want to use candles or a modernized electric version of your chosen style. Wired versions of different styles of lanterns are very useful for creating a "global" theme in a room and are available in several appropriate styles such as Chinese, African, Moroccan, Caribbean, and even South American lamps. Remember that certain colours and patterns have associations with particular countries. For example, a plain, pale-blue shade would be appropriate for a Nordic room, while a tartan shade would suit a Celtic-style room. Always associate the lighting with suitable ornamental references such as pottery, basketware, and wood carvings. However, you must be careful not to include to many elements which can visually overload the scene.

Far left Illustrating how well the right props work together, an entire still-life of Western Americana includes studded hide deed boxes, saddlery, and a bronco lamp with rawhide lampshade.

Top left This is a good choice of lamp for this African scheme. The plain black base works well with the parchment-style shade, which has a simple "stitched" edge.

Middle left This harmonious mixture of

furniture, textiles, and accessories overseen by an elegant bamboo lamp creates the right mood for this Far Eastern setting.

Bottom left Here, style and comfort are not compromised within this satisfying African-themed room, where the horned lamp not only illuminates but also stars as an artistic installation.

Below It is possible to produce a striking visual impact that is still easy to live with. Here, these

charming red, gold, and white lights complement the Chinese-style lacquer pieces. Grouping the pendant lights is a simple but effective idea. You do not need to limit yourself to using groups of identical lights; look for different shapes and colours that will work together to create an overall effect.

Modern Candles

Today, candles have become such an integral part of modern homes and their decoration, that a room without them almost looks as if something vital is missing. They are, of course, especially noticeable in the minimalist, modern interior scheme which has little extra ornamentation. The softening effect of candlelight can completely change a sharp, cool daytime look into an intimate mellow one, particularly when candles are used on different surfaces and levels to create a multi-level radiance. To create a harmonious and smart look, use candles of the same style grouped together, or group a few chunky candles in suitably sculptural holders for a dramatic look. The great range of candle styles and containers available means there is something to suit every decorative scheme and personal taste.

Candles are no longer used simply as a means of providing soft, intimate lighting. Now we can use them to scent the air as well. Scent, shape, and colour combine to enhance today's living style – this is a far reach from the foul-smelling, smoky tallow candles used in bygone years. Before you choose your candles, think carefully about what look you want to achieve and where in the room they will have the best effect. For example, a large scented candle lit in the entrance hall will present a welcoming aroma as you walk through, as well as providing a pleasant light, but you should avoid using scented candles in the dining room because they will create a conflict with food smells and tastes. Try to use appropriate styles of candle for each room and associate them with complementary objects – sit them among sea-shells in the bathroom; diffuse light through pierced parchment shades for a gentle look in the bedroom; or even embed night-lights in a platter of polished pebbles on the coffee table to create an interesting textural focus in the living room.

Far left Here, square containers in different sizes have been grouped together. This produces a stronger lighting effect and also concentrates the therapeutic quality of scented candles.

Left In a neutral decorating scheme textural changes are important, as is the occasional splash of vibrant colour. Here, the candles satisfy both requirements.

Above These bathroom candles are given added effect by being placed with the different textures of a sea-shell, glass, and wood. The reflective quality of the glass intensifies the light.

Right Colour contrasts in blues and greens look fresh and vibrant. These curvaceous candle holders have a clean, contemporary look.

Modern Electric Lighting

To make the most of the truly innovative range of modern electric lighting, you really need to start planning installation before you begin to decorate the room. However, not many of us have this luxury, so some sort of compromise is usually required. For example, you may have to live with a central hanging light, but you can ring the changes using spotlights or an interesting sculptural fitting, rather than a conventional shade. If the fixed light fittings do not provide the required ambience, add moveable table or standard lamps to complement the effect. Why not introduce some kinetic light in the form of a lava lamp or fibre-optic lamp for visual interest? Always match your lighting to its desired purpose. Directional downlighters, for example, are an ideal method of lighting a work space and highlighting decorative details, such as paintings and sculptures. Next, you need to consider the type of filament, wattage, and whether a dimmer switch is desirable and can be used. Always consider the function of the room. The dining area should have two flexible, independent lighting focuses – one on the table and the second around the perimeter of the room for more general light. The average living room combines various uses – as a social meeting point, an area for quiet relaxation, and a place for television viewing – so lighting needs to be versatile to accommodate all these needs. Include lots of generous-sized table lamps, low-wattage floor lights for the corners of the room, and functional reading lamps with extendable necks. Dimmer switches allow you to vary the mood and so are ideal in multi-purpose rooms. In the kitchen you could include the functional parts of the lighting system, such as the attachment methods and wiring, as decorative elements of an industrial-style room.

Top The importance of good lighting is illustrated in this streamlined kitchen where hidden downlighters provide practical and atmospheric lighting.

Above The strength of modern lighting design often lies in its simplicity and good proportion. Here, the light makes an impact without overpowering the room.

Top left This sculptural uplighter makes a decorative impact and casts a subtle, even light.

Top right The skeletal frame of this light fixture suits the strong, lean architectural lines of this modernist interior.

Above Lighting can play a creative role, used here to illuminate sculptured pots.

Right Stylish and neat, these squares of recessed light are a vital safety feature for the stairway, and are aesthetically pleasing as well.

Cushions

Cushions are an indispensable way of introducing a stylistic element to any interior, while adding comfort, and contributing to the room's decorative narrative. Cushions soften the hard edges of furniture and architectural elements, and can be used to reflect the main colours in the scheme, and accentuate the chosen period and style. They can also add texture and enliven a plain setting and are not limited to use in the living room. Choice of size and shape is related to the balance of scale and use, from tie-on seat squabs suitable for kitchens or dining rooms to elegant rounded bolsters, buttoned window seats, or delicate lace bed pillows. Size will also depend on use and the style of fabric motif. Cushion covers offer a great opportunity to add an individual touch to a decorative scheme. The choices for covers show great versatility, and range from pieces of antique material to stylized appliqué, embroidered monogram, stencils, quilted harlequin patterns, or charity-shop woollen jumpers.

Always back luxury materials and delicates such as organza, lace, and silk with a lining fabric or insert them into a stronger border of material. Bolster-shaped cushions can be simply wrapped in a generous quantity of material, securing the ends with cord or ribbon, in a Christmas cracker shape. These are easy to make and easy to change. Instead of furnishing fabrics, dress fabrics can be used in a wide range of elegant materials and designs from silks to ginghams. Silk head-scarves make unusual cushion covers, when wear and tear is minimal. Think about textural contrast between the body of the cushion and its border, or use a contrast material on the reverse side. A good finish is essential, whether simple piping cord or ornate fringe. You do not want a cushion to look squashed, so always use a good quality filler pad – down and feather is best as this combination is soft and keeps its shape with plumping.

Traditional Cushions

Using cushions and upholstery to add decorative embellishment and comfort to a room dates back to the Middle Ages, when cushions were placed on the floor for the ladies of the household to sit on, while the men sat on hard wooden seats. The loose cushion had its heyday prior to the invention of modern methods of upholstering sofas and chairs. During the sixteenth century, wooden seats were given a flat squab cushion, while from the seventeenth century onward, tie-on squabs were used on English, and later French, cane-seated dining chairs, Swedish Gustavian-style furniture, and rush-seated Dutch chairs. Use squab cushions to add comfort and style to plain wooden seating – they are ideal for embellishing chairs that are not used every day. In seeking to make beds and seat furniture more comfortable, eighteenth-century upholsterers even invented air cushions, firstly out of pigs' bladders and subsequently of oiled leather, and by 1842, India-rubber air cushions were being manufactured.

Use carefully chosen cushions in a purely decorative way to suggest a particular traditional style using appropriate fabrics and trimmings. Improvements in seat springing and the general use of thick upholstery in the nineteenth century allowed cushions to be included as a solely decorative addition. The decorative merits of cushions have always been recognized. In the seventeenth and eighteenth centuries, tapestry work, damask, and velvet panel cushions, ornamented with elaborate trimmings such as gold-threaded braid and heavy corner tassels, were included in decorative schemes as a sign of wealth and status. You could use any of these styles to create added decorative focus and sumptuous comfort within a period-style room.

Top left Attention to detail elevates a cushion into a work of art. These antique tapestry cushions are edged in a twisted-cotton rope border.

Top right Contrasting styles of work are exhibited with this sturdy tapestry-covered stool and a nineteenth-century cushion with delicate, appliquéd flowers.

Above Use tassels to further embellish your soft furnishings. This elegant silk cushion would be at home in the living room or in a bedroom.

Opposite Unaffected by time, the brilliant colours in this Victorian beadwork cushion are reflected in the specially made cording trim.

Above Here, a fragment of nineteenth-century Aubusson tapestry carpet has been made into an exquisite ornament with the addition of a fine bell-tassel fringe.

Opposite top This exquisite piece of nineteenth-century English embroidered linen has been given new life as a delicate, tasselled cushion.

Opposite left A subtle, self-coloured patterned fabric gives these cushions visual interest, but the pattern is not fighting with the stripes in the upholstery.

Opposite right If you want to add comfort and style without adding colour, choose fabrics that match or harmonize with the other soft furnishings within your scheme.

Antique tapestry cushions have become very popular and also expensive in recent years, but there are also many woven materials available that cleverly imitate needlepoint as well as weaves in the style of Aubusson and Savonnerie rugs. "Antiqued" fabrics – such as velvet, brocade, and "ready-faded" chintz – will contribute to the traditional style. Finish cushions with an edging trim as they will have far greater impact when given an appropriate finish. Needlepoint cushions need to have a trim of cord, fringe, or tasselling that picks up a tone from the pattern, usually from the lighter colours, so that the delicacy of the work is not lost. As antique fabrics are inclined to be fragile, and because it creates a smart look, the reverse side of the cushion should be of a plain material which complements the weight and colour of the antique fabric. Do not worry if your budget will not stretch to buying large quantities of fabric. Even if you only have a small scrap of old petit-point or silk velvet fabric, it can be incorporated into a larger cushion panel of plain material, accompanied by the necessary trimming or braiding to give it substance. Panels of antique lace can be stitched into ordinary pillow cases or mounted on a backing material which could either be white or coloured, to show off the intricate work. Choose a backing fabric that echoes another colour in the room. Lace is particularly appropriate for the bedroom, and a bed piled up with a variety of lace cushions and pillows looks sumptuous and comfortable.

Country Cushions

Cushions are a versatile means of creating accents of texture and pattern – both essential components of a country-style scheme. The soft furnishings you choose are vital as they are a simple way of adding country flavour to the room. In traditional country homes, piles of cushions, charming tablecloths, and other needlework items often adorned the home. As well as their practical use, these items provide an inexpensive form of decoration. Country-style cushions are versatile but can be utterly simple in design, using a small amount of luxurious material, in the make-do-and-mend tradition, or cleverly tailored in inexpensive cotton ticking for a true home-spun look. They can be trimmed and fringed, buttoned and embroidered, piled high in variety, or used singly as an eye-catching work of art. Do not limit yourself to using your cushions in the sitting room or bedroom. What could be nicer in a traditional country kitchen than a simple rocking-chair adorned with a comfortable seat-pad and one, or even a whole collection, of loose cushions? Seek out authentic pieces of traditional embroidery, patchwork, or even knitting or crochet to use on your cushions. Do not worry if the needlecraft is not perfect – slightly worn or naive stitching can look charming on cushions. Country-style soft furnishings also provide the perfect excuse for putting your own creative talents into practice. Look for suitable fabrics, trimmings, embroidery kits, or even knitting or crochet patterns to add a personal touch to your home.

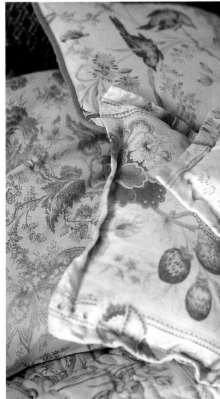

Opposite top A neat, buttoned, check seat-pad is complemented with a wonderful pictorial cushion. Use your soft furnishings to add texture to your decorative scheme. The woollen fruit in this charming rustic basket design add texture and a bright splash of colour.

Opposite left Traditional checks in lightweight fabrics are easy to sew

and inexpensive. You can also continue the theme around the room through curtains, tablecloths, and any other soft furnishings.

Opposite right Add comfort to a seat using seat pads and bolster cushions. Ticking suggests a country theme.

Above Piles of cushions decorated with glorious embroidery in rich colours and tactile materials

would work anywhere in the house. Always use good-quality cushion pads to keep your cushions looking their best.

Top right Elegant red and white stripes look fresh and are extremely versatile. This crisp fabric suits the pattern perfectly.

Middle right This ubiquitous gingham seat cushion is lent a feminine touch with a border of

lace. The red painted chair gives a modern slant on a country classic.

Right Fruits and flowers will always have a place in the country interior. These pretty red and white fabrics have a wonderful period feel.

Global Cushions

It does not take much material or expense to create characterful cushions to convey the style of a chosen global interior scheme. They can be as large or dainty as necessary, using pieces of tapestry or carpet, offcuts of material, left-over bits and pieces, or a plain fabric that relates to the rest of the interior by picking out a particularly effective colour in the dominant theme. Do not discard any little pieces of ethnic-style fabrics; even the tiniest scrap can help to hold the scheme together. For an Indian scheme, use different coloured silks – dress fabric will do – for front and back panels, and make lots of small cushions, grouping them together in a kaleidoscope of colour. North Africa is a rich source of ethnic materials and carpets in intricate, non-figurative patterns. Mix together many different designs and colours in strong earth and sunset shades to create the aura of a Moroccan souk, with cushions rich in textures and weaves and finished with beading, fringing, and leather trimming. Make large floor cushions to replace regular seating where possible. African textiles range from vibrant hand-blocked cottons to heavy woven fabrics in earthy pigment colours. You should stick to one type of fabric with the same weight and colour tones, and use textures related to other elements such as beaded basket-work, unglazed ceramics, and chunky carvings. The lineal design and warm colours of Celtic tartans, plaids, and checks make them easy to use in the form of cushions and pillows. They can be mixed and matched, with different borders of various fabrics, but always maintain a decorative rhythm by putting harmonious tones together.

Above left Warm, subtle colouring and various designs of tartans and plaids help to create a welcoming, cosy environment in this Celtic-style room.

Above right Stamped leather and dark, abstract fabric cushions from Africa afford dramatic textural and colour contrasts.

Opposite top Layers of colour and texture go a long way to promote a sense of place. Here, beads, bangles, and shells adorn a richly patterned cushion and carpet.

Opposite left Create a colourful, cosy den, full of textural Arabic artifacts and an assortment of Islamic motif cushions.

Opposite right Even worn bits of carpet can be turned into fun and useful floor cushions perhaps with a different, hard wearing fabric for the underside.

Modern Cushions

Cushions have become such an integral part of the modern interior decorative scheme that a room without them looks rather naked. Even the most pared-down, minimally accessorized room will look more complete with the addition of a few cushions of some sort. Cushions provide an inimitable finished and tailored look which softens the edge of hard furniture, picks up the thematic colours of the room, or adds highlights of texture and interest. In addition to this, they are also thoroughly comfortable and comforting. The contemporary look covers all types of materials and creative techniques. New life can be given to traditional cushion fabrics such as needlework and damask by mixing them with fashionable fabrics, including tickings and checks. Textured materials will add contrast to the body of the cushion design, picking up on details in other materials while also providing decorative rhythm by linking areas of texture and colour to each other. Mix luxury fabrics with contrasting materials or finishes to provide a useful method of including expensive materials in affordable quantities. For example, devouré velvet and cashmere, chenille and natural linen, and fake fur and silk will create an aura of sensual and tactile indulgence. Be discriminating in how cushions are placed together; it is a good idea to keep texture-biased fabrics segregated from patterned, colourful cushions. Using a limited range of unified trimmings and borders on all cushions can create a pleasing sense of symmetry.

Above left A tailored cushion looks smart and masculine nestling against the arm of an upholstered chair. A fabric with some sort of texture and weight is best for the job.

Left Clusters of pearl beads have been hand-sewn onto a cream linen pillow and finished with a light, piped edging for elegance and luxury. This will add valuable texture to the room.

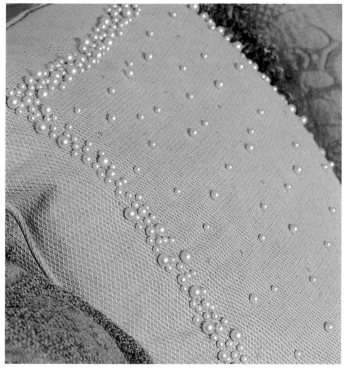

Above left Generous amounts of sumptuous fabrics will give your cushions a really luxurious feel. These tactile materials add instant comfort and are ideal for rooms where relaxation is important, such as bedroooms and sitting rooms. Colours can be subtle and harmonizing, or as bright and bold as you wish.

Above middle These striking check cushions make a strong visual statement. Alternatively, you could use broad lengths of ribbon woven together as a smooth-textured variation.

Above right Illustrating that it is possible to be innovative and creative, this cushion is trimmed with tiny sea-shells with holes drilled into them.

Below left Here, a piece of woven raffia is edged with a broad flap of natural linen to create a cushion with an unusual textural effect. Linen has an uncomplicated look that is ideal for a modern setting.

Below right Neutral colours are ideal for making cushions or pillows that will harmonize discreetly with the room's decorations, especially when there is already a lot of pattern and colour in the scheme. Here, an amusing decorative pocket on the front of the pillow conjures up the notion of an old-fashioned apron.

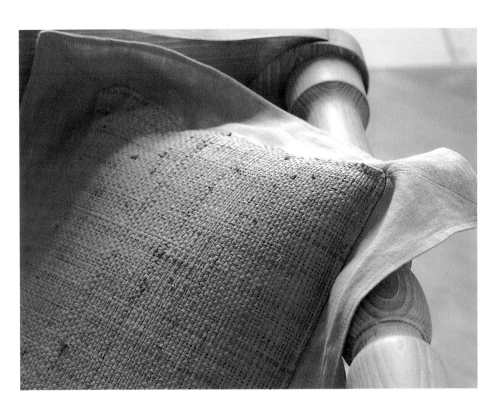

Vases & Containers

There are times when we take certain decorative items for granted, or at least do not afford them enough respect for their contribution to the interior finish. We often leave the odd vase or urn sitting in the same place on the mantelpiece or display shelf which it has always occupied, without the benefit of fresh flowers or new decorative pieces to give it renewed life. But these details really can help to bring a scheme together and create the focus of story and place which is so important to the final concept. Unlike other decorative embellishments, such as paintings, fixed lighting, rugs, and window dressing, these items can be moved and manipulated with great ease, and can be mixed with other pieces to create a complete *mise-en-scène*. Like a moveable feast, such decorative artifacts should be evolving all the time, and given new backgrounds and visual context when there is a need. The Zen ideology dictates that there should always be a single beautiful and harmonious item to contemplate and this is relevant to the use and placement of decorative containers and vases. Following this maxim, one beautifully elegant ebony vase holding a single branch of apple blossom means more to a room and to one's senses than a whole armful of bright roses.

Containers are not limited to vases. Antique decorative boxes that reflect the style of the room can look wonderful and provide valuable storage space in the modern home. Why not make a display of your jewellery boxes, souvenirs from an exotic trip, or even attractive boxes and baskets designed to hold photographs, magazines, or computer disks? You can even make a decorative feature of utilitarian items, such as china. Whatever you choose, show it off to its best advantage. Gather together a whole collection of a particular type of container and exploit its decorative merit by putting it in a dynamic context with contrasting materials and good atmospheric lighting.

Traditional Vases & Containers

As with all decorative objects, traditional vases, pots, and containers need to be carefully selected and thoughtfully placed within a room. You need to consider not just their visual impact, but also the function of the vessel. For instance, are you going to use your vases simply as objets d'art or will you fill them with wonderful flower arrangements, therefore bringing further colour and shape into the room? If you are going to use your containers to store much-needed items they must be positioned conveniently. Traditional containers are wonderfully varied in colour and form, from elegant classical vases to abstract Art Deco pieces.

Think about how you can make the most of your containers and what contribution they can make to the look of the room. A collection of a particular period and style of vase acquires stronger decorative merit when set against a backdrop of other artifacts of a similar epoch, so always consider the decorative scheme as a whole. Positioning your pieces in the right light is also beneficial, especially when the item to be displayed is glass or silver. Make the most of any reflective surfaces to welcome natural light into the room. A tall vase, filled with lilies and placed on a plinth in front of a window where the sun filters through the flowers and glass, will be gloriously cheerful, and more beneficial to the room than if it had been placed in a dark corner.

Any type of vessel can become decorative given the right setting and accessories: all it takes is a little imagination. A row of painted tea-glasses filled with delicate blossom or a single rose in each can look just as effective as any grand, formal flower arrangement. Place them down the centre of the dining table for a stunning effect. A Classical porcelain urn standing proudly alone on the mantelpiece has more decorative input than a massed collection of small trinkets huddled on a table. Containers of alll sorts are essential in most rooms, so celebrate them.

Opposite bottom This traditional, formal setting is lifted by the placement of a large elegant vase and simple flowers, adding height and luminosity to the scene.

Opposite top left Here, handsome nineteenth-century Classical vases are given a sense of place by associating them with a period picture and contrasting red damask.

Opposite top middle Use appropriate imagery, such as these Classical scenes, to emphasize the style of your room. These vases add style as well as giving period flavour.

Opposite top right This balanced composition is created by a casual arrangement of vases, one a lamp base, and companion pictures and frames.

Above This stunning blue and white vase is given added purpose by a pretty flower arrangement. The rounded shape of the vase is echoed in the shape of the blooms.

Country Vases & Containers

The traditional country kitchen would have included a wide variety of home-spun containers made from locally available materials. These would have included wooden storage bins and hessian sacks, wire-work egg and bottle holders, and woven baskets for fruit gathering, bent wood trugs for the vegetable garden, and earthenware storage jars for preserving the fruits of the harvest.

Today, we view these items in a different way, seeing their potential not only as practical items but as design artifacts, and we can manipulate their uses to suit modern practicalities and decorative tastes. The country theme incorporates many elements which have their foundation in the working rural environment but which now make a more aesthetic contribution to the home. The essence of these country-crafted items lies in their homespun charm, unique textures, and "lived-in" character, colour, or patina which adds another dimension to the country scheme. Relate the object to what it contains or to its surroundings to underline its contribution: fill vases with local flowers or paint vegetable trugs with pictures of the produce grown in your garden.

Experiment with colours and textures. Combine earthy textures, such as wood, hessian, and stone with a contrast of colour and feel, such as red rose petals or green apples for a striking, yet comfortable effect. Create a tableau using a stack of rough wooden bowls in different sizes, or a row of rugged terracotta flower pots filled with herbs, nuts, and dried fruits. Marry the colour and texture of the item with a contrasting or comparable background, using the same tones within the group or something utterly different, such as velvet beside unglazed pottery, or silk next to basket-work.

Top left Accentuate the texture of the vessel by pairing it with contrasting colour and texture, illustrated here by wood and apples.

Top middle Here, perfect colour unity is provided by lilac, pink, violet, and blue. Petals and greenery contrast well with the glazed pottery.

Top right Choose effective "props" to enhance your room. This blue and white room is complemented by a crate and a striped hat box.

Opposite bottom Why not decorate your containers to suit your decorative scheme? This painted creamware jug has been simply painted to suit its surroundings.

Above An aesthetic feel for colour, style, and lighting is illustrated by this stack of simple, paint-stained bowls.

Top right Use attractive earthenware bowls and jugs to give a warm and rustic feel to a room.

Bottom right Colours need not be harmonized as this combination of lavender, rose, and terracotta set against rough painted wood and sail-cloth shows.

Global Vases & Containers

It is often the detail which links the various elements within a decorative scheme, providing the last piece of the puzzle for a pleasingly complete and plausible finish. When travelling, look carefully, as you can sometimes find a truly authentic, aesthetic, or ingenious work that does credit to the maker, and the country. However, there are also opportunities to acquire suitable pieces closer to home. Try markets and craft fairs and look for shops that specialize in goods from your chosen country. Vases, pots, and containers are amongst the most easy of accessories to place at home. They are both practical and artistic and thus may be placed according to either usage. Colour and texture are always important and some pieces make fine illustrations of the benefits of mixing aesthetic textures together. For example, African clay pots – as dark and lustrous as ebony – make very handsome partners to woven containers and plates in subtle, earthy shades. They look sensational placed in a group against a rough, polished plaster wall or a backdrop banner of ethnic cloth. Any colourful pot, basket, or dish can be used to highlight the hues used elsewhere within the room and discreetly evoke the essence of the decorative style. The original, practical purpose for the piece might be ignored in favour of some unexpected use: a display of polished pebbles on a basket-weave plate, perhaps, or a bunch of mint leaves in a Moroccan coloured tea glass, or an arrangement of elegant silver-birch twigs placed in a terracotta storage pot.

Left Indian jewels and baubles glitter like a treasure trove within this brightly painted bowl. Set on an equally colourful painted background, this makes an intriguing – and tempting – display. When looking for vases and containers, think about what you can put in them for added interest.

Above Delicate, painted Moroccan tea glasses can be found in red, blue, or green with gold filigree decoration. They make a pretty display grouped on their own, or filled with tiny bunches of flowers or herbs. Glassware is also very useful for encouraging natural light into the room.

Above left A giant coloured cardboard and rattan basket acts as a foil to both the colour and the theme within this "modern-ethnic" sitting room. It also creates a stunning focal point. Such dominant items need the balance of strong form and colour, as here.

Above right Bright and fun, these woven bowls are actually made from telephone wire, and show the African ability to adapt ancient traditions to new methods without losing their aesthetic appeal. Although their original purpose is practical, these bowls can stand as works of art in their own right.

Right These African pots and baskets, with their abstract patterns, earthy colours, and aesthetically pleasing texture, make a rich and powerful display against the various pieces of ethnic fabric in this room. All the accessories in the room should combine to emphasize your chosen global theme. If necessary, combine appropriate pieces with very plain, simple objects that will not confuse the effect.

Modern Vases & Containers

Modern vases, pots, and containers can be as imaginative, innovative, and unusual as you can make them. Think beyond the original use and placing of a potential vessel and adapt it to suit your practical and decorative requirements. In a modern-style room you can let your creativity run wild when choosing vases and containers. Containers of all sorts have added purpose in a contemporary-style room, as modern, minimalist schemes demand clutter-free rooms, making storage key to the success of the scheme. Terracotta flower pots are particularly adaptable, whether painted or left with their original garden patination, they convert to toothbrush mugs, cutlery stands, and even pen holders. A massed gathering of drinking glasses of different shapes and sizes, stuffed with herbs, leaves, and simple flowers, makes a charming, informal table arrangement. For an extra decorative ingredient try tinting the water with paint, ink, or food colouring in shades that suit the flowers and interior scheme. On a more sophisticated level, sleek and glamorous new ways with glaze finishes have provided many stylistic, textural, and colour alternatives to the traditional forms of decorative containers. Updated designs in glassware have revitalized enthusiasm for its decorative contribution, and the brilliant, luminous colours available make perfect companions for youthful, bright and bold interiors. Dynamic modern ways of presenting flowers have resulted in a great interest for relating the container to the style of the flower, as opposed to thrusting an armful of dahlias into the nearest vase. Recently, there has been a move towards the Eastern approach to flower arranging, where a single branch or bloom in a vase creates a contemplative focus for the room. Within a modern setting, accord vases, pots, and containers the status of works of art in their own right and use them as a decorative foil and focus for your scheme.

Far left The "retro" look is exemplified here with a classic 1950s Knoll cabinet surmounted by three modern glass vases that suit both 1950s and modern style.

Left A chrome finish gives the plant container a sleek and modern dimension and acts as a lively counterpoint to bright flower colours.

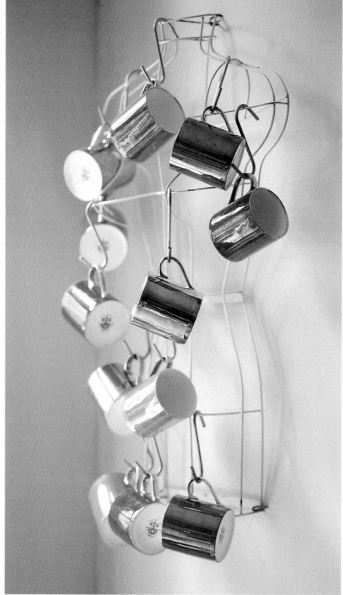

Above Grouping objects together gives them extra impact, here making a focus of their vivid colour which can act as a contrasting highlight.

Above right These unusual clear-glass wall vases offer a really modern way of displaying flowers. The strong wall colour works well with the transparent glass.

Right Here, a dressmaker's skeletal dummy is hung with mugs, making an effective modern sculpture which is decorative and practical.

JOSEPH BEUYS NATUR MATERIE FORM Schirmer/Mosel

Frames & Mirrors

Pictures and paintings make a tremendous impression on the style of a room, not just in their content but also in their hanging. The smallest print or inexpensive poster can provide great decorative merit if it is given the right frame and placed in an appropriate context. Auctions, antique markets, and art schools will invariably provide something affordable and pleasing, whether it be a work of art or a good frame. Apart from paintings and prints, the subject could be a beautiful scrap of needlework or an unusual piece of fabric. Whatever the subject within, the framing is vital. Be over-generous with space, leaving a good border area to emphasize the subject and overall impact on the wall. Group smaller frames together in blocks, laying them out on the floor to see the effect before hanging. Generally, hang pictures low on the wall. If you hang pictures too high, it will actually emphasize the wall's bareness, rather than fill it.

One of the most effective ways of creating the illusion of space and to reflect light within a room is to use mirrored glass. For hundreds of years candlelight and firelight were the prime sources of lighting and were often enhanced by placing candles or candle brackets in front of mirrors or reflective surfaces. Mirrors can alter the proportions of a room by giving the illusion of depth and of widening narrow spaces. There are five ways of placing mirrors; as the overmantel, the decorative wall-hung mirror, the free-standing table mirror, the full-length chevalier dressing mirror, or the mirrored insert used as part of the room's decorative architecture. From the elegant sinuous scrolls of gilded and painted Rococo mirrors to the heavily carved Victorian Gothic fantasy overmantels and sleek minimalism of Art Deco, mirrors have played an integral part in period rooms. Although the elemental purpose may be to reflect light and create a sense of space, the mirror has become a work of art in its own right.

Traditional Frames & Mirrors

Frames and mirrors are an essential part of the scheme for many period styles. In order to place pictures and mirrors in an integrated way with period decoration, it is useful to understand how and where they were used, and what the quintessential types for each period were. During the seventeenth century, paintings were frequently hung on tapestry-lined walls and the frames were simple in construction, usually black and gilt, but sometimes silvered with red or blue detailing. In grand houses, large paintings fitted the dimensions of the fireplace overmantel or were hung above interior doorways. For a room in the style of the early eighteenth century, choose gilded frames hung on chains disguised with ribbon. By the 1760s, there was a great fashion for engravings and sheets of printed frames, garlands, and ornaments which were sold as cut-outs to paste directly onto papered or painted walls and doors to create entire print rooms. For an early-nineteenth-century look, choose rectangular carved and gilded frames. Hang them on plain cord or chain, or cord disguised with silk sleeves and rosettes. From the mid-nineteenth century, groups of framed paintings, prints, cameos, and silhouettes were hung in tight groups. To recreate the crowded ornamentation of the late-Victorian interior use an abundance of ornamental silver frames.

Mirrors too should be treated according to their period. Remember that the reflective qualities of mirrors were invaluable for welcoming natural light into dark period interiors. During the seventeenth century, looking-glasses, and some paintings, were often hung canted forward, perhaps so they should better catch the candlelight. From about 1670, quantities of mirror glass were inserted into decorative panelling in French and Italian interiors, and by the early eighteenth century the pier-glass arrangement of a mirror above a built-in table between windows was fashionable. Above the fireplace is the appropriate location for mirrors of a number of periods. Ornately decorative Rococo mirrors should be given pride of place over the fireplace – perhaps accompanied by candle sconces or brackets to match. Silver and mercury glass becomes patinated by age, and this will add to the period look. The palm frond is an emblem of sleep popular in the nineteenth century, so look out for mirrors with palm carving that will be ideal for the bedroom. Mirrors are also an essential part of the overmantel in the Chinese or Gothic style. In a Regency-style room choose mirrors with vertical architectural lines or gilt-framed oval and round mirrors with eagles, wreaths, trophies, and baubles. Convex glass was an innovation of the time, so mirrors of this type are also suitable. The Victorian period produced a broad range of overmantel mirrors – often relating to the various Revival styles with ornate heavy carving, niches, and tiers to hold ornaments. For an Art Deco look, choose mirrors that are stepped or circular in shape, unframed, or finished with beautiful etched detailing.

Above The arrangement of objets d'art, furniture, and painting perfectly reflects the atmosphere of the mid-eighteenth century in this restored French château. The gilt oval frame is typical of the period and suits the framework of panelling painted in soft green, grey, and gold.

Below This cluster of photographs is given balance and harmony by the collection of similar ornate, silver Victorian frames, and a solid contrasting background of striped wallpaper, two nineteenth-century busts, an ebony frame, and a pair of amaryllis.

Above left A beautifully carved giltwood frame in the mid-eighteenth-century manner, incorporating C-scrolls and S-scrolls with acanthus leaves and stems. This mirror has been hung over a second plain panel to "frame" it in turn and reflect the room more effectively.

Above middle This typically French mid-eighteenth-century Rococo door panel has blue-grey paint and gilded mouldings. Use mirrored door panels to expand the illusion of space and reflect light. It is a simple idea to imitate in any interior, especially when wall space is limited.

Above right This Regency-period mirror is typical of its type. The round, convex mirror is balanced by a sturdy frame with simple detailing and a string of small baubles and slim candles. Mirrors should be hung fairly low, as here, so that the light and reflection can be fully appreciated.

Below Etruscan-style ornamentation was made popular by Robert Adam around 1775. This was based on ancient Greek vase decoration, much of which was in red and black. Here, the idea has been adapted to a modern interior, using mid-eighteenth to early nineteenth-century pictures in simple black and gold frames. Architectural and decorative stencils link the pictures and create a balanced symmetry.

Country Frames & Mirrors

The traditional cottager would not have had the resources to adorn his walls with luxuries, least of all expensive paintings and ornate mirrors. The most likely ornamentation would be in the form of an arrangement of treasured cooking pots and utensils, or earthenware plates displayed on a dresser. Today, however, we see the cottage interior as a place of cosiness and comfort, and barren wall surfaces would not suit this atmosphere. Much can be made of the room's building material, whether it is rough, colourwashed plaster, or rough-cut stone, brick, or timber, so frames should be chosen to complement the character and nature of this as well as the decorations. For example, a simple frame made of pewter, or a wide-painted fruit-wood frame, would be natural companions for a country scheme and would reflect the rural environment. An old pine mirror will sit far better in a country bathroom than a streamlined modern one. Choose a picture to enhance your chosen scheme and to complement your frame: fruit and vegetables in the kitchen, "foody" prints in the dining room, or flowers and needlework samplers in the sitting room. Hang pictures, collections, and mirrors in an informal way, or simply lean them against the mantelpiece, shelves, or dresser to provide a flexible decorative element. Mirrors and romantic lighting always make good companions, so place mirrors where candlelight will be seen to double its effect.

Opposite top Mirrors can be used simply for their geometric shape as a counterbalance to other objects. Here, a plain, antique-pine mirror is set beside a pair of patinated bronze candlesticks while supporting a pair of miniature paintings. The contrast of colour and texture are fundamental to creating a traditional, rustic style.

Opposite left Vinegar-graining has been used on frames, objects, and furniture for hundreds of years. It simulated the figuring and grain of exotic hardwoods on plain softwoods, particularly Bird's-eye maple. This modern example associates well with the Victorian-style basin and antique bed.

Opposite right Here traditional materials have been used to create a luxury bathroom in a converted barn. Pine panelling creates a shelf on which to place the simply made but generous mirror.

Right The bronze effect of the mirror suits the muted tones of the fireplace and adds a glamorous note to the colourwashed walls. The objects on the marble mantelpiece, and the creamware jug complete the country aura.

Global Frames & Mirrors

Mirror and picture frames can make so much difference to the look of an ethnic room because the right choice can really hold the look together. Some global styles are easier to recreate than others, of course, so do not set yourself impossible targets of authenticity, but rather go for the overall allusion to the ethnic style. Look for frames that could be adapted to create the look you want. If your chosen global style is particularly associated with a colour or pattern, why not transform a plain frame yourself? For example, a simple wooden frame painted cool blue would be perfect in a Nordic-style room, and the clashing Mexican colour palette is easy to adopt for a mirror or picture frame. For an African theme, you could simply paint an earthy undercoat on a frame, add a topcoat of matt black, and then, while the paint is still wet, inscribe a simple design. If you are feeling more adventurous you can create more complex frames. Short lengths of bamboo cane bunched together with raffia can be used to make a basic frame for an Asian-style room, or you might make some pierced tin frames in the style seen in Indian decoration. Another idea is to cut out an attractive Moorish arch shape in heavy card, stick it within a rectangular mirror frame, and paint the two parts the same colour. Look for authentic pieces that can be converted for use on frames, such as small, carved shutters. Even suitable pieces of needlework can be used to achieve the right global look.

Opposite top A collection of native American and American Indian artifacts and furniture has a rustic look, with photographs framed in the same raw style.

Opposite bottom The colours of this Mexican room are echoed in the frame, which is as dynamic as the picture.

Above It is easy to recreate a North African mirror like this, using stiff card cut to fit within a rectangular mirror.

Right The intricate decoration of this Persian fire surround needs little embellishment, but the antique bronze and a richly ornamented mirror illustrate the room's style.

Far right Indian wood craftsmen carve intricate window surrounds which are now frequently adapted for mirrors, as here, giving them a new decorative contribution.

Modern Frames & Mirrors

In a modern setting works of art go a long way beyond paintings or photographs. Diverse images include fabric scraps, wire-work, multi-media montage, and nature's treasures such as feathers, and sea shells. The frames are the key to effectiveness and should suit the image they hold as well as reflecting the flavour and proportions of the room. Bear in mind that their distribution will affect the room's visual geometry. Any frame should be partnered with a generous border to contain and emphasize the work of art within. Sometimes a frame is so beautiful on its own that it will not need anything inside. Traditional-style frames are always useful because they have a decorative curvaceousness that makes its own interest, even within a modern setting. Alternatively, an unglazed frame could surround some object fixed to the wall, such as sea-worn driftwood or a personal collection. As well as traditional materials, frames can be made from perspex, glass, fabric, even concrete. Frames create an informal group sitting on the mantelpiece, where they can be moved about or interchanged. Pictures of the same size can be alternated with pieces of mirror to create a contemporary slant on the overmantel. Modern mirrors are usually simple and dynamic, and they maximize light and space. Be generous with size, even if you hang a picture on top of the mirror, but avoid placing one immediately opposite the entrance to a room as this can have a very unsettling effect.

Opposite top left The oversized photographs are displayed to good effect, as if seen through a real window. The spotlight casts fake sunshine shadows on the wall.

Opposite top right Balance the scale and style of pictures with your look, as with these slim frames and wide mounts in a simple bedroom.

Opposite left In this informal dressing room, this stylish metallic frame creates another reflective surface to welcome in the light. Lean the mirror for a casual look.

Above The clean lines and simplicity of a generous mirror can be used to reflect the room and create a greater sense of space and light.

Above right Paintings and frames are used as a focus above the fireplace, suitably combining classic and modern. Alternate images to suit your mood.

Right Boxed insects make a startling and suitable foil above witty rope "sculptures" that have been inspired by primitive cultures.

Collections

A collection can consist of anything you want it to, from a plethora of Victorian treasures to a display of well-loved photographs or even CDs. A decorative collection will contribute greatly to any interior scheme by providing a point of decorative reference which draws the eye as you enter a room. Choosing what sort of collectable to assemble is a matter of personal preference, expense, and will depend on the setting. Whatever the choice, the resulting collection should be strong and defined by a balanced and considered method of display. A single collection could be placed at the focal point in the room, which will probably be over the fireplace, on either side of the overmantel mirror, or it could partner the most dominant piece of furniture.

The most effective display has a cohesive thread holding it together, without being entirely uniform. Examples are a collection of beadwork bags drawn from several periods, or a tableau of silver frames, boxes, and different objects placed together. Equally, an arrangement of blue and white china looks most dramatic when a great variety of styles are massed together. The background is important as a foil for the collection, even if it has to be manipulated with the addition of a contrasting cloth or painted panel. Good lighting will enhance any arrangement and should be directed and controlled. Colour and texture play a part in this scene, too, and need to be experimented with to maximize their potential for creating contrast and focus. Your collection can be as dominant or as subtle as you wish. Victorian collections gave the room a busy, cluttered appeal, but while this can work well in a traditional, country, or even a global setting, a more restrained approach may be desired in a modern or modern-style room. However, you can incorporate your treasures in a modern scheme – a small, stylish collection can help to add visual interest in a minimalist room.

Traditional Collections

The vogue for collecting was instigated in Europe by the economic and cultural advances of the mid-nineteenth century, by which time there was more leisure travel than ever before, thanks to the expanding British Empire and improved transport. A wide choice of potential collectables became available to a broader public, especially through the Great Exhibitions of the second half of the century that took place in Britain, the colonies, Europe, and America, at a time when so many desirable and innovative artifacts were being introduced. Such was the passion for collections that even in a modest household, every surface, cabinet, and receptacle would hold some sort of display, often because the Victorians believed that interesting objects promoted conversation. They frequently favoured collections of classical or contemporary objects, subjects from nature, such as shells, eggs, and taxidermy, and sometimes quite bizarre curiosities. To recreate this effect, look for objects from nature, or display your treasured objects. The Arts and Crafts movement promoted the desirability of beautifully made houseware that was both functional and aesthetic. Whether your preference is for the finest porcelain or commemorative mugs, traditional collections should complement, rather than dominate, the room's decorative scheme. The colour and texture of the background is an important consideration and the display should be spaced so as not to diminish individual merit. Coloured and engraved glass both look spectacular placed against natural light, while delicate antique glass benefits from association with highly polished wood or silver against a plain, dark backdrop. Place small items, such as silver trinkets or enamelled boxes, at a level where their detail can be admired from above.

Opposite top Create a neat and balanced presentation of some eighteenth- and nineteenth-century silver objects on a period side table. The lamp and vase of sweet peas add vertical emphasis.

Opposite left This collection of nineteenth-century scent bottles is prettily displayed on a marble-topped dressing table which is in keeping with its situation and period.

Opposite right Light your collections sympathetically for the best effect. Here, the light behind an eclectic assortment of Brazilian glass and animals, candlesticks, and tortoiseshell boxes allows the glassware to glow.

Above Background and lighting are vital to a collection. This ghostly arrangement of bone collectables has been placed against a dark background with filtered light.

Right Victorian ladies were always busy crafting pretty things for the home and as gifts. These lovely shell boxes and scallop inkwell were made in North America, some as souvenirs of past travels. A simpler version of the idea works just as well for the modern interior.

Country Collections

The words "country collection" immediately bring to mind an image of a stripped-pine dresser, groaning under the weight of a great assortment of china and pottery, mugs and plates, tureens, and platters. The ideal cottage image, complete with warming Aga and wet dog at the flagstone hearth, conveys the importance of dressing a scene with well-loved, colourful, and decorative items which give a sense of place and personality. Make your country collections artless and rustic, highly crafted and delicate, or simply relate them to the everyday items used in the rural environment which have been given a more decorative interpretation. There are the obvious choices, such as floral china and rustic wooden bowls, but now there is so much more to creating the homely, artistic aura that practically anything can be adopted and arranged in a "collectable" manner. Whatever the collection, from corn dolls to baking moulds, place them with care. Position them within a relative context as this helps to underline their contribution to the overall decorative scheme. For example, if you are displaying some old baskets, give them content, rather than hanging them up on a pole where they are out of place and not used. Fill them with old French linen tea-towels, or gingham napkins, dried lavender, or pinecones. Purposefully paint a wall in an antiqued finish as a backdrop for old garden implements or pewter ware. Rustic items are normally hardwearing and should provide practical as well as decorative uses.

Above left Here, rich patina and colour are brought together with an eclectic mixture of kitchen articles catching the evening light.

Left Fill every inch of a classic country dresser with a kaleidoscope of shape and colour, mixing practical with decorative uses.

Above A collection of nesting boxes made by an American artist around 1950 are associated with rustic furniture and a clapboard background.

Above right This unusual collection of old American and Shaker wooden items, some of which are painted, others stained, works well because of the companionable tones and textures.

Right Use an antique cutlery storage box to house a collection of old patchwork pin cushions and colourful rag dolls.

Global Collections

It is very tempting to collect glorious items from around the world, especially if they evoke memories of a treasured holiday. Amassing collectable global objects could present a logistical problem if you fall for a particular style of basketware from Bali, or soapstone statuary from the heart of Africa, given the distances and expense that obtaining more from the source will involve. More importantly, it is too easy to be seduced into buying a touristic trophy when on holiday that looks wonderful when infused by the magic and romance of its original situation, but, when brought home, looks sadly lost. Therefore, global collections need to be brought together and placed with dedication and a discerning eye. Somehow, ethnic items collected with diligence and patience over a period of time make a much more significant contribution than an instant bulk-buy. Mixing similar materials together often works well, even if they are not from the same country, as they will visually strengthen each others' craftsmanship. Just as colours are chosen to work in harmony, so you should select ethnic pieces which will complement each other. Setting the global collection within the right room and display context is very important too. Pottery, china, or porcelain can be arranged in textural and colour associations in the kitchen and dining room, either integrated with more domestic necessities, or set a little apart to give them distinction as decorative pieces. Often items from other cultures have different colours, patterns, and textures to items found in your own culture. Think about the jewel-bright colours of Indian textiles and decorations, the restrained elegance of Japanese decorative items, or the wonderful texures to be found in many African pieces and bring out these differences when displaying your collections. You could look for pieces that emphasize your existing global or colour-orientated scheme, or use your collection to inject a burst of colour into an otherwise neutral or muted room.

Opposite bottom The background is nearly as important as the collection itself. This evocative statuette is the perfect home for these bold African beads.

Opposite top left Highly decorative, these luminous and richly textured painted eggs are from Eastern Europe and are generously displayed in lustrous heaps set against the lustrous gold colouring of the painting and the candlestick.

Opposite top right The North American Indian tribes each had their craft speciality, amongst which are these naive-painted pots, ornate basket-ware, and glass beadwork pieces. Navajo blankets add their subtle colours to the background.

Above top left Creating an appropriate setting for the style and country, these Japanese and Chinese artifacts are contained within a fine lacquered desk with an ornamental bamboo scroll background.

Above left An eclectic mixture of secular and religious artifacts form a collection that evokes Eastern culture. Always use an appropriate setting – here colourful fabrics – to set the scene.

Above right In African culture, nothing is wasted and the decorative potential is realized in everything, as shown by these ornately carved and stained calabashes or gourds.

Modern Collections

Many collections are purely decorative, especially collections found in a modern-style setting. For a modern collection, choose items because you like the style, because they provoke a memory, or simply because they go well with the decoration. A collection does not have to have intrinsic value or artistic worth, as long as it contributes to the scene and has wit or sentiment. Modern collections can be conjured from unlikely objects which might be as whimsical, narrative, and surprising as you like. In the contemporary interior, with its propensity for pared-down, textured quality, decisions about what to put on display relate to how much room or requirement there is for extra ornamentation. You can even make an attractive decorative statement using the practical items in your room, including books and magazines, or CD's. Within the sleek, uncluttered scheme, no matter what shape it takes, a collection needs to be displayed in an almost Zen-like way, as a contemplative focus, with lots of empty space around it. Alternatively, storage itself can become part of the collective display. Choose an innovative storage method, such as a basket made of industrial metal sheeting or bookends of moulded coloured perspex, for example. Quite ordinary items will be spontaneously transformed into a collection when presented in an artistic manner. Examples are postcards displayed on a sleek noticeboard, pieces of driftwood mounted in unglazed frames, and sea shells or beads filling sculptured glass vases. With a bit of lateral thinking and imaginative presentation a modern collection can make a novel addition to any room.

Above left Create an ever-changing collection with a well placed pin-board and whatever cards and clippings are flavour of the moment.

Left Glass topped display boxes could be turned into a desk-with-a-view, or incorporated into a window ledge or around the bath.

Above Keeping up with the times, modern collections can be idiosyncratic – like this display of characterful clocks set against a neutral backdrop.

Above right Even in minimalist interiors, CDs have to be stored within reach. This smart pierced plastic basket marries storage and display.

Right Make a collection of the things you love. Here, an elegant glass bowl houses a colourful collection of waterlillies. The ornamental fish continues with the aquatic theme.

Directory

This spread by spread breakdown gives you the name and details of all the swatches shown throughout the book, including a price guide. Contact details for manufacturers or distributors are given in the Addresses section.

Key to Symbols

These symbols show you at a glance what type of material is illustrated in the swatch.

 Paint

 Fabric

 Wallpaper

Tiles

Flooring

At Home with Heraldry

1. The Silk Gallery/Fleur Weave
Colourway: antique gold and green
Composition: 68% silk, 32% polyester
Width: 127cm/50in, Repeat: 6cm/2½in
Suitable for windows and upholstery

2. G. P. & J. Baker/Caliph Chenille J0235-74
Colourway: green, red and blue
Composition: 100% cotton
Width: 145cm/57in, Repeat: 57cm/22½in
Suitable for loose covers, windows and upholstery

3. G. P. & J. Baker/ Heraldic Damask W0113-02
Colourway: 02, Width: 52cm/ 20½in
Length: 10m/11yd, Repeat: 53cm/21in

4. Carocim/Gothic, Colourway: red and grey
Composition: ceramic, Size: 20 x 20 x 1cm/
8 x 8 x ¾ in, Suitable for walls and floors

5. Three Shires/Pava S101
Colourway: pava, Composition: 100% sisal
Width: 4m/4½ yd

Gothic Inspiration

1. The Silk Gallery/Demeter
Colourway: gold/beige, Composition: 100% silk
Width: 127cm/49¾ in Repeat: 50cm/19½ in
Suitable for windows

2. Stuart Interiors/Darnley
Colourway: ivory
Composition: 60% wool, 40% cotton
Width: 125cm/49in, Repeat: 30cm/11¾in
Suitable for loose coverings, windows, bedcovers, upholstery and walls

3. Zuber/Alcove Chambre de la Reine 9222
Colourway: gold, terracotta and grey
Width: 51cm/20in, Length: 9m/10yd
Repeat: 88cm/34½ in

4. Stonell/Bamboo
Colourway: grey with rust streak
Composition: slate
Size: 20 x 20 x 1.2cm/8 x 8 x ½ in
Suitable for floors; available in other sizes

5. Victorian Wood Works/Chantilly
Colourway: AA, Composition: oak
Width: to order

Classical Lessons

1. Lewis & Wood/Vauxhall Gardens-Aqua
Colourway: green on white
Composition: 100% cotton
Width: 140cm/55in
Repeat: 62cm/24¼in
Suitable for windows and upholstery

2. Marvic Textiles/Empire
Colourway: red on sand
Composition: 100% cotton,
Width: 140cm/55in
Repeat: 78cm/30¾in
Suitable for loose covers, bedcovers and walls

3. Elizabeth Eaton/Muslin 9550/3837
Colourway: white, Composition: 100% cotton
Width: 150cm/59in, Repeat: 11cm/4¼ in
Suitable for windows

4. Sinclair Till/Greek Key Border
Colourway: natural
Composition: walnut, maple
Width: 28.5cm/11in

5. Brintons/Golden Serenade 116/4700
Colourway: 116, Composition: 80% wool
20% nylon, Width: 4m/4½ yd
Repeat: 100cm/39¼in

1. Marvic Textiles/Emilio F. R. 1302
Colourway: red, black and gold
Composition: 63% viscose, 37% modacrylic
Width: 140cm/55in, Repeat: Width of stripe
Suitable for upholstery

2. Lelièvre/Lampas Abeilles-Rouge 4023-02
Colourway: red and gold
Composition: 60% viscose, 40% acetate
Width: 130cm/51in, Repeat: 8cm/3in
Suitable for upholstery

3. Scalamandré/Prestwould Saloon Dado
WB81504, Colourway: document
Width: 53cm/21in

4. Berti Pavimenti Legno/Todeschini Border
Colourway: natural
Composition: doussie, walnut, gatambu, wenge
Width: to order

5. Hugh Mackay/Ribbon 100089-910953
Colourway: multi, Composition: 100% wool
Width: 69cm/27in, Repeat: 11cm/4 ¼in

Victorian Romance

1. Apenn/Hampton linen LN 476-8/9
Colourway: red-blue,
Composition: 100% linen, Width: 125cm/49in
Repeat: 20cm/8in
Suitable for windows and upholstery

2. Gainsborough Silk Weaving Co. Ltd/S6851
Colourway: red, Composition: 100% silk
Width: 127cm/49¾in, Repeat: 68cm/26½ in
Suitable for windows and upholstery

3. Scalamandré/Amazonia 16232
Colourway: 001
Composition: 100% cotton
Width: 140cm/55in, Repeat: 91.5cm/36in
Suitable for windows and upholstery

4. Sanderson/Rococo BL6420/1.
Colourway: off-white
Composition: 100% cotton
Width: 122cm/48in
Repeat: 60cm/23¾in
Suitable for windows

5. Stark/Houles, Colourway: floral black
Composition: 100% wool
Width: 3.66m/4yd
Repeat: 99cm/39in

1. Monkwell/Plain 5446
Colourway: 811
Composition: 91% cotton, 9% modacrylic
Width: 120cm/47in
Suitable for windows

2. Borderline/Juniper 2528a
Colourway: red, Composition: 100% wool
Width: 137cm/54in
Repeat: 44cm/17¼in
Suitable for loose coverings, windows, upholstery

3. Cole & Son/Owen Jones 52/7040
Colourway: red
Width: 53cm/21in, Length: 10m/11yd
Repeat: 7cm/2¾ in,

4. Minton Hollins/Ivy Link UIL5
Colourway: multi, Composition: ceramic
Size: 15 x 15cm x 8mm/6 x 6 x ½ in
Suitable for walls

5. LASSCO/Herringbone
Colourway: natural
Composition: Rhodesian teak
Width: to order

Arts and Crafts Style

1. Belinda Coote Tapestries/Jacobean Brocade
Colourway: beige and terracotta
Composition: 66% viscose, 34% cotton
Width: 136cm/53½ in
Repeat: 61cm/24in
Suitable for loose covers, windows, upholstery

2. Sanderson/Fruit PR8048/2
Colourway: multi, Composition: 100% cotton,
Width: 137cm/54in
Repeat: 64cm/25in
Suitable for windows and upholstery

3. Liberty/Burnham 1061036
Colourway: L, Composition: 100% cotton
Width: 137cm/54in
Repeat: 32cm/12½ in
Suitable for windows and upholstery

4. Sanderson/Willow Boughs WM7614/1.
Colourway: Morris 5
Width: 53cm/21in
Length: 10.5m/11½ yd
Repeat: 46cm/18in

5. Original Style/Rose & Trellis 6970A
Colourway: multi
Composition: ceramic
Size: 15 x 15cm x 7mm/6 x 6 x ¼ in
Suitable for walls

In the Mackintosh Mood

1. Liberty/Ianthe 1069604
Colourway: E, Composition: 100% cotton
Width: 137cm/54in
Repeat: 31cm/12in
Suitable for windows, upholstery

2. Bradbury & Bradbury/Thistle Wall
Colourway: THW-970
Width: 68.5cm/27in, Length: to order
Repeat: 53cm/21in

3. Original Style/Rose and Bud
Colourway: Colonial white, Composition: ceramic
Size: 15 x 15 x 7mm/6 x 6 x ¼in (5-tile panel)
Suitable for walls

4. Graham & Brown/Shantou 96273
Colourway: Green, Width: 10cm/4in
Length: 5m/5½ yd

5. Minton Hollins/Baroque ANFI
Colourway: blue, Composition: ceramic
Size: 15 x 15cm x 8mm/6 x 6 x ½ in
Suitable for walls

Country Home Chintz

1. Warner Fabrics/Edwardian Roses CS 336910
Colourway: pink/blue/cream
Composition: 100% cotton
Width: 137cm/54in
Repeat: 64cm/25in
Suitable for windows and loose covers

2. Lee Jofa/Floral Bouquet 88903
Colourway: 03
Composition: 100% cotton
Width: 129cm/51in, Repeat: 84cm/33in
Suitable for windows and upholstery

3. Lee Jofa/Southdown Rose 909403
Colourway: 03
Composition: 100% cotton
Width: 132cm/51¾in
Repeat: 45cm/17½ in
Suitable for windows and upholstery

4. Brunschwig & Fils/Suffield Arabesque 15690.06
Colourway: white,
Width: 57cm/22½ in, Length: 4.5m/5yd,
Repeat: 55cm/21½ in

5. Axminster Carpets/Persian Panel 34/01397
Composition: 100% wool
Width: 3.66m/4yd, Repeat: 85cm/33½ in

Jazz Age – Art Deco

1. Brunschwig & Fils/Jazzywoven Damask
6033.02
Colourway: camel
Composition: 100% cotton
Width 137cm/54in, Repeat 53cm/21in
Suitable for upholstery

2. The Silk Gallery/Chenille II
Colourway: Henna and Gold
Composition: 83% cotton, 17% silk
Width: 127cm/50in
Suitable for upholstery

3. Lelièvre/Velours Fourrure Serval 610-01
Colourway: serval
Composition: 68% cotton, 32% viscose
Width: 135cm/53in, Repeat: 39cm/15¼ in
Suitable for upholstery, bedcovers
and cushions

4. Chatsworth/White Tiger
Colourway: black and white
Composition: 100% nylon, Width: 3.66m/4yd
Repeat: 90cm/35½ in

5. Original Style/Salmon
Colourway: multi, Composition: ceramic
Size: 15 x 15cm x 7mm/6 x 6 x ¼ in
Suitable for walls

Antique Inspiration
1. Chelsea Textiles/Grapes Fine Crewelwork FO32
Colourway: multi
Composition: 100% cotton with wool crewelwork
Width: 150cm/59in, Repeat: 96cm/37¾ in
Suitable for curtains, bedcovers, upholstery

2. Manuel Canovas/La Source 11349/89
Colourway: ficelle, Composition: 100% cotton
Width: 136cm/53½ in, Repeat: 74cm/29in
Suitable for curtains, walls

3. The Design Archives/Liaisons 54044
Colourway: brown on cream
Composition: 100% cotton
Width: 137cm/54in Repeat: 46cm/18in
Suitable for curtains, upholstery

4. Bernard Thorp & Co/Lucien
Colourway: multi
Composition: 58% flax, 42% cotton
Width: 120cm/47in, Repeat: 37cm/14½ in
Suitable for windows

5. Crucial Trading/Tortoiseshell E924
Colourway: green, Composition: 100% sisal
Width: 4m/4½ yd

Shaker Style
1. Ian Mankin/Empire 1,
Colourway: Air Force
Composition: 100% cotton, Width: 137cm/54in
Suitable for windows and upholstery

2. Abbott & Boyd/Voile de Lin, Colourway: 07
Composition: 100% linen, Width: 150cm/59in
Suitable for windows

3. Sanderson/Foursome BL6437/1.
Colourway: cream, Composition: 100% cotton
Width: 150cm/59in, Repeat: 4cm/1½ in
Suitable for windows

4. John Wilman/Traviata 170259
Colourway: green, Width: 52cm/20½ in
Length: 10m/11yd

5. Kalon/BS4800 Colour Range
Colour: Westmorland 12B21
Composition and finish: water-based matt and
satin, oil-based gloss and satin
Suitable for walls and woodwork

1. Ian Sanderson/Pym Stripe
Colourway: brick, Composition: 100% cotton,
Width: 140cm/55in
Suitable for windows, loose covers, bedcovers
and upholstery

2. Colefax and Fowler/Maplehurst Check F1305/03
Colourway: green
Composition: 48% cotton, 44% Velicren, 8% linen
Width: 140cm/55in
Repeat: 6cm/2½ in
Suitable for windows and upholstery

3. Brats/Mediterranean Palette 113
Colour: Amalfi
Composition and finish: water-based matt
Suitable for walls

4. Finnaren & Haley/Roasted Pepper AC116N
Composition and finish: water-based low lustre
and semi-gloss, oil-based high gloss
Suitable for walls, woodwork and exterior use

5. Warwick/Washcott Fairford 118192414580
Colourway: dusk 20
Composition: 100% cotton
Width: 137cm/54in
Repeat: 15cm/6in
Suitable for windows and upholstery

Homey Checks
1. Lelièvre/Satin Milleraies 4164
Colourway: blue and cream
Composition: 100% viscose
Width: 130cm/51in
Suitable for windows and upholstery

2. Ian Sanderson/Box Check
Colourway: cornflower
Composition: 100% cotton
Width: 140cm/55in, Repeat: 2.5cm/1in
Suitable for windows and upholstery

3. Baer & Ingram/DaisyDSF13
Colourway: raspberry
Composition: 100% cotton
Width: 140cm/55in
Repeat: 11cm/4¼ in
Suitable for windows and upholstery

4. Hill & Knowles/Foursquare Fabric 21174F
Colourway: blue and white
Composition: 100% cotton
Width: 137cm/54in
Repeat: 2.5cm/1in
Suitable for windows and upholstery

5. Ramm, Son & Crocker/Cheltenham E7525
Colourway: multi
Composition: 100% cotton
Width: 140cm/55in, Repeat: 27cm/10½ in
Suitable for windows

Faded Florals
1. Jason D'Souza/Blenheim
Colourway: plum/rust
Composition: 64% linen, 36% cotton
Width: 135cm/53in, Repeat: 92cm/36in
Suitable for windows, bedcovers
and upholstery

2. Jason D'Souza/Medici MED03
Colourway: burgundy/blue
Composition: 70% linen, 30% cotton
Width: 136cm/53½ in, Repeat: 49.5cm/19½ in
Suitable for upholstery

3. Montgomery/Damask Rose Colour No. 4
Colourway: green on beige
Composition: 100% cotton satin
Width: 137cm/54in
Repeat: 63.5cm/25in
Suitable for windows, loose covers
and upholstery

4. Old World Weavers/Vera Shear B/1886S0108
Colourway: multi
Composition: 100% cotton
Width: 139cm/54¾ in,
Repeat: 97cm/38¼ in
Suitable for windows

5. Stark/Filigrane et Fleurs
Colourway: pastel
Composition: 100% wool
Width: 101cm/40¼ in
Repeat: 131cm/52¼ in

Rustic Weaves
1. Jim Thompson/Mirage Check P4011
Colourway: taupe
Composition: 100% silk
Width: 122cm/48in, Repeat: 4cm/1½ in
Suitable for windows and upholstery

2. Old World Weavers/Cubic PWO 0930005
Colourway: rust/putty
Composition: 60% cotton, 40% rayon
Width: 140cm/55in
Suitable for upholstery

3. Interdesign/Ric Api 230109, Colourway: 03
Composition: 100% linen
Width: 160cm/63in
Repeat: 12cm/4¾ in
Suitable for windows and bedcovers

4. Andrew Martin/Raffia Medium
Colourway: natural, Width: 76cm/30in
Length: 6m/6½ yd

5. The Alternative Flooring Co/Buckingham
Basketweave AFC 102, Colourway: natural
Composition: 100% Indian grass
Width: 4m/4½ yd

Relaxed Country
1. Abbot & Boyd/Abeto 50054-2
Colourway: beige and cream
Composition: 81% rayon, 19% polyester
Width: 137cm/54in
Repeat: 32cm/12½ in
Suitable for curtains and upholstery

2. Baer & Ingram/Daisy Paper DSW04
Colourway: yellow, Width: 52cm/20½ in
Length: 10m/11yd, Repeat: 4.5cm/1¾ in

3. Osborne & Little/Piggy W1195-04
Colourway: green, Width: 52cm/20½ in
Length: 10m/11yd, Repeat: 53cm/21in

4. Donghia Textiles/Housepets 0450/5850-8
Colourway: beige & taupe
Composition: 100% cotton, Width: 137cm/54in
Repeat: 34cm/13 ¼ in
Suitable for upholstery

5. Lewis & Wood/Chelsea Check LW3911
Colourway: red and white
Composition: 100% cotton,
Width: 140cm/55in, Repeat: 2cm/ ¾ in
Suitable for windows and upholstery

At Home in Provence
1. Lewis & Wood/Pimlico Stripe LW1738
Colourway: multi
Composition: 100% cotton herringbone,
Width: 140cm/55in
Suitable for windows and upholstery

2. Scalamandré/Caprice des Dames 16229M-5
Colourway: multi, Composition: 100% silk
Width: 135cm/53in, Repeat: 73.5 cm/29in
Suitable for upholstery

3. Hamilton Weston/Bedford Stripe
Colourway: 303, Width: 52cm/20½ in
Length: 10m/11yd, Repeat: 15cm/6in

4. Lee Jofa/Fleur Plaid 970061-919
Colourway: multi, Composition: 100% cotton,
Width: 137cm/54in, Repeat: 14cm/5½ in
Suitable for upholstery

5. Brunschwig & Fils/Aix 69222.06
Colourway: blue, Width: 69cm/27in
Length: 4.5m/5yd, Repeat: 6cm/2½ in

Travels in Tuscany
1. Scalamandré/Adriatic Antique Taffeta 5870-028
Colourway: maize, Composition: 100% silk
Width: 142cm/55¾ in

2. Crowson/Palazzo 03097 PO2
Colourway: red and gold
Composition: 56% viscose, 44% polyester
Width: 137cm/54in, Repeat: 68cm/26¾ in
Suitable for curtains and upholstery

3. Brunschwig & Fils/Angelina Figured
Texture 53591.01, Colourway: shell
Composition: 60% cotton, 20% silk, 20% polyester
Width: 132cm/51¾ in, Repeat: 11cm/4¼ in
Suitable for upholstery

4. Elon/Saltillo Square
Colourway: terracotta
Composition: terracotta
Size: 30 x 30 x 2cm/11¾ x 11¾ x ¾in
Suitable for floors and walls

5. Liz Induni, Colour: terracotta
Composition and finish: limewash
Suitable for walls, floors and woodwork

Moroccan Magic
1. Donghia Textiles/Righe
Colourway: red and gold
Composition: 100% silk
Width: 140cm/55in, Repeat: 2cm/¾ in
Suitable for upholstery

2. Jab/Maharadscha 6943-211
Colourway: orange
Composition: 100% silk, Width: 122cm/48in
Suitable for windows

3. Zimmer & Rohde/Peking 8326-98
Colourway: rust
Composition: 50% silk
25% cotton, 25% polyester
Width: 140cm/55in
Suitable for upholstery

4. Hill & Knowles/Troubadour
Colourway: green and red
Composition: 100% cotton
Width: 137cm/54in, Repeat: 32cm/12½ in
Suitable for upholstery and windows

5. Kenneth Clark Ceramics/Plain Colours D6
Colourway: sienna, Composition: ceramic
Size: 10 x 10cm x 7mm /4 x 4 x ¼ in
Suitable for walls

Safari Style

1. Scalamandré/Daktari 26270
Colourway: 002, Composition: 65% cotton
30% rayon, 5% polyester
Width: 137cm/54in, Repeat: 41cm/16in
Suitable for upholstery

2. Jab/Bardera 1.-8057, Colourway: 174
Composition: 100% cotton, Width: 140cm/55in
Repeat: 32cm/12½ in
Suitable for windows and upholstery

3. Sahco Hesslein/Uris 50271
Colourway: natural
Composition: 55% viscose, 24% cotton,
21% linen, Width: 155cm/61in
Suitable for windows

4. Crowson/ Rima 37550R05
Colourway: 10, Width: 52cm/20 ½ in
Length: 10m/11yd

5. Sinclair Till/Giraffe, Colourway: giraffe
Composition: 100% sisal, Width: to order

Indian Spice

1. Abbott & Boyd/Elefantes 47654
Colourway: 2, Composition: 100% cotton
Width: 145cm/57in, Repeat: 56cm/22in
Suitable for windows and upholstery

2. Designers Guild/Kashipur F517/03
Colourway: fuchsia, Composition: 100% cotton
Width: 137cm/54in, Repeat: 41cm/16in
Suitable for upholstery

3. Marvic Textiles/Bhatinda 1204-2
Colourway: multi
Composition: 55% cotton 45% wool
Width: 130cm/51in
Repeat: 40cm/15½ in
Suitable for windows, bedcovers and cushions

4. Liz Induni, Colour: pale pink
Composition and finish: limewash
Suitable for walls, floors and woodwork

5. Tiles of Stow/Heraldic Star
Colourway: multi, Composition: ceramic
11 x 11cm x 7mm /4¼ x 4¼ x ¼ in
Suitable for windows

Asiatic Elements

1. Sahco Hesslein/Caprice 50262
Colourway: gold, Composition: 50% viscose
21% silk, 15% acrylic, 14% linen
Width: 140cm/55in

2. Monkwell/Batumi 09358
Colourway: 5, Composition: 100% cotton
Width: 137cm/54in, Repeat: 62cm/24¼ in
Suitable for windows and upholstery

3. Andrew Martin/Raffia Medium
Colourway: natural, Width: 76cm/30 in
Length: 6m/6½ yd

4. Attica/Ancient Rhythm Fresco
Colourway: multi, Composition: ceramic
Size: 15 x 15 x 1cm/6 x 6⅛ in

5. Waveney Apple Growers/Rush Medieval Matting
Colourway: natural, Composition: 100% rush
Width: to order

Zen from Japan

1. Brunschwig & Fils/Canton Cotton Print 79512.04
Colourway: blue fish on white
Composition: 100% cotton,
Width: 134cm/52½ in, Repeat: 64cm/25in
Suitable for windows and upholstery

2. Zimmer & Rohde/Idris 6991-556
Colourway: blue, Composition: 100% silk
Width: 135cm/53in

3. Maya Romanoff/Washi Tsuchikabe
Colourway: suede beige
Width: 93cm/36in, Length: to order

4. Donghia/Grasscloth G946-04
Colourway: 04 seaweed
Width: 91cm/35¼ in
Length: 3.5m/3¾ yd

5. The Alternative Flooring Co/Sisal Panama
AFC 503, Colourway: Donegal
Composition: 100% sisal
Width: 4m/4½ yd

Nordic Style

1. Nina Campbell/Violet Plaid NCF3131
Colourway: 01, Composition: 100% cotton
Width: 140cm/55in, Repeat: 9cm/3¼ in
Suitable for windows and upholstery

2. Sherwin Williams/Preservation Palette
Colour: Burma jade SW 2862
Composition and finish: water-based matt,
satin, semi-gloss; oil-based semi-gloss
Suitable for walls, ceilings and woodwork

3. Anna French/Rupert Check Voile V73
Colourway: green, Composition: 100% cotton
Width: 110cm/43in, Repeat: 13cm/5in

4. Zoffany/Hopetoun Flower 7704004
Colourway: 04, Width: 52cm/20½ in
Length: 10m/11 yd, Repeat: 26.5/10½ in

5. LASSCO/Sycamore Boards
Colourway: natural, Composition: sycamore
Width: to order

1. Nice Irma's/Blue Stripe Voile
Colourway: blue and white stripe
Composition: 100% cotton
Width: 100cm/39¼ in
Suitable for windows

2. Baer & Ingram/Daisy Border DSB16
Colourway: blue, Width: 10cm/4in,
Length: 10m/11 yd Repeat: 9cm/3½ in

3. Paint Magic/Liming Paste, Colour: natural
Composition and finish: water-based matt
Suitable for woodwork

4. Zoffany/Pastiche, Colourway: spindrift
Composition: 100% wool
Width: 4m/4½ yd
Repeat 5cm/2in

5. Ceramiche Eurotiles/Listello Gazebo
Colourway: rosa, Composition: ceramic
Size: 20 x 10cm x 7mm/8 x 4 x ¼ in
Suitable for walls

Celtic Connections

1. The Isle Mill/Kildonan STR016
Colourway: multi, Composition: 100% wool
Width: 140cm/55in
Repeat: 14cm/5½ in
Suitable for loose covers and bedcovers

2. The Isle Mill/Dress Gordon S5863
Colourway: multi, Composition: 100% wool
Width: 137cm/54¾ in, Repeat: 33cm/13¼ in
Suitable for loose covers and bedcovers

3. Zoffany/Venetian Grill V43405
Colourway: 05, Width: 52cm/20½ in
Length: 10m/11yd, Repeat: 8cm/3in

4. Tiles of Stow/Check
Colourway: green and purple
Composition: ceramic
Size: 10 x 10cm x 5mm/4 x 4 x ⅕ in
Suitable for walls

5. Stark/Kenshire
Colourway: gold/green
Composition: 100% wool, Width: 68.5cm/27in
Repeat: 18cm/7in

A Taste of Tex-Mex

1. Sahco Hesslein/Dundee 12073
Colourway: 445, Composition: 60% viscose,
25% cotton, 15% polyacrylic,
Width: 140cm/55in
Repeat: 15cm/6in

2. Watts of Westminster/Flame F0007-02/J17
Colourway: gold, Composition: 51% cotton,
29% lumiyarn, 20% rayon
Width: 124cm/48¾ in
Repeat: 21cm/8¼ in
Suitable for windows and upholstery

3. John Willman/Rio 500. Colourway: Papaya
Composition: 100% cotton
Width: 137cm/54in, Repeat: 7cm/2¾ in,

4. Dulux/Trade Colour Palette
Colour: 09YR 11/476
Composition and finish: water-based matt, silk,
soft sheen; oil-based dead flat, eggshell, gloss
Suitable for walls and ceilings

5. Lowitz & Co/Talisman Panel Beginnings Border
Colourway: white, Composition: ceramic
Size: 15 x 10cm x 7mm/6 x 4 x ¼ in
Suitable for walls and exterior use

Minimal Mood

1. Jab/Sylt 1.-6002, Colourway: 255
Composition: 100% cotton
Width: 140cm/55in
Suitable for windows

2. Garin Pling 1532, Colourway: white
Composition: 64% cotton, 36% linen
Width: 150cm/59in
Suitable for windows

3. John Wilman/Aida 170549
Colourway: green
Width: 52cm/20½ in, Length: 10m/11yd
Repeat: 1.5cm/⅝ in

4. Jane Churchill, Colour: primrose 12
Composition and finish: water-based matt
Suitable for walls, floors and
woodwork

5. Pratt & Lambert/Interior Wall & Trim
Colour: princely blue 1148
Composition and finish: water-based matt,
satin, eggshell, semi-gloss, gloss
Suitable for walls, floors and
woodwork

Bright and Bold

1. Seamoor Fabrics/Kaleidoscope
Colourway: crushed rose
Composition: 100% cotton
Width: 122cm/48in
Suitable for windows

2. Elizabeth Eaton/Lanka Check
Colourway: pink, Composition: 100% cotton
Width: 127cm/50in, Repeat: 2.5cm/1in
Suitable for windows and upholstery

3. Designer's Guild/Diagonale F563/11
Colourway: green, Composition: 100% cotton
Width: 140cm/55in
Suitable for upholstery

4. J. W. Bollom, Colour: mandarin 06E51 JWB74
Composition and finish: water-based matt, silk;
oil-based eggshell, gloss
Suitable for walls, ceilings and woodwork

5. Louis de Poortere/Byzance 330
Colourway: yellow
Composition: 100% polyamide
Width: 4m/4½ yd

1. Zoffany/Ticking Stripe 36KT03
Colourway: 03
Width: 52cm/20½ in, Length: 10m/11yd

2. Olicana/Calypso
Colourway: paradisian pink
Composition: 100% cotton,
Width: 145cm/57in
Suitable for windows, walls and upholstery

3. Brunschwig & Fils/Amandine Glazed Chintz
77730-04, Colourway: multi on white
Composition: 100% cotton
Width: 132cm/51¾ in, Repeat: 85.5cm/33½ in,
Suitable for windows

4. John Oliver, Colour: kinky pink
Composition and finish: water-based matt
oil-based eggshell, gloss
Suitable for walls and woodwork

5. Scalamandré/Georgian 1225M-044
Colourway: rose and burgundy
Composition: 100% silk, Width: 140cm/55in
Repeat: 61cm/24in
Suitable for windows and upholstery

Purely Pale

1. Sahco Hesslein/Akka 04614
Colourway: cream, Composition: 100% cotton
Width: 140cm/55in

2. Brunschwig & Fils/Brendan Woven Texture
Colourway: 02, Composition: 100% cotton
Width: 137cm/54in, Repeat: 9cm/3½ in
Suitable for windows and upholstery

3. Ian Sanderson/Donovan
Colourway: natural
Composition: 65% cotton, 35% linen
Width: 137cm/54in
Suitable for upholstery

4. Zoffany/Viola Plain V21704
Colourway: 04, Width: 52cm/20½ in
Length: 10m/11yd, Repeat: 13cm/5in

5. Fired Earth/Roman Mosaic Natural Floor
Colourway: white, Composition: stone
Size: 20 x 20 x 1.2cm/8 x 8 x ½ in

Contemporary Geometrics
1. G. P. & J. Baker/Gallery J0242
Colourway: 755 Composition: 100% silk,
Width: 140cm/55in, Repeat: 18cm/7in
Suitable for windows and upholstery

2. Baumann Fabrics/Bristol
Colourway: 186, Composition: 90% cotton,
10% polyester, Width: 150cm/59in
Repeat: 3.5cm/1¼in
Suitable for loose covers, bedcovers

3. Zimmer & Rohde/Nomen 1264-707
Colourway: green/yellow
Composition: 80% cotton, 20% viscose
Width: 140cm/55in, Repeat: 9cm/3½ in
Suitable for windows and upholstery

4. Brunschwig & Fils, Altena Velvet 53293
Colourway: 01
Composition: 78% polyester,
22% cotton, Width: 140cm/55in
Repeat: 23cm/9in
Suitable for upholstery

5. Zoffany/Fresco Check VA3604
Colourway: 04, Width: 52cm/20½ in
Length: 10m/11yd, Repeat: 10.5cm/4in

New Ways with Texture
1. Northwood Designs/Hibiscus
Colourway: miel
Composition: 100% cotton
Width: 2.8m/3ft,
Repeat: 34cm/13 ¼ in

2. Nice Irma's/Rosemary CWF 39
Colourway: pastels on cream
Composition: 100% cotton with wool crewelwork
Width: 132cm/51¾ in, Repeat: 95cm/37in
Suitable for windows, bedcovers, walls

3. Interdesign/Studio Quasar - Fiore
Colourway: natural,
Composition: 100% cotton
Width: 160cm/63in, Repeat: 12cm/4¾in
Suitable for windows

4. Bruno Triplet/Stella Color
Colourway: cream
Composition: 40% linen
33% cotton, 23% polyester
Width: 20cm/47in
Repeat: 8cm/3in
Suitable for loose covers and windows

5. Fired Earth/VM Travertino
Colourway: travertino
Composition: Venetian marble
Size: 10 x 10 x 2cm/4 x 4 x ¾ in
Suitable for floors

Florals Updated
1. Hodsoll McKenzie/English Crewelwork 220/107
Composition: 60% spun rayon, 40% cotton
Width: 130cm/51in, Repeat: 62cm/24½ in
Suitable for windows and upholstery

2. Ralph Lauren Home Collection/Fab Yvette Floral
Composition: 100% cotton
Width: 135cm/53in, Repeat: 90cm/35¼ in
Suitable for upholstery and curtains

3. Ramm, Son & Crocker/Tulips E9948
Colourway: green, Composition: 100% cotton
Width: 140cm/55in, Repeat: 50cm/19½ in
Suitable for windows and upholstery

4. Jane Churchill/Tulip Sprig JY67W-02
Colourway: blue on white
Width: 52cm/20½ in, Length: 10m/11yd
Repeat: 13cm/5in

5. Cath Kidston/Rose Bouquet RB02
Width: 52cm/20½ in, Repeat: 46cm/18in

Neutral Entrance
1. Knowles & Christou/Amphora
Colourway: stone, Composition: 100% cotton,
Width: 132cm/51¾ in, Repeat: 30cm/1¾ in
Suitable for windows

2. Bentley & Spens/New Geometrics
Colourway: beige
Composition: 52% velicron modacrylic,
37% cotton, 11% nylon, Width: 144cm/56½ in
Repeat: 49cm/19¼ in
Suitable for windows, upholstery and walls

3. Akzo Nobel/Italian Renaissance RD 1952
Colourway: white, Width: 52cm/20½ in
Length: 102cm/40in, Repeat: 102cm/40in

4. Osborne & Little/Glissando W1443/01
Colourway: silver, Width: 52cm/20 ½ in
Length: 10m/11yd

5. Kahrs/Rotterdam Diagonal Pattern 3215 0B 50
Colourway: natural, Composition: birch/oak
Width: 15cm/6in

Neutral Living
1. Ian Mankin/Striped Jacquard
Colourway: natural, Composition: 100% cotton
Width: 137cm/54in
Suitable for windows, loose covers,
bedcovers and upholstery

2. Zimmer & Rohde/Plumito 7008 91
Colourway: 1
Composition: 57% viscose
23% linen, Width: 140cm/55in
Repeat: 62cm/24¼ in
Suitable for windows and upholstery

3. Maya Romanoff/Patina MR-T35-176-G
Colourway: golden taupe
Width: 2m/2½ yd, Length: to order

4. Afia/Matto,
Colourway: 235, Composition: 100% paper
Width: 76cm/30in, Length: to order

5. Stark/Dover,
Colourway: stock
Composition: 100% wool, Width: 3.66m/4yd
Repeat: 30.5cm/12in

1. Donghia/Double Diamond 0259/8200-08
Colourway: natural oyster
Composition: 60% linen, 40% cotton
Width: 137cm/54in, Repeat: 50cm/19½ in
Suitable for windows and upholstery

2. Sahco Hesslein/Akkord 04625
Colourway: cream
Composition: 68% cotton, 32% viscose
Width: 140cm/55in, Repeat: 13cm/5in
Suitable for upholstery

3. Hill & Knowles/Canbury
Colourway: banana, Composition: 100% cotton
Width: 130cm/51in, Repeat: 36cm/14in
Suitable for windows and upholstery

4. Cuprinol/Interior Quick Drying Woodstain
Colourway: brown mahogany
Composition and finish: oil based, semi-
transparent satin

5. The Alternative Flooring Co, Sisal Panama
Colourway: Donegal, Composition: 100% sisal
Width: 4m/4½ yd

Neutral Bedroom
1. Jab/Murano 1-6050-122,
Colourway: gold
Composition: 54% viscose, 46% cotton
Width: 130cm/51in
Suitable for windows, loose covers and walls

2. Donghia/Rugose 0556/6480-10
Colourway: cavolo-cream
Composition: 80% viscose, 12% polyester,
8% polyacrylic, Width: 133cm/52in
Repeat: 9cm/3½ in

3. Northwood Designs/Scala 001
Colourway: natural
Composition: 55% polyester, 45% cotton
Width: 3m/3.2yd, Repeat: 19cm/7½ in
Suitable for windows and walls

4. Crowson/Rima 37550R05
Colourway: 10, Width: 52cm/20½ in
Length: 10m/11yd

5. Colefax and Fowler/New Paris 7603/10
Colourway: stone, Width: 52cm/21in
Length: 10m/11yd

Neutral Bathroom
1. Bentley & Spens/Shells B5044 Voile
Colourway: bronze, silver, white
Composition: 67% polyester, 33% cotton
Width: 134cm/52½ in, Repeat: 67cm/26¼in
for windows

2. Anya Larkin/Moondust Teapaper
Colourway: 236 pueblo, Width: 102cm/40in
Length: 3m/3½ yd

3. Maya Romanoff/Grecian Crystal MR-W54-482
Colourway: dusty lilac, Width: 77cm/30¼ in
Length: 3.5m/3¾ yd

4. The Alternative Flooring Co./Panama AFC612
Colourway: bleached, Composition: 100% jute
Width: 4m/4½ yd

5. Kievel Stone/Fossil Stone
Colourway: cream, Composition: limestone
Size: 40 x 20cm x 7mm/15¾ x 8 x ¼ in
Suitable for floors

Neutral Dining
1. Dovedale/Yale, Colourway: 02,
Composition: 100% cotton
Width: 143cm/56in, Repeat: 63cm/24¾ in
Suitable for windows and upholstery

2. Pecheron/Lampas – Les Abeilles
Colourway: 1
Composition: 63% cotton
37& viscose, Width: 130cm/51in
Repeat: 14cm/5½ in
Suitable for windows and upholstery

3. The Old-Fashioned Milk Paint Co.
Colour: oyster white
Composition and finish: milk paint
Suitable for woodwork and plasterwork

4. The Stulb Company
Colour: fancy chair yellow 74.2000.1.
Composition and finish: milk paint
Suitable for walls, floors and woodwork

5. LASSCO/Sycamore Boards
Colourway: natural, Composition: sycamore
Width: to order

Neutral Kitchen
1. Galliards/Francesco
Colourway: beige and brown
Composition: 100% cotton
Width: 137cm/54in
Repeat: 16cm/6¼ in
Suitable for windows and upholstery

2. Scalamandré/Newport Damask
Colourway: cream,
Composition: 100% silk
Width: 140cm/55in, Repeat: 47cm/18½ in
Suitable for upholstery and walls

3. Ian Mankin/Pacific Plain
Colourway: spice
Composition: 100% cotton
Width: 137cm/54 in
Suitable for windows and upholstery

4. Nobilis-Fontan/Papiers Bois Couleur PBC103
Colourway: yellow, Width: 125cm/49in
Length: to order

5. Stonell/Bamboo
Colourway: grey with rust streak
Composition: slate
Size: 10 x 10 x 1.2cm/4 x 4 x ½ in
Suitable for floors

1. De Le Cuona Designs/Herringbone Natural
LL103212, Colourway: natural
Composition: 100% linen
Width: 114cm/44¾ in
Suitable for windows and upholstery

2. Zimmer & Rohde/Tana 1269-832
Colourway: beige
Composition: 85% cotton, 15% viscose
Width: 140cm/55in, Repeat: 6cm/2¼ in
Suitable for windows and upholstery

3. Hamilton Weston/Richmond Trellis
Colourway: 8162, Width: 53cm/21in
Length: 10m/11yd, Repeat: 17.5cm/7in
Hand-blocked or hand-printed

4. Wendy Wilbraham/Cornish Slate Tiles
Colourway: stone
Composition: stone and cement
Size: 20 x 15 x 1.5cm/8 x 6 x ⅝ in

5. DLW/Marmorette 121-70
Colourway: 70, Composition: linoleum
Width: 2m/2⅕ yd

Hot Entrance
1. Warwick/Marseille 105461506620
Colourway: burgundy
Composition: 100% cotton
Width: 137cm/54in, Repeat: 64cm/25in
Suitable for windows and upholstery

2. Northwood Designs/Chambord Rubis
Colourway: 05
Composition: 55% cotton, 45% viscose
Width: 138cm/54in, Repeat: 70cm/27½ in
Suitable for windows, upholstery, walls

3. Scalamandré/Brighton 16121-002
Colourway: multi on framboise
Composition: 100% cotton, Width: 137cm/54in
Repeat: 101cm/39¾in
Suitable for windows

4. Harlequin/15011,
Colourway: terracotta, Width: 52cm/20½in,
Length: 10m/11yd

5. Bradbury & Bradbury/Roland RLW-130
Colourway: 130, Width: 68cm/26¾in
Length: 4.5m/5yd, Repeat: 27cm/10½ in
Hand-blocked or hand-printed

1. Jab/Maharadscha 6943-211
Colourway: orange, Composition: 100% silk
Width: 122cm/48in
Suitable for windows

2. Zimmer & Rhode/Peking
Colourway: red
Composition: 56% viscose, 44% polyester
Width: 137cm/54in, Repeat: 68cm/26¾in
Suitable for windows and upholstery

3. Liz Induni
Colourway: Terracotta
Composition: limewash, distemper

4. Dulux/Trade Colour Palette
Colour: 09YR 11/476
Composition and finish: water-based matt, silk, soft sheen; oil-based dead flat, eggshell, gloss
Suitable for walls and ceilings

5. Victorian Wood Works/Jacobean Oak Plank
Colourway: Jacobean oak stain
Composition: oak, Width: 20cm/8in

Hot Living
1. Lelièvre/Lotus 929 01
Colourway: 12
Composition: 95% cotton, 5% polyamide
Width: 146cm/57½ in, Repeat: 27cm/10½ in
Suitable for upholstery

2. Liberon Waxes
Colourway: Fontainebleu
Composition and finish: spirit based satin sheen

3. Watts of Westminster/Holbein F0012-21/Q4
Colourway: purple
Composition: 100% silk
Width: 124cm/48¾ in, Repeat: 33cm/13in
Suitable for windows

4. Osborne & Little/Adagio W1444/05
Colourway: yellow,
Width: 52cm/20½in
Length: 10m/11yd

5. Cole & Son, Colourway: Etruscan
Composition and finish: water-based matt
Suitable for walls and ceilings

1. Garin/Janini 96455041
Colourway: rojo, Composition: 69% cotton, 21% viscose, 10% linen, Width: 150cm/59in
Repeat: 56cm/22in
Suitable for windows and upholstery

2. Cole & Sons/Owen Jones 52/7040
Colourway: red, Width: 53cm/21in
Length: 10m/11yd, Repeat: 7cm/2¾ in

3. Ramm, Son & Crocker/Oakley 14661.06
Colourway: red,
Width: 52cm/20½ in, Length: 10m/11yd,
Repeat: 26cm/10¼ in

4. J. W. Bollom/Bromel,
Colour: RAL 4005
Composition and finish: water-based matt, silk; oil-based gloss
Suitable for walls, ceilings and woodwork

5. Bill Amberg/Leather Floor (Tile)
Colourway: light tan, Composition: leather
Width: to order

Hot Bedroom
1. Seamoor Fabrics/Kaleidoscope
Colourway: crushed rose
Composition: 100% cotton
Width: 122cm/48in
Suitable for windows

2. Olicana/Calypso
Colourway: paradisian pink
Composition: 100% cotton,
Width: 145cm/57in
Suitable for windows, upholstery and walls

3. Designers Guild/Marquetry F542
Colourway: 14,
Composition: 44% cotton
41% modacrylic, 15% polyacrylic
Width: 137cm/54in, Repeat: 14cm/5½ in
Suitable for upholstery

4. Colefax and Fowler/Sudbury Park 7046/01
Colourway: pink, Width: 53cm/21in
Repeat: 7½ cm/3in

5. Ulster Carpet Mills/Turkestan 10/2381
Colourway: red
Composition: 80% wool,
20% nylon, Width: 3.66m/4yd
Repeat: 94cm/36½ in

Hot Bathroom
1. Olicana/Yachting Cotton
Colourway: red rag, Composition: 100% cotton
Width: 137cm/54in
Suitable for windows, upholstery and walls

2. Paint Library, Colour: Elizabethan red
Composition and finish: water-based matt, silk; oil-based dead flat, gloss
Suitable for walls, floors, stonework, exterior use

3. Pittsburgh Paints/Designacolor System
Colour: Naples 4035
Composition and finish: water-based matt, satin, eggshell, gloss; oil-based satin, gloss
Suitable for walls, floors and exterior use

4. Rustins/Colorglaze, Colour: yellow
Composition and finish: oil-based satin
Suitable for woodwork and exterior use

5. Amtico/Maple W684,
Colourway: maple, Composition: vinyl
Width: 3.66m/4yd

Hot Dining
1. Marvic Textiles/Misa Moire Plain 6565
Colourway: daisy
Composition: 52% linen, 48% viscose
Width: 140cm/55in
Suitable for windows, upholstery and walls

2. Jim Thompson/Image 1023
Colourway: 07, Composition: 100% cotton
Width: 137cm/54in
Suitable for windows and upholstery

3. Scalamandré/Lampa – Rosecliff Laurel 20221-007
Colourway: cranberry, Composition: 100% silk
Width: 140cm/55in, Repeat: 17cm/6¾ in
Suitable for windows and upholstery

4. G. P. & J. Baker/Heraldic Damask W0113-02
Colourway: 02
Width: 52cm/20½ in, Length: 10m/11yd,
Repeat: 53cm/21in

5. Zuber/Rayures à Auge
Colourway: 190 jaune
Width: 47cm/18½ in,
Length: 10m/11yd

Hot Kitchen
1. Designers Guild/Latika F538/05
Colourway: red, Composition: 100% cotton
Width: 137cm/54in, Repeat: 64cm/25in
Suitable for upholstery

2. Ottilie Stevenson/Monty Check VF0052
Colourway: mustard
Composition: 100% cotton
Width: 137cm/54in
Suitable for windows and upholstery

3. Dulux/Trade Colour Palette
Colour: MYR 13/558
Composition and finish: water-based matt, silk, soft sheen; oil-based dead flat, eggshell, gloss,
Suitable for walls and ceilings

4. Elon/Carrillo Plain
Colourway: red, Composition: ceramic
Size: 10 x 10cm x 7mm/4 x 4 x ¼ in
Suitable for walls and floors

5. DLW/Marmorette 121-18
Colourway: 18, Composition: linoleum
Width: 2m/2⅕ yd

Cool Entrance
1. Scalamandré/Province 154-007
Colourway: yellow and pale blue
Composition: 100% silk
Width: 127cm/50in
Repeat: 2.5cm/1in
Suitable for windows and upholstery

2. Dedar/Manon
Colourway: cream and black
Composition: 58% cotton, 23% viscose, 19% polyester, Width: 140cm/55in
Suitable for windows

3. Crowson/Cashel 03097 CC9
Colourway: 11
Composition: 67% polyester, 33% cotton
Width: 137cm/54in
Suitable for windows

4. Tor Coatings/Ardenbrite,
Colour: black enamel
Composition and finish: spirit-based satin
Suitable for woodwork, metalwork and exterior use

5. Pittsburgh Paints/Designacolor System
Colour: deep marine 7090
Composition and finish: water-based matt, satin, eggshell, gloss enamel; oil-based satin, gloss
Suitable for walls, floors and exterior use

Cool Living
1. Ian Mankin/Ticking II Navy
Colourway: navy and off-white
Composition: 100% cotton, Width: 120cm/47in
Repeat: width of stripe
Suitable for windows and upholstery

2. Passinari & Chatel/Les Lyres 1511
Colourway: 01
Composition: 100% silk
Width: 130cm/51in, Repeat: 22cm/8½ in
Suitable for upholstery

3. Cole & Son/Georgian Rope Trellis 52/7030
Colourway: gold on eau de nil, Width: 48cm/19in
Repeat: 47cm/18½ in

4. Zoffany/Brittany 36BY03
Colourway: 03, Width: 52cm/20½ in
Length: 10m/11yd Repeat: 8cm/3in

5. Cuprinol/Quick Drying Wood Dye
Colour: light oak, Composition and finish: oil-based semi-transparent satin
Suitable for woodwork

1. Zoffany/Vine 347706
Colourway: Swedish blue
Composition: 45% modacrylic, 41% cotton, 14% nylon, Width: 137cm/54in
Repeat: 10cm/4in
Suitable for windows and upholstery

2. Elizabeth Eaton/Muslin 9550/3837
Colourway: white, Composition: 100% cotton
Width: 150cm/59in, Repeat: 11cm/4¼ in
Suitable for windows

3. Mary Fox Linton/Marquis 8351
Colourway: blue and yellow
Composition: 100% silk, Width: 140cm/55in
Repeat: 12cm/4¾ in
Suitable for windows

4. Northwood Designs/Senza
Colourway: blue, Width: 90cm/35½ in
Length: to order

5. Baer & Ingram/Ticking Paper TKW11
Colourway: black, Width: 52cm/20½ in, Length: 10m/11yd, Repeat: 4.5cm/1¾ in

Cool Bedroom
1. Ian Mankin/Ticking I
Colourway: spruce, Composition: 100% cotton
Width: 120cm/47in
Suitable for windows, loose covers, bedcovers and upholstery

2. Bentley & Spens/Animal Magic Sheer BS204
Colourway: white on white
Composition: 67% polyester, 33% cotton
Width: 135cm/53in, Repeat: 106cm/41½ in
Suitable for windows

3. Hamilton Weston/Archway House
Colourway: white, green, black on grey
Width: 52cm/20½ in, Length: 10m/11yd
Repeat: 9cm/3½ in

4. John Oliver
Colour: Betty II blue
Composition and finish: water-based matt
Suitable for walls and woodwork

5. Stark/Small Star
Colourway: cobalt blue
Composition: 100% wool
Width: 3.66m/4yd, Repeat: 15cm/6in

1. Pierre Frey/Rivoli 2150
Colourway: anthracite
Composition: 77% viscose, 23% cotton
Width: 130cm/51in
Repeat: 2cm/¾ in
Suitable for windows and upholstery

2. Brunschwig & Fils/Coraux Glazed Chintz
Colourway: blueberry, Composition: 100% cotton
Width: 140cm/55in, Repeat 14cm/5½ in
Suitable for windows

3. Akzo Nobel/Berkeley RD125
Colourway: white, Width: 52cm/20½ in
Length: 10m/11yd, Repeat: 13cm/5in

4. Dulux/Heritage Colours
Colour: 0710 Y10R
Composition and finish: water-based matt, silk,
soft sheen; oil-based dead flat, eggshell, gloss
Suitable for walls and ceilings

5. The Old Fashioned Milk Paint Co
Colour: oyster white
Composition and finish: milk paint
Suitable for woodwork and plasterwork

Cool Bathroom
1. Jab/Syit 1-6002, Colourway: 255
Composition: 100% cotton
Width: 140cm/55in,
Suitable for windows

2. Bentley & Spens/Shells Voile
Colourway: bronze, silver and white
Composition: 67% polyester, 33% cotton
Width: 134cm/52½ in, Repeat: 67cm/ 26¼ in
Suitable for windows

3. Mosquito/Sparkle Tile
Colourway: Cobalt blue
Composition: ceramic, glass
Size: 20 x 20 x 1.5cm/8 x 8 x ⅝ in

4. Kenneth Clarke Ceramics/Plain colours G3
Colourway: crazed white, Composition: ceramic
Size: 15 x 15cm x 7mm/6 x 6 x ¼ in

5. Marble Flooring Specialists/
Labrador Blue Pearl,
Colourway: blue pearl, Composition: quartzite,
Size: 30 x 30 x 1cm/11¾ x 11¾ x ⅜ in

Cool Dining
1. Ian Mankin/Pavilion, Colourway: natural
Composition: 100% cotton, Width: 137cm/54in
Repeat: 2cm/¾ in
Suitable for windows and upholstery

2. Joanna Wood/Classic Stripe LW35/53
Colourway: summer blue, Width: 52cm/20½ in
Length: 10m/11yd

3. Sanderson/Spectrum
Colour: pheasant's feather 2-23M
Composition and finish: water-based matt, silk;
oil-based eggshell, gloss
Suitable for walls and exterior use

4. Nutshell Natural Paints/Casein Milk Paint
Colour: spinell turquoise
Composition and finish: milk paint
Suitable for walls, woodwork, stonework
and plasterwork

5. Atlas Carpet Mills/Cipriani 35
Colourway: R947 Lapis
Composition: 100% nylon
Width: 3.66m/4yd
Repeat: 2cm/¾ in

Cool Kitchen
1. Jab/Maharadscha 6943-252
Colourway: silver, Composition: 100% silk
Width: 122cm/48in
Suitable for windows

2. Abbott & Boyd/Voile de Lin
Colourway: 07, Composition: 100% linen
Width: 150cm/59in
Suitable for windows

3. Harlequin/95002,
Colourway: pastel, Width: 52cm/20½ in,
Length: 10m/11yd

4. Amtico/Norwegian Slate SN36
Colourway: silver, Composition: vinyl
Width: 30.5 x 30.5cm/12 x 12in
Available in other sizes

5. Paint Magic/Liming paste, Colourway: natural
Composition and finish: water based

Fresh Entrance
1. Crowson/Script 02579S97
Colourway: 02
Composition: 67% polyester, 33% cotton
Width: 137cm/54in, Repeat: 64cm/25in
Suitable for windows

2. Andrew Martin/Tang
Colourway: red and gold on cream
Composition: 100% cotton, Width: 132cm/52in
Repeat: 137cm/54in
Suitable for upholstery

3. Dulux Heritage Colours
Colour: eau de nil 15GY44268
Composition and finish: water-based matt, silk,
soft sheen; oil-based dead flat, eggshell, gloss
Suitable for walls and ceilings

4. Fired Earth/Circulaire
Colourway: black and white
Composition: encaustic
Size: 20 x 20 x 2cm/8 x 8 x ¾ in
Suitable for floors

5. Corres Mexican Tiles/Fruit and Veg no.76
Colourway: multi, Composition: ceramic
Size: 10 x 10cm x 7mm/4 x 4 x ¼ in

Fresh Living
1. Elizabeth Eaton/Saighton
Colourway: green on white
Composition: 100% linen
Width: 122cm/48in
Repeat: 5cm/2in
Suitable for windows and upholstery

2. Lelièvre/Harmonie-Anis 3503-1.
Composition: 65% cotton, 35% viscose
Width: 145cm/57in, Repeat: 45cm/17½ in
Suitable for upholstery

3. Farrow & Ball/National Trust Range
Colour: pea green 33
Composition and finish: water-based distemper,
matt; oil-based dead flat, eggshell
Suitable for walls and exterior use

4. Fired Earth/Victoria & Albert Museum
Colour: terre vert 16
Composition and finish: water-based distemper,
matt; oil-based dead flat, eggshell
Suitable for walls, ceilings and woodwork

5. Ollerton Hall/Grain
Colourway: sea green,
Composition: 100% wool
Width: 4m/4½ yd

1. Brunschwig & Fils/Amandine Glazed
Chintz 77730-04,
Colourway: multi on white
Composition: 100% cotton
Width: 132cm/51¾in,
Repeat: 85.5cm/33½in
Suitable for windows

2. Manuel Canovas/Vita 4424
Colourway: pêche, veronse
Composition: 58% viscose, 42% cotton
Width: 130cm/51in, Repeat: 4cm/1½ in
Suitable for windows and upholstery

3. Osborne & Little/Shagreen WSH09
Colourway: light green and cream
Width: 52cm/20½ in,
Length: 10m/11yd

4. Jane Churchill
Colour: primrose 12
Composition and finish: water-based matt
Suitable for walls, floors and woodwork

5. Brintons/Golden Serenade 116/4700
Colourway: 116
Composition: 80% wool, 20% nylon
Width: 4m/4½ yd, Repeat: 100cm/39¼ in
Available in other sizes

Fresh Bedroom
1. Passinari & Chatel/Diane 1555
Colourway: 03,
Composition: 100% silk
Width: 130cm/51in, Repeat: 28.5cm/11in
Suitable for windows and upholstery

2. Lee Jofa/Rose Stripe Weave 845015
Colourway: blue/cream/multi
Composition: 100% cotton
Width: 142cm/55¾ in, Repeat: 8cm/3in
Suitable for upholstery

3. Scalamandré/Simbolo 90010-001
Colourway: multi on peach
Composition: 100% silk,
Width: 127cm/50in
Repeat: 43cm/17in
Suitable for windows and upholstery

4. Cole & Son/Victorian Star 55/3021
Colourway: gold on eau de nil
Width: 52cm/20½ in,
Repeat: 5cm/2in

5. Osborne & Little/Couronne
Colourway: pale green
Width: 52cm/20½ in
Length: 10m/11yd

Fresh Bathroom
1. Marvic Textiles/Les Amours 5330-007
Colourway: blues on off-white
Composition: 100% cotton
Width: 140cm/55in
Repeat: 53cm/21in
Suitable for windows and bedcovers

2. Brunschwig & Fils/West Indies Toile Cotton
79522.04, Colourway: blue on white
Composition: 100% cotton
Width: 134cm/52½ in
Repeat: 87cm/34¼ in
Suitable for windows

3. Colefax and Fowler/Lincoln 2061/03
Colourway: cream and aqua
Composition: 60% linen, 20% cotton,
20% modacrylic
Width: 137cm/54in
Repeat: 45.5cm/18in
Suitable for windows and upholstery

4. Attica/Moss Green
Colourway: moss green,
Composition: ceramic
Size: 18 x 13 x 1.5cm/7 x 5 x ⅝ in
Suitable for walls and floors

5. Amtico/Napoleon Marble
Colourway: tan, Composition: vinyl
Size: 30.5 x 30.5 cm/12 x 12in

1. Harlequin/95002
Colourway: pastel
Width: 52cm/20½ in

2. Celia Birtwell/Classical Stripe French Voile
Colourway: yellow and white
Composition: 67% polyester, 33% cotton
Width: 140cm/55in
Repeat: 64cm/25in
Suitable for windows and bedcovers

3. Walker Zanger/Toltec Sol
Colourway: clear
Composition: glass
Width: 4m/4½yd

4. Nutshell Natural Paints/Casein Milk Paint
Colourway: spinnell turquoise
Composition: milk paint

5. Fired Earth/Roman Mosaic Natural Floor
Colourway: white
Composition: stone
Size: 20 x 20 x 1.2cm/8 x 8 x ¼ i

Fresh Dining
1. Brunschwig & Fils/Sycamore Floral Plaid 53373.01, Colourway: mandarin plaid
Composition: 100% cotton
Width: 130cm/51in
Repeat: 16cm/6¼ in
Suitable for upholstery

2. Baumann Fabrics/Sinfonia
Colourway: 730
Composition: 100% polyester
Width: 3m/3.2yd
Suitable for windows

3. Thomas Dare/Cavalli Ocean 199125/120
Colourway: blue and green
Composition: 100% silk
Width: 120cm/47in
Repeat: 2cm/¾in
Suitable for windows

4. Colefax and Fowler/Candy Stripe 7409/02
Colourway: pink,
Width: 52cm/20½ in
Length: 10m/11yd

5. Ulster Carpets/Velvet W9205
Colourway: seascape
Composition: 80% wool, 20% nylon
Width: 3.66m/4yd

Fresh Kitchen
1. Designers Guild/Bellagio F814
Colourway: apple
Composition: 45% modacrylic, 41% cotton, 14% nylon
Width: 140cm/55in
Repeat: 5cm/2in
Suitable for windows and upholstery

2. Lelièvre/Alderbaran M1 - Peuplier
Colourway: green
Composition: 100% polyester trevira
Width: 140cm/55in, Repeat: 9cm/3¼ in
Suitable for upholstery

3. Hodsoll McKenzie/English Ribbon 223/101-108, Colourway: blue
Composition: 61% spun rayon, 39% cotton
Width: 127cm/50in,
Repeat: 20.5cm/8in
Suitable for windows, upholstery and walls

4. Ace Royal/Interior Wall Paint
Colour: bouquet yellow
Composition and finish: water-based matt, eggshell, semi-gloss
Suitable for walls

5. Attica/San Marco Pavement
Colourway: multi
Composition: terracotta, slate and stone
Size: 15 x 15 x 2cm/6 x 6 x ¾ in
Suitable for floors

Muted Entrance
1. Liberty/Sutrana, Colourway: sky
Composition: 56% viscose, 33% cotton 11% nylon, Width: 135cm/53in
Repeat: 52cm/20½ in

2. Hill & Knowles/Trefoil – Cornelia
Colourway: green
Composition: 57% linen, 43% cotton
Width: 137cm/54in, Repeat: 21cm/8¼ in
Suitable for windows and upholstery

3. Dulux/Heritage Colours
Colour: French grey 16BB50066
Composition and finish: water-based matt, silk, soft sheen; oil-based dead flat, eggshell, gloss
Suitable for walls and ceilings

4. Jack Lenor Larsen/Luminescence
Colourway: topaz, Composition: 66% metal, 22% cotton, 12% polyester,
Width:140cm/55in, Suitable for windows

5. Formica/Sylva 1069
Colourway: olive wood
Composition: resin laminate
Width:30.5 x 12 cm/12 x 4¾ in

Muted Living
1. Donghia Textiles/Magic 0392/5725-03
Colourway: cream, Composition: 100% silk
Width: 140cm/55in, Repeat: 11cm/4¼ in
Suitable for upholstery

2. Zimmer & Rohde/Myra 6999
Colourway: 642
Composition: 72% cotton, 28% silk
Width: 130cm/51in
Suitable for windows and upholstery

3. Paint Library
Colour: blue gum
Composition and finish: water-based matt; oil-based dead flat, eggshell
Suitable for walls and woodwork

4. The Old Fashioned Milk Paint Co
Colour: mustard
Composition and finish: milk paint
Suitable for woodwork and plasterwork

5. Auro Organic Paints/Woodstains
Colour: grau
Composition and finish: oil-based satin
Suitable for woodwork and exterior use

1. Jason D'Souza/Riccio RICO4
Colourway: peach
Composition: 50% linen, 50% cotton
Width: 136cm/53½ in, Repeat: 17cm/6¾ in
Suitable for bedcovers and upholstery

2. Jack Lenor Larsen/Solace
Colourway: coral
Composition: 52% viscose, 48% polyester
Width: 130cm/51in, Repeat: 33cm/13in
Suitable for upholstery

3. Dulux/Heritage Colours
Colourway: 90RR22/227
Composition and finish: water-based matt, silk, soft sheen; oil-based dead flat, eggshell, gloss
Suitable for walls and ceilings

4. Colourman Paints/Reproduction Colours
Colourway: 115, Composition: 100% wool
Width: 69cm/27in

5. Bosanquet Ives/Trellis
Colourway: olive and khaki
Composition and finish: water-based matt
Suitable for walls and woodwork

Muted Bedroom
1. Brunschwig & Fils/89286-050
Colourway: cream, Composition: 100% linen
Width: 142cm/56in, Repeat: 107cm/42in
Suitable for windows and upholstery

2. Old World Weavers/Shantung Albatross SB14862201, Colourway: multi
Composition: 100% silk
Width: 140cm/55in
Repeat: 34cm/13¼ in
Suitable for windows and upholstery

3. Antico Setificio Fiorentino/Tela di Seta T1
Colourway: green/gold,
Composition: 100% silk
Width: 120cm/47in
Suitable for windows, loose covers, upholstery and walls

4. Finnaren & Haley/Shades of 76
Colour: Saybrook ivory 520800
Composition and finish: water-based matt, satin, semi-gloss, gloss; oil-based semi-gloss
Suitable for walls, woodwork and exterior use

5. DLW/Marmorette 121-78
Colourway: 78, Composition: linoleum
Width: 2m/2⅕ yd

Muted Bathroom
1. Warner Fabrics/Versailles Marble CS 336220
Colourway: celadon and apricot
Composition: 100% cotton, Width: 137cm/54in
Repeat: 64cm/25in

2. Colefax and Fowler/Maplehurst Check F1305/03, Colourway: green
Composition: 48% cotton, 44% Velicren, 8% linen, Width: 140cm/55in
Repeat: 6cm/2½ in
Suitable for windows and upholstery

3. Nutshell Natural Paints/Casein Milk Paint
Colour: spinell turquoise
Composition and finish: milk paint
Suitable for walls, woodwork, stonework and plasterwork

4. Stonell/Bamboo
Colourway: grey with rust streak
Composition: slate
Size: 10 x 10 x1.2cm/4 x 4 x ½in
Suitable for floors; available in other sizes

5. Fired Earth/VM Travertino
Composition: Venetian marble
Size: 10 x 10x 2cm/4 x 4 x ¾ in

Muted Dining
1. Brunschwig & Fils/Involve Silk Texture
Colourway: grey and gold
Composition: 24% cotton, 76% silk
Width: 140cm/55in, Repeat: 30cm/11¾in
Suitable for light upholstery

2. Abbott & Boyd/Ajedrez Listada 49881-2
Colourway: blue, multi, checker stripe
Composition: 100% cotton
Width: 140cm/55in, Repeat: 8.5cm/3¼ in
Suitable for windows and upholstery

3. The Silk Gallery/Three-inch Stripe Antique Gold WW, Colourway: red and gold
Composition: 100% silk, Width: 127cm/49¾ in
Repeat: width of stripe
Suitable for windows

4. Hill & Knowles/Canbury
Colourway: banana, Composition: 100% cotton
Width: 130cm/51in, Repeat: 36cm/14in
Suitable for windows and upholstery

5. Maya Romanoff/Patina MR-T35-176-G
Colourway: golden taupe, Width: 76cm/30in
Length: to order

1. Apenn/Hayward AV469-1
Colourway: green
Composition: 100% cotton
Width: 121cm/47½ in, Repeat: 8cm/3in
Suitable for windows and upholstery

2. Garin/Vinanoz 66754891
Colourway: beige
Composition: 70% cotton, 30% viscose
Width: 140cm/55in, Repeat: 39cm/15¼ in
Suitable for upholstery

3. Auro Organic Paints/Emulsion Paint
Colour: cranberry
Composition and finish: water-based matt
Suitable for walls, floors and stonework

4. The Old Fashioned Milk Paint Co
Colour: Lexington green
Composition and finish: milk paint
Suitable for walls, floors and woodwork

5. Wicanders/Terracotta and River Cork LS05 & LS09
Colourway: terracotta, river
Composition: cork,
Width: 30.5 x 30.5cm/12 x 12in

Muted Kitchen
1. Pierre Frey/Rivoli 2150
Colourway: anthracite
Composition: 77% viscose, 23% cotton
Width: 130cm/51in,
Repeat: 2cm/¾ in
Suitable for windows and upholstery

2. Celia Birtwell/Beasties, Colourway: green
Composition: 100% cotton
Width: 140cm/55in
Repeat: 64cm/25in
Suitable for windows and uholstery

3. Shaker
Colourway: cabinet maker blue
Colourway: blue and green
Composition and finish: milk paint

4. Dulux/Heritage Colours
Colourway: pearl 34GY69077
Composition and finish: water-based matt, silk and soft sheen, oil-based dead flat, eggshell, gloss

5. DLW Marmorette 121-70
Colourway: 70
Composition: linoleum
Width: 2m/2⅕ yd

Addresses

All items in the book are available either via a distributor or a store, or by mail order. If a stockist in your area is not listed, please contact the head office address (shown beneath the company name). Before visiting suppliers please telephone, since not all outlets are available to the public.

A

Aalto Country Colour
8 Railway Street, Newmarket, Auckland
New Zealand, Tel: 9 522 2019
And
29 Leslie Hills Drive
Christchurch, Auckland, New Zealand
Tel: 3 348 8015
(*Distributors of Farrow & Ball*)

Abbott & Boyd
Chelsea Harbour Design Centre
London SW10 0XE, UK Tel: 020 7351 9985
(*see also Brunschwig & Fils*)

Akzo Nobel Decorative Coatings Ltd
PO Box 37, Crown House
Hollins Road, Darwen, Lancs BB3 0BG, UK
Tel: 01254 704951
And
Bentley Brothers
2709 South Park Road, Louisville
KY 40219, USA Tel: (502) 969 1464
And
Decorlux, 7733 Bordeaux Ville La Salle,
Que, Canada, Tel: (514) 367 4522
And
Decoroll Homewares
121 Wetherill Street, PO Box 6005, Silverwater,
NSW 2128, Australia, Tel: 9 748 7799
And
Pacific Wallcoverings Ltd, Private Bag 50-907
Porirua, New Zealand, Tel: 4 237 8029

The Alternative Flooring Company
14 Anton Trading Estate, Andover, Hants
UK, Tel: 01264 335111

Altfield Ltd
Chelsea Harbour Design Centre
London SW10 0XE, UK Tel: 020 7351 5893
(*distributor of Maya Romanoff and Scalamandré*)
And
942 Third Avenue, New York, NY 10022 USA,
Tel: (212) 980 3888
And
Passementeries Ltd, 131 Wilson Street,
Newton NSW, Australia, Tel: 2 550 5510

The Amtico Company Ltd
Kingfield Road, Coventry CV6 5PL
UK, Tel: 01203 861400
And
Amtico Studio, 200 Lexington Avenue
32nd Street, Suite 809, New York, NY 10016
USA, Tel: (212) 545 1127
And
86-88 Dickson Avenue, Antarmon, Sydney
NSW 2064, Australia Tel: 2 9901 4199
And
Electric Plus Ltd, G/F 158 Lockhart Road
Wanchai, Hong Kong
Tel: 5 111 115
And

Taaf Hamman Trading Ltd
22 Dublin Road, Bramley View, Ext 6 2090
Johannesburg, South Africa
Tel: 11 882 1000

Andrew Martin International Ltd
200 Walton Street, London SW3 2JL, UK
Tel: 020 7225 5100
And
Kravet Fabrics Inc
225 Central Avenue South, Bethpage
Long Island, NY 11714, USA
Tel: (516) 293 2000
And
Unique Fabrics Ltd
19 Garfield Street, PO Box 37692
Parnell, Auckland, New Zealand Tel: 9 377 8444
And
Marquis Furniture Gallery Ltd
134 Joo Seng Road, Nobel Design House
Singapore 368359, Tel: 3 830 120
And
Halogen International Ltd, PO Boz 52599
Saxonwold 2132, Johannesburg
South Africa, Tel: 11 448 2060

Anna French
343 Kings Road, London SW3 5ES, UK,
Tel: 020 7351 1126
And
Classic Revivals Inc, Suite 534
5th Floor, 1 Design Centre Place
Boston, MA 02210, USA Tel: (617) 574 9030

Antico Setificio Fiorentino
Via L Bartolini 4, 50124 Florence, Italy
Tel: 55 21 38 61

Anya Larkin
8th Floor, 39 West 28th Street
New York, NY 10001, USA, Tel: (212) 532 3263

Apenn
33 Kensington Park Road, London W11 2EU
UK, Tel: 020 7792 2457

Atlas Carpet Mills
2200 Saybrook Avenue, Los Angeles
CA 90040, USA
Tel: (800) 372 6274

Attica
543 Battersea Park Road, London SW11 3BL
UK, Tel: 020 7738 1234

Auro Organic Paints
Unit 1, Goldstones Farm, Ashdon,
Saffron Walden, Essex CB10 2LZ, UK
Tel: 01799 584888
And
Sinan Company, PO Box 857
2202 Muir Woods Place, Davis
CA 95617, USA, Tel: (916) 753 3104

Axminster Carpets Ltd
Axminster, Devon EX13 5PQ, UK
Tel: 01297 32244
And
919 3rd Avenue, New York, NY 10022, USA
Tel: (212) 421 1051

B

Baer & Ingram
273 Wandsworth Bridge Road
London SW6 2TX, UK, Tel: 020 7736 6111
And
Davan Industries, 144 Main Street

Port Washington NY 11000, USA
Tel: (516) 944 6498

Baumann Fabrics
41/42 Berners Street, London W1P 3AA
UK, Tel: 020 7637 0253
And
114 North Center Avenue, Rockville
Rockville Center, NY 11570, USA
Tel: (516) 764 7431

Belinda Coote Tapestries
Unit 3/14, Chelsea Harbour Design Centre
London SW10 0XE, UK, Tel: 020 7351 0404

Bentley & Spens
1 Mornington Street, London NW1 7QD, UK
Tel: 020 7837 7374
And
Christopher Hyland inc, D&D Building
Suite 1714, 979 Third Avenue
New York, NY 10022, USA, Tel: (212) 688 6121
And
Designers International
77a Parnell Road, Auckland
New Zealand, Tel; 9 309 1589
And
E&Y Co. Ltd, Milles Roches B1
5-3-5 Minami-Aoyama
Minato-Ku, Tokyo 107, Japan
Tel: 3 5485 8461

Bernard Thorp & Co
53 Chelsea Manor Street, London SW3 3ST, UK
Tel: 020 7352 5745
(*see also Stark Carpet Corp*)

Berti Pavimento Legno
Via Rettilineo 83,, 35010 Villa del Conte
Padua, Italy, Tel: 49 93 25 011
And
PM Hardwoods, 5 Nelson Street
Southend-on-Sea, Essex SS1 1ES
Tel: 01702 348877

Bill Amberg
The Shop, 10 Chepstow Road,
London W2 5BD UK, Tel: 020 7727 3560
And
The Workshops, 23 Theatre Street
London SW11 5ND, UK, Tel: 020 7924 4296

Bosanquet Ives
3 Court Lodge, 48 Sloane Square,
London SW1 8AT UK, Tel: 020 7730 6241

Bradbury & Bradbury,
PO Box 155, Benicia, CA 94510, USA
Tel: (707) 746 1900
(*See also Hamilton Weston*)

Brats Paints
281 Kings Road, London SW3 5EW, UK
Tel: 020 7351 7674
And
624c Fulham Road, London SW6 5RS UK
Tel: 020 7731 6915

Brintons Ltd
PO Box 16, Exchange Street
Kidderminster, Worcs DY10 1AG, UK
Tel: 01562 820000
And
Brintons Carpets (USA) Ltd, E-210 Route 4
Paramus, NJ 07652, USA
Tel: (201) 368 0080

Brunschwig & Fils
10 The Chambers
Chelsea Harbour Design Centre
London SW10 0XF, UK, Tel: 020 7351 5797
And
979 Third Avenue, New York
NY 10022-1234, USA, Tel: (212) 838 7878
(*distributor of Abbott & Boyd*)
and
St James Furnishings Pty Ltd
164 Burwood Road, Hawthorn
Vic. 3122, Australia, Tel: 3 9819 1569

C

Carocim
BP 10,1515 Route du Puy, Sainte Rèparade
13540 Puyricard, France, Tel: 4 42 92 20 39

Cath Kidston
8 Clarendon Cross, London W11 4AP UK
Tel: 020 7221 4000

Celia Birtwell
71 Westbourne Park Road, London W2 5QH
UK, Tel: 020 7221 0877

Chatsworth Carpets
227 Brompton Road, London SW3 2JD UK
Tel: 020 7584 1165
And
1125 Globe Avenue, Mountainside
NJ 07092 USA, Tel: (908) 233 5645

Cole & Son
17 Church Street, Rickmansworth
Herts WD3 1DE, UK, Tel: 01923 710041
And
910 Chelsea Harbour Design Centre
London SW10 0XE, Tel: 020 7376 4628

Colefax and Fowler Group plc
19-23 Grosvenor Hill
London W1X 9HG, UK, Tel: 020 8874 6484
(*Distributor of Jane Churchill*)
And
110 Fulham Road
London SW3 6RL, UK, Tel: 0207 244 7427

Colourman Paints
Coton Clanford, Stafford
Staffs ST18 9PB, UK, Tel: 01785 282799

Crowson
Crowson House, Bellbrock Park
Uckfield, E. Sussex TN22 1QZ, UK
Tel: 01825 761044

Cuprinol
Adderwell Road, Frome
Somerset BA11 1NL, UK, Tel: 01373 465151

D

DLW
Centurion Court, Milton Park, Abingdon, Oxon
OX14 4RY, UK, Tel: 01235 831296

De Le Cuona Designs
1 Trinity Place, Windsor, Berks SL4 3AP, UK
Tel: 01753 830301

Dedar (*see Mary Fox Linton*)

Designers Guild
267-277 Kings Road
London SW3 5EN, UK, Tel: 020 7243 7300

Donghia
23 Chelsea Harbour Design Centre
London SW10 0XE, UK, Tel: 020 7823 3456
(*Distributors of Anya Larkin and David Bonk*)
And
485 Broadway, New York, NY 10013 USA
Tel: (212) 925 2777

Dovedale (*See Hill & Knowles*)

Dulux
Wexham Road, Slough, Berks, SL2 5DS, UK
Tel: 01753 550000

E

Elizabeth Eaton
85 Bourne Street, London SW1W 8HF, UK
Tel: 020 7730 2262

Elon
66 Fulham Road, London SW3 6HH UK
Tel: 020 7460 4600

F

Farrow & Ball
Uddens Trading Estate, Wimborne
Dorset BH21 7NL, UK, Tel: 01202 876 141

Finnaren & Haley
901 Washington Street, Conshohocken
PA 19428, USA, Tel: (610) 825 1900

Fired Earth plc
Twyford Mill, Oxford Road
Adderbury, Oxon, OX17 3HP, UK
Tel: 01295 812088
And
117-119 Fulham Road, London SW3 6RL UK
Tel: 020 7589 0489
(*Distributor of Froyle Tiles*)

G

G.P. & J. Baker
PO Box 30, West End Road, High Wycombe
Bucks HP11 2QD, UK, Tel: 01494 467400
(*Distributor of Fardis*)

Gainsborough Silk Weaving
Alexandra Road, Sudbury, Essex CO10 6XH UK
Tel: 01787 372081

H

Habitat
196 Tottenham Court Road, London W1 9LD, UK
Tel: 020 7255 2545

Hamilton Weston Wallpapers
18 St Mary's Grove, Richmond,
Surrey TW9 1UY, UK Tel: 020 8940 4850
(*Distributor of Bradbury & Bradbury*)
And
Classic Revivals Inc
1 Design Center Place, Suite 545, Boston
MA 02210, USA, Tel: (617) 574 9030

Hill & Knowles
2/15 Chelsea Harbour Design Centre
London SW10 0XE, UK, Tel: 020 7376 4686

Historic Floors of Oshkosh
911 East Main Street, Winneconne
WI 45986 USA, Tel: (920) 582 9977

Hodsoll McKenzie
52 Pimlico Road, London SW1W 8LP UK
Tel: 020 7730 2877

And
Clarence House
111 8th Avenue, New York, NY 10011 USA
Tel: (212) 752 2890
And
Charles Radford Furnishings
8-18 Glass Street, Burnley
Vic. Australia, Tel: 3 9429 6122

Hugh Mackay
PO Box 1, Durham City, Durham, DH1 2RX UK,
Tel: 0191 386 4444
And
Roman House, Wood Street
London EC2Y 5BU, UK, Tel: 020 7606 8491

I

Ian Mankin
109 Regents Park Road, London NW1 8UR UK
Tel: 020 7722 0997
And
Coconut Company, 129-131 Greene Street
New York, NY10012, USA, Tel: (212) 539 1940
And
The Natural Textile Company Inc
2571 West Broadway, Vancouver, BC V6K 2E9
Canada, Tel: (604) 736 2101

Ian Sanderson
PO Box 148, Newbury, Berks RG15 9DW UK
Tel: 01635 33188

Interdesign UK Ltd
Chelsea Harbour Design Center
London SW10 0XE, UK, Tel: 0171 376 5272

The Isle Mill Ltd
Tower House, Ruthurenfield Road
Inveralmond, Perth PH1 3UN UK
Tel: 01738 609 090

J

J.W. Bollom
PO Box 78, Croydon Road
Beckenham, Kent BR3 4BL, UK
Tel: 020 8658 2299

Jab International Furnishings Ltd
1/15-16 Chelsea Harbour Design Center
London SW10 0XE, UK Tel: 020 7349 9323
(*Distributor of Stroheim & Romann*)
and
155 East 56th Street, New York
NY 10022, USA, Tel: (212) 486 1500
And
326 Davenport Road, Toronto
Ont. M5R 1K6, Canada, Tel: (416) 927 9192
And
Seneca Textiles Ltd
10-12 Adolph Street, Richmond
Vic. 3121, Australia, Tel: 3 428 5021
And
14 Heather Street, PO Box 37-702
Parnell, Auckland, New Zealand, Tel: 9 309 6411
And
The Fabric Library
Stand 61, Old Pretoria Road, PO Box 912
Halfway House 1685, South Africa
Tel: 11 805 4211

Jack Lenor Larsen
233 Spring Street, New York NY 10013 USA
Tel: (212) 462 1300

Jane Churchill
151 Sloane Street, London SW1X 9BX

Tel: 020 7730 9847
(*See also Colefax & Fowler*)

Jason D'Souza
Chelsea Harbour Design Centre
London SW10 0XE, UK, Tel: 020 7351 4440
And
Nancy Corzine
5871 Rodeo Road, Los Angeles CA 90016, USA
Tel: (310) 559 9051

Jaymart Rubber & Plastics Ltd
Woodlands Trading Estate
Westbury, Wilts BA13 3QS UK

Jim Thompson (*See Mary Fox Linton*)

Joanna Wood
Lewis & Wood, 48a Pimlico Road
London SW1W 8LP, UK Tel: 020 7730 5064

John Wilman
Heasandford Industrial Estate
Burnley, Lancs BB10 2TJ UK Tel: 01232 617777

K

Kalon
Huddersfield Road, Birstall
West Yorks WF17 9X4 UK, Tel: 01924 354000

Karndean Ltd
Ferry Lane, Offenham, Evesham
Worcs WR11 5RT, UK Tel: 01386 49902
And
Karndean International pty Ltd
Unit 1, 4 Samantha Court
PO Box 15, Knoxfield, Vic. 3180
Australia Tel: 3 9764 9466
And
Unit A, 73 Greenmount Drive
East Tamaki, Auckland, New Zealand
Tel: 9 273 5430

Kievel Stone
Lower Farm, Ampfield, Hants SO51 9BP UK
Tel: 01794 368865

Knowles & Christou
Chelsea Reach, 79-89 Lots Road
London SW10 0RN, UK
And
Davan Industries, 144 Main Street
Port Washington, NY 11050 USA
Tel: (516) 944 6498

L

Lee Jofa
919 Chelsea Harbour Design Centre
London SW10 0XE, UK, Tel: 020 7351 7760
And
201 Central Avenue South
Bethpage, NY 11714, USA, Tel: (516) 752 7600
(*Distributor of The Design Archives, Firifiss,
Monkwell and Mulberry*)

Lelièvre
1/19 Chelsea Harbour Design Center
London SW10 0XE, UK, Tel: 020 7352 4798
And
Telio & Cle, 1407 rue de la Montagne
Montreal, H3G 1Z3, Canada
Tel: (514) 842 9116
And
Order Imports Ltd, 11a Boundary Street
Ruscutter Bay, NSW 2011, Australia
Tel: 2 9360 3565

Lewis & Wood
5 The Green, Uley, Glos, GL115SN UK
Tel: 01453 860 080

Liberon Waxes
Mountfield Industrial Estate, Learoyd Road
New Romney, Kent TN28 8XU UK
Tel: 01797 367555

Liberty plc
Regent Street, London, W1R 5LA UK
Tel: 020 7734 1234
(*See also Osborne & Little*)

Liz Induni
11 Park Road, Swanage, Dorset BH19 2AA UK
Tel: 01929 423 776

Louis de Poortere
Rue de la Royenne 45, B-7700 Mouscron
Belgium Tel: 56 39 31 11
And
136 Cass Street, Adairsville, GA 30103 USA,
Tel: (770) 773 7934

M

Marvic Textiles
G26 Chelsea Harbour Design Center
London SW10 0XE, UK, Tel: 020 7352 3119
And
Roger Arlington Inc
D&D Building, Suite 1411, 979 Third Avenue
New York, NY 10022, USA Tel: (212) 752 5288

Mary Fox Linton
Chelsea Harbour Design Centre
London SW10 0XE, UK, Tel: 020 7351 9908
(*distributor of Dedar, Glant and Jim Thompson*)

The Maya Romanoff Corporation
170 West Greenleaf, Chicago
IL 60626, USA, Tel: (312) 465 6909
(*See also Altfield*)

Metropolitan Tile Co
Lower Audley Centre, Kent Street
Blackburn, Lancs BB1 1DE UK
Tel: 01254 695 111

Monkwell
10-12 Wharfdale Road, Bournemouth
Dorset BH4 9BY, UK Tel: 01202 752944
(*See also Lee Jofa*)

Montgomery Tomlinson Ltd
Broughton Mill Road, Bretton
Chester CH4 0BY, UK, Tel: 01244 661363

N

Nice Irma's
46 Goodge Street
London W1P 1FJ, UK, Tel: 020 7580 6921

Nina Campbell (*See Osborne & Little*)

Nobilis-Fontan
93 Chelsea Harbour Design Centre
London SW10 0XE, UK Tel: 020 7351 7878
And
57a Industrial Road, Berkeley Heights
NJ 07922 USA Tel: (980) 464 1177
And
Crown Wallpapers
88 Ronson Drive, Rexdale, Ont. M9W 1B9
Canada Tel: (416) 245 2900
And

Redelman & Son Pty Ltd
96 Dalmeny Avenue, Roseberry NSW 2018
Australia, Tel: 2 313 6811
And
Vivace, Studio 6, 125 The Strand
PO Box 90664 Parnell, Auckland
New Zealand Tel: 9 309 6271
And
Source Interiors Ltd, 205 Wilson House
13 Wyndham Street, Central, Hong Kong
Tel: 2 5216214
And
Macromac, PO Box 76178
12d Kramer Road, Wendywood
Johannesburg, South Africa, Tel: 11 444 1584

Northwood Designs
Trinity Gask, Auchterarer, Perthshire PH3 1LG
UK Tel: 01764 683334

Nutshell Natural Paints
10 High Street, Totnes UK, Tel: 01364 642892

O

The Old Fashioned Milk Paint Co
436 Main Street, PO Box 222, Groton
MA 01450, USA, Tel: (978) 448 6336
And
Nitty Gritty Reproductions
163 Queen St East, Toronto
Ont. M5A 1S1, Canada, Tel: (416) 364 1393

Old World Weavers
D&D Building, 979 Third Avenue
New York, NY 10022, USA, Tel: (212) 752 9000

Olicana Textiles
Brook Mills, Crimble, Slaithwaite
Huddersfield, West Yorks HD7 5BQ UK
Tel: 01484 847666
And
Domus, 1919 Piedmont Road, Atlanta
GA 30324-4116 USA, Tel: (404) 872 1050

Ollerton Decor
Ollerton Hall, Knutsford, Cheshire WA16 8SF
UK Tel: 01565 650222

Original Style
Falcon Road, Sowton Industrial Estate
Exeter, Devon EX2 7LF UK, Tel: 01392 474058

Osborne & Little plc
49 Temperley Road London SW12 8QE UK
Tel: 020 8675 2255
(Distributor of Liberty and Nina Campbell)
and
90 Commerce Road, Stamford
CT 06902, USA, Tel: (203) 359 1500
(Distributor of Designers Guild and Liberty)

Ottilie Stevenson
101 Bethnal Green Road, London E2 7DG, UK

P

Paint Library
5 Elystan Place London SW3 3NT UK
Tel: 020 7823 7755

Paint Magic
48 Golbourne Road, London W10 5PR UK
Tel: 020 7354 9696

Pierre Frey
253 Fulham Road, London SW3 6HY UK
Tel: 020 7376 5599

And
D&D Building, 979 Third Avenue NY 10022
USA Tel: (212) 355 7200

Pittsburgh Paints
PPG Industries, 1 PPG Place
Pittsburgh, PA 15272 USA, Tel: (888) 774 1010

Pratt & Lambert
PO Box 22, Buffalo, NY 14240 USA
Tel: (800) 289 7728

R

Ramm, Son & Crocker
G28 Chelsea Harbour Design Center
London SW10 0XE, UK, Tel: 020 7352 0931

Rustins
Waterloo Road, London NW2 7TX, UK
Tel: 020 8450 4666
And
The Woodsmith Pty Ltd
1 Burgess Road, North Bayswater Road
Vic. 3153, Australia
Tel: 3 761 4622

S

Sahco Hesslein
G24 Chelsea Harbour Design Centre
London SW10 0XE, UK
Tel: 020 7352 6168
And
Bergamo Fabrics
37-20 34th Street, Long Island City
NY 11101, USA, Tel: (718) 392 5000

Sanderson
112-120 Brompton Road, London SW3 1JY UK
Tel: 020 7584 3344
And
The Patriot Center, 285 Grand Avenue, Englewood
NJ 07631, USA, Tel: (201) 894 8400

Scalamandré Silks
300 Trade Zone Drive, Ronkonkoma
NY22779-7381, USA, Tel: (516) 467 8800
(see also Altfield)

Seamoor Fabrics
2 Seamoor Road, Westbourne
Dorset BH4 9AJ, UK Tel: 01202 768768

Shaker Ltd
322 Kings Road, London SW3 5DU UK
Tel: 020 7352 3918

Sherwin Williams
202 Prospect Street, Cleveland, OH 44115,
USA , Tel: (216) 566 3140

The Silk Gallery
25 Chelsea Harbour Design Centre
London SW10 0XE, UK Tel: 020 7351 1790

Sinclair Till
793 Wandsworth Road
London SW8 3JQ, UK
Tel: 020 7720 0031

Stark Carpet Corporation
Chelsea Harbour Design Centre
London SW10 0XE, UK, Tel: 020 7352 6001
And
D&D Building 979 Third Avenue
New York 10022 USA, Tel: (212) 752 9000

Stonell
Forstal House, Beltring
Paddock Wood, Kent TN12 6PY
Tel: 01892 833500

The Stulb Company
PO Box 597, Allentown, PA 18105, USA

T

Thomas Dare
341 Kings Road, London SW3 5ES UK
Tel: 020 7351 7991
And
979 Third Avenue, New York, NY 10022 USA
Tel: (212) 755 6700
And
The Silk Company, PO Box 1738
Parkland 2121, South Africa, Tel: 11 4 828073

Tiles of Stow
Langston Priory Workshops, Station Road
Kingham OX7 6UP UK, Tel: 01608 658951

U

Ulster Carpet Mills
Castleisland Mill, Portadown
N.I. BT62 1EE, UK, Tel: 01762 334433
And
Ulster Carpet Mills North America Inc
212 Church Street
Marietta, GA 30060, USA
Tel: (770) 514 0707
And
Ulster Carpet Mills Pty Ltd
PO Box 72253, Mobemni 4060
South Africa Tel: 31 912 1310

V

Victorian Wood Works
International House
London International Freight Terminal
London E15 2ES UK, Tel: 020 8534 1000

W

Walker Zanger
8901 Bradley Avenue, Sun Valley
CA 91352, USA Tel: (818) 504 0235
And
World Mosaic Ltd 1665 West 7th Avenue
Vancouver BC V6J 1S4, Canada
Tel: (604) 736 8158

Wardlaw Pty Ltd
230-232 Auburn Road, Hawthorn
Vic. 3122, Australia, Tel: 3 9819 4233
And
St Leger & Viney Pty Ltd
PO Box 55508, Northlands 2116
Gauteng, South Africa, Tel: 11 444 6722

Warner Fabric plc
Talbot House, 17 Church Street
Rickmansworth UK, Tel: 01923 710 300
And
Whittaker & Woods
5100 Highlands Parkways, Smyrna,
GA 30082, USA, Tel: (770) 435 9720
And
Anne Starr Agencies, Suite 100
611 Alexander Street, Vancouver BC V6A 1E1
Canada, Tel: (604) 254 3336

Warwick Fabrics UK Ltd
Hackling House, Bourton Industrial Park
Bourton-on-the-Water, Glos GL54 2EN
UK Tel: 01451 822383

Watts of Westminster
2/9 Chelsea Harbour Design Centre
London SW10 0XE UK Tel: 020 8376 4486
And
Christopher Norman Inc
41 West 25th Street, New York 10010 USA
Tel: (212) 647 0303
And
Hazleton House, 234 Davenport Road, Toronto,
Ont. M5R 1JB Canada, Tel: (416) 925 4779
And
Boyac Decorative Furnishings
234 Auburn Road, Melbourne
Vic. 3122, Australia, Tel: 3 9818 5300

Waveney Apple Growers Ltd
Common Road, Aldeby, Beccles
Suffolk NR34 0BL, UK, Tel: 01502 677345

Wicanders
Star Road, Partridge Green, W. Sussex
RH13 8RA, UK, Tel: 01403 710001

Z

Zimmer & Rhode
15 Chelsea Harbour Design Centre
London SW10 0XE, UK Tel: 020 8351 7115
(distributor of Jack Lenor Larsen)
And
D&D Building, 979 Third Avenue,
New York, NY 10022 USA Tel: (212) 758 5357
And
Primavera Interior Accessories Ltd
160 Pears Avenue, Suite 210, Toronto, Ont.
Canada, Tel: (416) 921 3334
And
Mokum Textiles Ltd, Suite 1.
15-19 Boundary Street, Rushcutters Bay
Sydney, NSW 2011, Australia
Tel: 2 9380 6188
And
Mokum Textiles Ltd
11 Cheshire Street, Parnell, Auckland
New Zealand, Tel: 9 379 3041
And
Home Fabrics, PO Box 5207
Halfway House, Midrand 1685
South Africa, Tel: 11 805 0300

Zoffany
Talbot House, 17 Church Street
Rickmansworth, Herts WD3 1DE UK
Tel: 01923 710041
and
G10 Chelsea Harbour Design Centre
London , UK Tel: 020 376 4628
And
Whittaker & Woods
5100 Highlands Parkway, Smyrna, Georgia
30082, USA, Tel: (800) 395 8760

Zuber & Cie
42 Pimlico Road, London SW1W 8LP, UK
Tel: 020 7824 8265
And
D&D Building, 979 Third Avenue, New York
NY 10022 USA ,Tel: (212) 486 9226

Telephone numbers and addresses are
supplied by the listed companies; neither the
publisher not the companies can be held
responsible for errors or subsequent changes.

Index

Acknowledgments

Page 6 © Octopus Publishing Group Ltd. (OPG)/Tim Clinch; 8 © OPG/James Merrell 9 Houses & Interiors/Jake Fitzjones; 10 © OPG/James Merrell; 11 © OPG/James Merrell; 12 OPG/Dominic Blackmore; 13 The Interior Archive/Ken Hayden/Jonathan Reed 14-15 Ianthe Ruthven; 16 © OPG/James Merrell; 18 © OPG/James Merrell; 18-19 © OPG/James Merrell; 20 © OPG/James Merrell/Stuart Interiors, Barrington Court (Ken Peterkin); 20-21 © OPG/James Merrell/Lee Anderson; 22 above Ianthe Ruthven/Desiré Short; 22 below Elizabeth Whiting & Associates/Brian Harrison; 23 Ianthe Ruthven/Gordon Watson; 24 © OPG/Tim Clinch/Yves Gastou; 24 above Elizabeth Whiting & Associates/Tom Leighton; 24 below OPG/Tim Clinch/Frédéric Méchiche; 26 © OPG/James Merrell/Suzanne Henderson L.A.; 27 © OPG/James Merrell/Second House Museum (Gilmartin); 28 © OPG James Merrell; 28 © OPG/James Merrell/Marshall; 30 © OPG/James Merrell; 31 © OPG/James Merrell; 32-33 The Interior Archive/Fritz von der Schulenburg/Charles Rennie Mackintosh; 33 Ianthe Ruthven/Charles Rennie Mackintosh; 34 The Interior Archive/Simon Upton/Cath Kidston; 34-35 The Interior Archive/Christopher Simon Sykes; 36 above © OPG/James Merrell/Geffrye Museum; 36 below © OPG/James Merrell; 37 © OPG/James Merrell/Marshall/Schule Associates; 38 © OPG/James Merrell/Manoir de Leret upholstery; 40-41 © OPG/James Merrell/Ratcliffe & Barber; 41 © OPG/James Merrell/Robert Young; 42 © OPG/James Merrell; 42-43 © OPG/James Merrell; 48 The Interior Archive/Herbert Ypma; 44-45 © OPG/James Merrell/Jacomini, Houston; 46 left © OPG/James Merrell/Roger Banks-Pye; right © OPG/James Merrell/Sasha Waddell; 46-47 © OPG/James Merrell/Anna Thomas; 48 above © OPG/James Merrell; 48-49 © OPG/James Merrell; 49 below © OPG/James Merrell; 50 © OPG/James Merrell/Nancy Braithwaite; 50-51 © OPG/James Merrell/Nancy Braithwaite; 52 © OPG/Simon Upton; 53 © OPG/Dominic Blackmore/Ditch Cottage; 54 The Interior Archive/Simon Brown/Rebecca Hossack; 56 © OPG/James Merrell/Chateau de Montuert and Petit; 57 © OPG/James Merrell; 58 © OPG/James Merrell; 59 © OPG/James Merrell; 60 © OPG/James Merrell; 60-61 © OPG/James Merrell/François Gilles; 62 © OPG/James Merrell/David Champion; 62-63 © OPG/James Merrell; 64 Elizabeth Whiting & Associates/Nick Carter; 64-65 Ianthe Ruthven; 66 © OPG/James Merrell; 66-67 Elizabeth Whiting & Associates/Tom Street-Porter/Putu Suarsa (Bali); 68-69 © OPG/James Merrell; 68 © OPG/James Merrell/Issey Miyake; 69 © OPG/James Merrell/Jack Lenor Larson; 70 © OPG/James Merrell; 71 © OPG/James Merrell; 72 Houses & Interiors/Mark Bolton; 73 Ianthe Ruthven/designed by Nick & Limma Groves-Raines the Edinburgh based architects; 74 © Dominic Blackmore; 74-75 © OPG/James Merrell; 76 © OPG/James Merrell/Tyler Beard; 77 © OPG/James Merrell; 78 © OPG; 80 Elizabeth Whiting & Associates/Rodney Hyett; 81 © OPG/Simon Upton; 82 © OPG/Simon Upton; 82-83 © OPG/Dominic Blackmore; 84 © OPG/James Merrell; 84-85 © OPG/James Merrell; 86-87 © OPG/James Merrell; 87 © OPG Ltd./James Merrell; 88 © OPG/James Merrell/ Cheney - Atlanta; 88-89 © OPG/James Merrell/Mary Drysdale; 89 © OPG/James Merrell; 90 © OPG/James Merrell/Mariette Gomez; 91 © OPG/James Merrell/Annie Martin; 92-93 © Ebury Press/from Vintage Style/Cath Kidston; 93 © Ebury Press/from Vintage Style/Cath Kidston; 94-95 Arcaid/Simon Kenny/Belle/Paul Donohoe; 96 © OPG/Dominic Blackmore; 98 © OPG/Dominic Blackmore/Well Cottage; 98-99 © OPG/Tim Clinch/Michael Graves; 99 © OPG/James Merrell/Mary Drysdale; 100 above © OPG/James Merrell/Nancy Braithwaite; 100 below © OPG/James Merrell/Mary Drysdale; 101 © OPG/James Merrell/Mary Drysdale (Rosso/Alvarez); 102 © OPG/James Merrell/Cheney - Atlanta; 103 © OPG/James Merrell/Nancy Braithwaite; 104-105 © OPG/Simon Upton; 105 above © OPG/Dominic Blackmore/Bankside; 105 below © OPG/James Merrell/ Stephanie Vatelot/Chateau de Reignac; 106 © OPG/James Merrell/showhouse Kim de Pole; 107 above © OPG/Dominic Blackmore/Andrea Spencer flat; 107 below © OPG/James Merrell/Stephanie Vatelot; 118-109 © OPG/James Merrell/Mary Drysdale; 109 © OPG/James Merrell/Mary Drysdale; 110-111 © OPG/Simon Upton; 111 © OPG/Dominic Blackmore; 112 © OPG Ltd./James Merrell/Melanie Martin, Marin County; 112-113 © OPG/Simon Upton; 114 The Interior Archive/Nadia Mackenzie/Lisa Guild; 116 © OPG/James Merrell; 116-117 © OPG/Dominic Blackmore; 118-119 Arcaid/John Edward Linden/designed by Justin De Syllas, Avanti Architects; 119 Arcaid/David Churchill/architect Stickland Coombe, Urban Cookie Collective Apartment; 120 above Houses & Interiors/Verne; 120 below P van Robaeys; 121 Camera Press/Niels Hansen; 122 Camera Press/Sarie; 122-123 Camera Press/M Jolibois/Ponopresse; 124 Narratives/Jan Baldwin; 125 Camera Press/Max Jourdan; 126 C P Hart; 126-127 © Collins & Brown; 128-129 © OPG/Dominic Blackmore; 128-129 below The Interior Archive/Simon Brown/artist Rebecca Hossack; 129 The Interior Archive/Henry Wilson/Ian Dew; 130 © OPG/Dominic Blackmore/Great Putney Street; 131 © OPG/Dominic Blackmore; 132 The Interior Archive/Henry Wilson/Denise Lee; 134 © OPG/Simon Upton; 135 above The Interior Archive/Fritz von der Schulenburg; 135 below Arcaid/Richard Bryant/Courtesy of Hancock Shaker Village; 136 © OPG/James Merrell/Anna Thomas; 137 © OPG/Simon Upton; 138-139 Arcaid/Mark Burgin/Belle/Jeremy Salmon; 139 Narratives/Jan Baldwin; 140 © OPG/James Merrell/Second House Museum (Gilmartin); 141 Arcaid/Mark Burgin/Belle/Jeremy Salmon; 142 © OPG/James Merrell/Roger Banks-Pye; 142-143 Camera Press/Schöner Wohnen; 144 © OPG/Simon Upton; 144 © OPG/Simon Upton; 145 Arcaid/Willem Rethmeier/Belle/ Larcombe & Solomon; 146 Ianthe Ruthven; 148-149 Elizabeth Whiting & Associates/Andreas von Einsiedel; 148 © OPG/James Merrell; 149 © OPG/Simon Upton; 150 The Interior Archive/Simon Upton/Sasha Waddell; 152 Camera Press/Schöner Wohnen; 153 © OPG/James Merrell; 154 Camera Press/Schöner Wohnen; 154-155 © OPG/James Merrell/Sasha Waddell; 156-157 © OPG/Dominic Blackmore/Doughty Mews; 157 © OPG/James Merrell; 158 Narratives/Jan Baldwin/Roger Oates Design; 159 © OPG/James Merrell; 160-161 © OPG/James Merrell; 161 © OPG/James Merrell/ Anna Thomas; 162 Camera Press/Schöner Wohnen; 162-163 © OPG/Dominic Blackmore; 164 © OPG/James Merrell; 165 Arcaid/Petrina Tinslay; 166-167 © OPG/James Merrell; 167 © OPG/James Merrell; 168 © OPG/James Merrell/ Mary Drysdale; 170-171 © OPG/James Merrell; 172-173 Ianthe Ruthven/green living room with green 'marble' fireplace; 173 © OPG/James Merrell/Stephanie Vatelot; 174 © OPG/Jan Baldwin; 174-175 The Interior Archive/Ken Hayden/Jonathan Reed; 176-177 Arcaid/Simon Kenny/Belle/architect Daryl Gordon; 177 © Collins & Brown; 178 © OPG/Simon Upton; 178-179 The Interior Archive/Henry Wilson/Colin Duckworth; 180 © OPG/James Merrell/ Jacomini; 181 © OPG/James Merrell; 182 © OPG/James Merrell/Cheney, Atlanta; 182-183 © OPG/James Merrell; 184-185 © OPG/Dominic Blackmore; 185 © OPG Ltd./Simon Upton; 186-187 Arcaid/Eric Sierins/Belle/Alan Steiner; 188 Camera Press/Brigitte; 190 above left © OPG/James Merrell; 190 above right © OPG/James Merrell/Nancy Braithwaite; below © OPG/James Merrell/Anna Thomas; 191 above left © OPG/James Merrell/Vincent Wolf; above right © OPG/James Merrell; below © OPG/Simon Upton; 192 above right © OPG/James Merrell; left © OPG/James Merrell; right © OPG/James Merrell; 193 above left © OPG/Tim Clinch; below right © OPG/James Merrell; centre right © OPG/James Merrell; 194 above left © OPG/James Merrell; below left © OPG/James Merrell; below right Camera Press/Brigitte; 195 above left Houses & Interiors/Steve Hawkins/Teresa Ward; above right © OPG/James Merrell; below Arcaid/Alan Weintraub/Terrence O'Flaherty; 196-197 © OPG/James Merrell; 197 above left © OPG/James Merrell; below left Arcaid/Alan Weintraub/Sandra Sakata; below right Narratives/Jan Baldwin; centre left © OPG/James Merrell; 198 centre Narratives/Jan Baldwin; left Elizabeth Whiting & Associates/Mark Luscombe-Whyte; 198-199 Camera Press/Schöner Wohnen; 199 The Interior Archive/Nadia Mackenzie/Paula Pryke; 200 above left Richard Glover/Fiona Feeley; above right Arcaid/Paul Raftery; below © OPG/Dominic Blackmore; 201 above left Arcaid/Nicholas Kane/Gary Webb; above right © OPG/Dominic Blackmore; below © OPG/Dominic Blackmore; 202 Houses & Interiors/Jake Fitzjones; 204 above left © OPG/James Merrell/ Nancy Braithwaite; above right © OPG/James Merrell/Sadouin + Monflguin; below © OPG/James Merrell/Thiviers La Brugere; 205 © OPG/James Merrell/Manoir de Leret - accessories; 206 © OPG/James Merrell; 207 above © OPG/James Merrell/Thiviers La Brugere; below left © OPG/James Merrell; below right © OPG/James Merrell; 208 above © OPG/James Merrell/Gervaise; below left © OPG/James Merrell/Roger Banks-Pye; below right © OPG/James Merrell; 209 above © OPG/James Merrell/Manoir de Leret; above right © OPG/James Merrell; below right © OPG/James Merrell/Sadouin + Monflaguin; centre right © OPG/James Merrell/Sasha Waddell; 210 © OPG/James Merrell; 210-211 © OPG/James Merrell; 211 above right © OPG/James Merrell; below left © OPG /James Merrell/François Gilles; below right © OPG/James Merrell/Manoir de Leret; 212 above © OPG/James Merrell/Mary Drysdale; below © OPG/James Merrell/Mariette Gomez; 213 above centre © OPG/James Merrell/Nancy Braithwaite; above left © OPG/Neil Mersh; above right © OPG/James Merrell; below left © OPG/James Merrell/Stephanie Vatelot, Chateau de Reignac; below right © OPG/Debi Treloar; 214 © David Parmiter Photography; 216 above centre © OPG/Tim Clinch; above left © OPG/Tim Clinch; above right © OPG/Tim Clinch/Peggy Rollins; below © OPG/James Merrell; 217 © OPG/James Merrell; 218 above centre © OPG/James Merrell; above left © OPG/James Merrell; above right © OPG/Simon Upton; 219 above right © OPG/James Merrell; below right © OPG/James Merrell; centre right © OPG/James Merrell; left © OPG/James Merrell; 220 left © OPG/James Merrell; right © OPG/James Merrell; 221 above left © OPG/James Merrell; above right © OPG/James Merrell; below © OPG/James Merrell; 222 left © OPG/Simon Upton; right Richard Glover/Fox-Linton & Campbell Grey; 222-223 Narratives/Jan Baldwin; 223 above right The Interior Archive/Nadia Mackenzie/Paula Pryke; below right © OPG/Simon Upton; 224 Camera Press/Brigitte; 226 above © OPG/Tim Clinch/Lillian Williams; 226-227 © OPG/James Merrell; 227 above centre © OPG/Tim Clinch/Lillian Williams; above left © OPG/Tim Clinch; above right © OPG/Tim Clinch; below © OPG/Peter Marshall; 228 above © OPG/James Merrell; below left © OPG/James Merrell; below right © OPG/James Merrell; 229 © OPG/James Merrell; 230 above © OPG/James Merrell; below © OPG/James Merrell; 231 above left © OPG/James Merrell; above right © OPG/James Merrell; below © OPG/James Merrell; 232 above © OPG/Simon Upton; above right © OPG/James Merrell; below © OPG/James Merrell/Mary Drysdale; 233 above left © OPG/Dominic Blackmore; above right © OPG/Dominic Blackmore; below © OPG/Simon Upton; 234 © OPG/Simon Upton; 236 above © OPG/James Merrell, Jane Churchill Designs Ltd.; below left © OPG/James Merrell; below right © OPG/James Merrell; 237 left Arcaid/Alan Weintraub; right © OPG/James Merrell; 238 above © OPG/James Merrell; below © OPG/James Merrell; 239 above left © OPG/James Merrell; above right © OPG/James Merrell; below © OPG/James Merrell; 240 above left © OPG/James Merrell; above right © OPG/James Merrell; 240 below © OPG/James Merrell; 241 above left © OPG/James Merrell; 241 below left © OPG/James Merrell; 241 right © OPG/James Merrell; 242 above © OPG/Simon Upton; 242 below © OPG/Simon Upton; 243 Camera Press/Brigitte.